MACHINE
MACHINE
TIMES

contents

essays and interviews

projects

MACHINE TIMES

"Now" lasts for approximately 0.3 seconds. This is the time it takes the various centers and sections of our brain to find a synchronous rhythm which we experience as the present. As cognitive research into the phenomenon of time progresses, it is becoming more and more obvious that time is not an objective quantity which can be measured by chronometers and divided up into seconds and everything beyond. Time is a personal and therefore emotional experience, controlled by social rhythms – a process which starts in the womb. Time is never only natural or only historical, only subjective or only objective: it is always both at the same time.

Paul Virilio once differentiated between "extensive" and "intensive" time. Extensive time is the time of durability and presence, the time of archives and memory, the time also of the city with its spatial and historical continuity. It is a time that has a certain slowness and viscosity, a time inextricably bound up with physical activities such as motion and movement, transformation and geography, perception, interpretation. Here, time and space are still continuous.

Intensive time is very different. In intensified time, more and more appears to fit into a second. It is the extreme time of acceleration – from here to New York in seven days, in six hours, in two and a half hours, in one and a half seconds, in real-time. Intensive time is time which, in the end, is beyond experience, because it lies below the 0.3-second threshold. It is the time of e-mail and surfing, the time which eliminates space: arrival and departure occur in the same moment in real-time and the road traveled in between is no longer relevant. Intensive time is the time that exists only in machines and between them, the context of the slow human "now." A millisecond is quite a long period for a computer or a network. We cannot observe it directly, but it turns our living and working environments, our social and cultural life, upside down.

Introduction

Time has become the factor which defines the content, information and knowledge contained within technical media like film, television, radio and video, as well as digital media like the Internet. Time enables our shared experience of these media: find a common hour and the geographical space separating media users is no longer relevant. "Change the world, stay home" (Adilkno). All the same, electronic machines such as video recorders, televisions and the Internet are most definitely linked to our historical sense of time – our extensive time. These devices even reinforce this historical awareness, because they function as a collective memory; they are machines of the "living dead," as Gregory Whitehead called them. Electronic media reinforce (process and manipulate) our notion of time; they are all time machines producing machine time. Our sense of past, present and future is part of this machine time.

DEAFOO, as well as this book of essays, interviews and art projects which doubles as a catalogue for the exhibitions and program, explores the latitude that machine time allows us in the physical, artistic, musical, cultural, scientific, biological and economic senses. Temporal structures are built into technological apparatuses, from industrial machines to radio frequencies and computers with their ever-increasing processing speeds. But our bodies are also time machines, with biological cycles and cellular aging mechanisms. Illness brings with it an awareness of time. Movement in time is the way in which we perceive, maybe even constitute space, and the most radical boundary of nature is made up of the speed of light, beyond which we transgress into the utopian terrain of time travel: back into history, forward into the future, or down into the depths of the "now."

DEAFOO/V2_Organisation

An interview with Francisco Varela

by Arjen Mulder

THE DEEP NOW

In your essay The Specious Present, *you propose a theory of the present as an embodied now: the now as a corporeal, neurological, cognitive experience. What is this now, this present?*

The question of the now, taken in its most immediate sense – a sense that is not necessarily scientific – is a perennial topic for mankind. Every human culture has grappled with the question: what is this temporality? It is a tremendous paradox that we live now, and yet time, the future and the past, seem so present and so important. In the West we have been so gripped by the physics of the notion of time as something that is ticked away by the clock, and that time is an arrow, and divided in equal seconds, that it is very good to realize that even in our tradition there has been somebody like Saint Augustine – and before him Aristotle – who put his finger on the fact that the now has a certain depth. Saint Augustine made it clear that for humans the quality of life depends on understanding how much the now, the present, is a deep and living thing. He centered some of his meditations in the Confessions on the exploration of this now, which eventually led him to view his relation to the divinity within the richness of the present. He had a tremendous influence.

This notion resurfaces only centuries later in America with William James, when he says the flow of consciousness

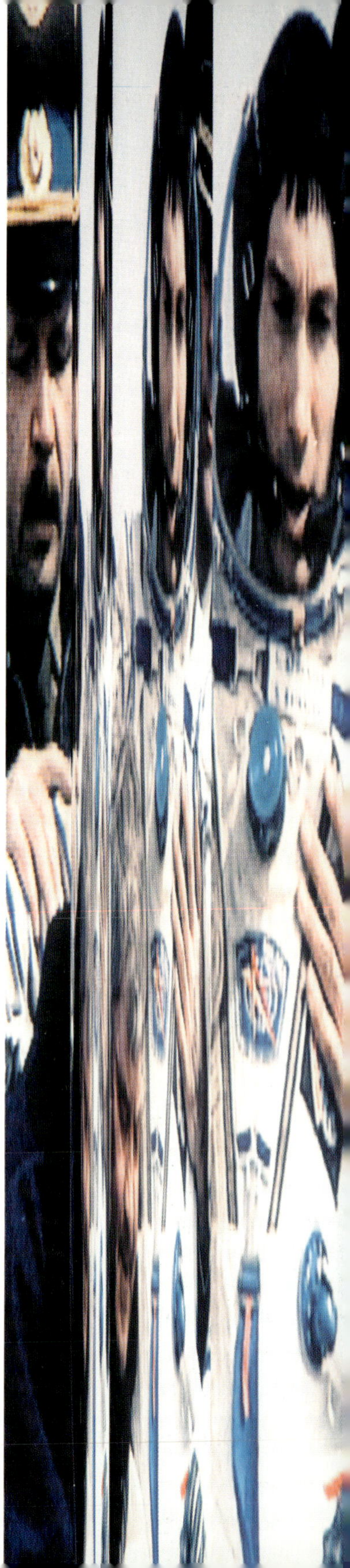

is what man is all about, and the now is what the flow of consciousness is about. This now he called the "specious present," that is, the slippery, tricky present. At the same time, in Europe, Husserl and the phenomenologists invented the term the "living present." That is exactly the same kind of understanding, that only when you break away from the spell of time as a sequence of instants one can measure by the clock, and you come back to your own depth of experience, you realize that what you live right now is almost like a cloud, like a whole, like a span, like a flash, which is far from a dot. The now is like an enormous matrix from which you can grow the quality of who you are. If the quality of that now is flat, your life is flat, and you have a life in which one appointment follows the other. It's hurry here and hurry there; it has no depth. Everything that has quality requires the reassessment, the reinvention of the now, whether it is in aesthetics, in love, in sensuality, eating or playing or sport.

So the question of the now is a very profound topic in understanding what human life is and what human consciousness is. In the end, the mystery of consciousness is in the depth of the now. That's where it appears as most central. I should mention here that this idea of coming back to the now as the center of learning how to be more human, in the sense of the development of attentiveness, is the center of the Buddhist tradition. The Buddhist tradition has made exactly the same discovery as Saint Augustine and William James and Husserl, et cetera. Ever since the time of the historical Buddha the idea has been to learn how to appreciate the quality of life through the now. Meditation is essentially that: it's stopping the hurriedness and the tick-tick-tick of the clock, to reassess the now. And the beautiful thing about the Buddhist tradition is that it has a method or a technique to actually give the statement "the now is fundamental" the necessary force: it's more than an opinion, it's a procedure. It's a how-to. I see all this as the same strand in human thinking in different cultures.

That was to situate the question of the now and the present. When we talk about consciousness and the temporality of the now, we're not talking about some minor thing but addressing a fundamental question. The last ten years or so, I've tried to work and think slightly differently than I previously did and most people still do. I try to bring together in a more clearly intrinsic relationship the part of what we study which belongs to our experience – what you might call the first person, which is something we have direct access to – with the scientific side, what you might call the third person, the external approach. We know we can study time from the third-person perspective, and we know time is something we live, as it has this quality of nowness. But these two aspects appear completely separated. We could say exactly the same about colors or memory or imagination. They're all dimensions of mind, experience or consciousness, and always possess what I would call a hybrid quality. It is simultaneously first-person and third-person. It's simultaneously something that has a lived quality and an objective quality. I want to bring these two aspects together intrinsically, and I'm not the only one doing this. A whole movement of people are trying to develop a "neurophenomenology," as I call it. It's a funny hybrid: studying something from the neural point of view as well as from the way it manifests itself. It asks: how can I live it and how can I study it? Neurophenomenology is a research pro-

gram, not a theory or a concept, but a direction for work. It says the lived approach and the objective approach are not just correlated, they actually shape each other mutually. There's no complete understanding of a thing like time without understanding how the brain works with respect to time, nor without understanding how my lived experience of time is. These two aspects constrain each other, guide each other.

We can go a little further and stretch the phenomenology by saying that the now is spacious, it has an extension, it's like an incompressible cloud. The cloud has the quality of containing the present and the just-past, because the present always points to the past. In the description of phenomenology we call that the "retention," the now is like a glob that moves and thus leaves a trail behind. That trail shows you that things are simultaneously in the present and already in the past. Retention is not memory: memory happens now. I remember the face of my wife now. Remembering in the now has its own retention. The paradoxical quality of retention is that it is the past now: it belongs to the past, but is still happening now. And then there's the side of the now that is the expectation or the construction of the future, which we call the "protention." One has to examine one's experiences carefully, for this trail of retention and this stream of protention are very subtle, but very important. As you see, the lived experience teaches you that time has

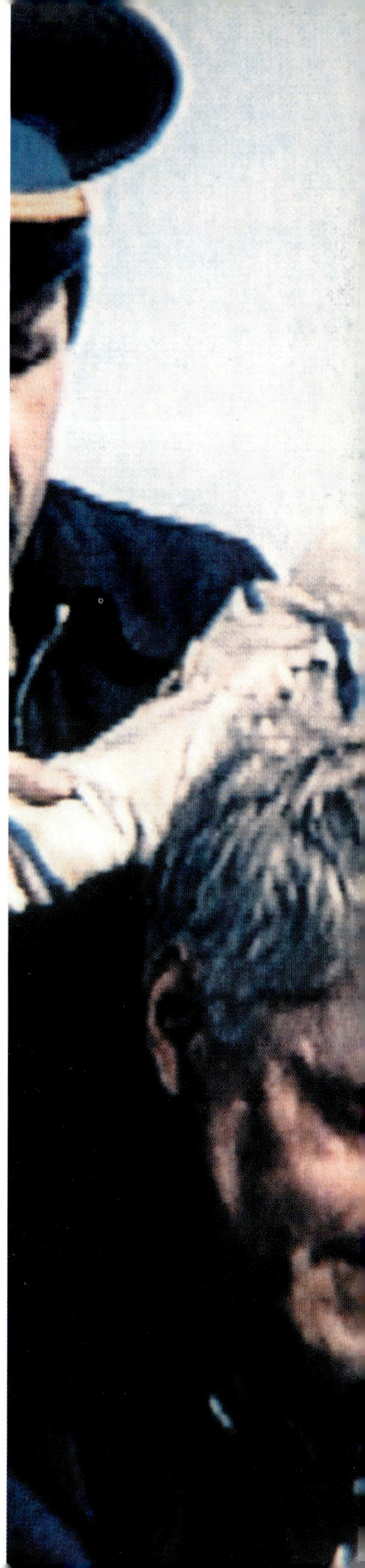

Out of the Present

Andrei Ujica

From their timeless world the gods once looked down upon all the teeming ants on earth. *Out of the Present* is a 92-minute film about the space station Mir made from documentary footage from 1991 and 1992, when the Soviet Union was falling apart, communism was discarded and for a while people had other things on their minds than astronauts high above the earth. The Russian cosmonaut who was thus forced to orbit the earth for 310 days – in 92-minute laps – was asked by a journalist, "When you left, the Soviet Union still existed and Gorbachev was still in power. Now Leningrad, your hometown, is called St. Petersburg. Which change impressed you the most?" Silence in the space station.

Then the cosmonaut answered: "It's hard to say. So many things have changed. But what amazes me the most is: just now it was night, and now it is day and the seasons just fly by. I'd say that is the most impressive thing you see from up here." Nature comes before history, says this astronaut: that is what you see from the vantage point of the gods. Andrej Ujica: "Space travel is a metaphysical project. There is no other reason for keeping a permanent space station in orbit but the continuation of the meta or outer-historical position." Timelessness has been technologically realized, literally over our heads.

But what a mess it is in those godly spheres! *Out of the Present* confronts our clean image of space travel with the chaotic reality of it. At the same time it confronts our image of space travel as a scientific enterprise with the euphoric primeval experience evoked by zero gravity. Ujica: "In a state

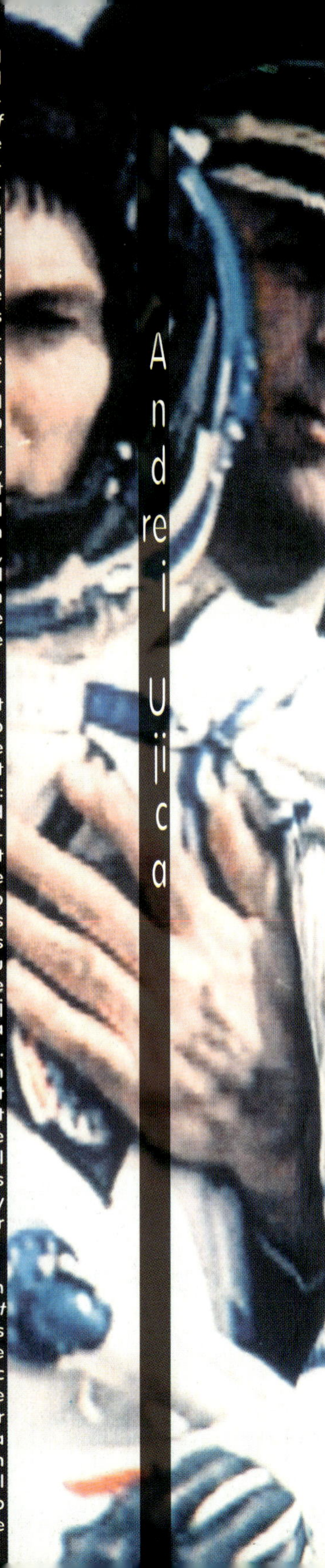

THE DEEP NOW

Francisco Varela

a three-part structure – now, retention, protention.

For years my scientific colleagues who work with an information-processing point of view have analyzed the operation of the brain with respect to time as you would in an information-processing model. There is an internal clock that ticks, you count the number of ticks, and this counting is the accumulator that gives you a sense of time. When you look at a well-known model like that, and then take the lived description, you have a strong example of where the first person can invalidate the third-person description. The first person says: this model has to be wrong. We must take a closer look and recover the three-part structure of time that the lived experience taught us. Within cognitive science there is a bit of a revolution going on, and the information-processing notions – which are based on an account of time like in physics – are being

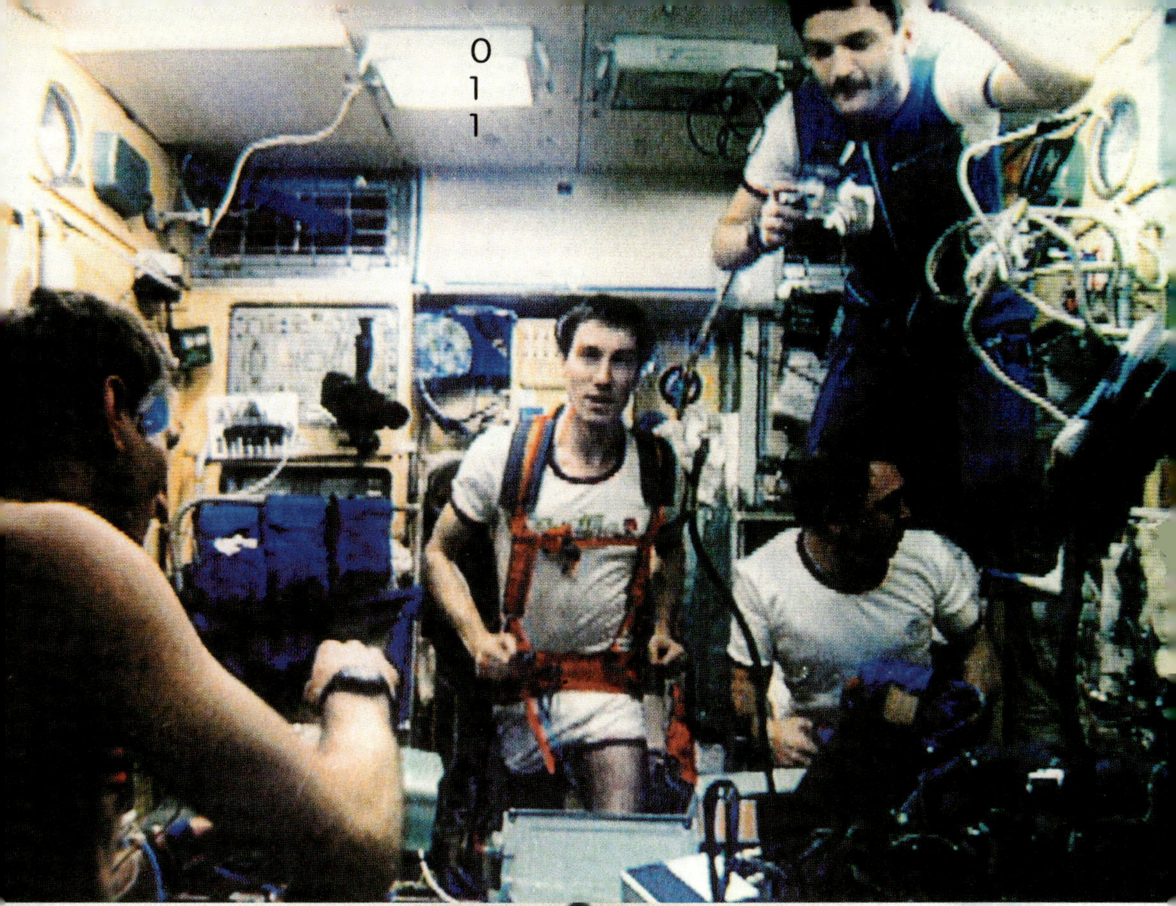

replaced by what one might call a dynamical approach. This dynamical approach is not based on the idea of the discreteness of time – tick-tick-tick – but on the idea of the evolution of trajectories. In the image of the trajectory the brain's functioning is seen in dynamical terms. The brain functions as a universe, and all the different parts of the brain are every moment brought together in a dynamical assemblage. The notion of dynamical assemblage is a very strong idea that has come entirely from the third-person approach, from studying animal nervous systems and single neurons and so on. It is a strong hypothesis about how the brain actually works. All these different bits, cortex this and cortex that and brain stem this and front lobe that, are not just separate things; they all work in harmony somehow. It is the dynamical view that they find each other in synchrony, in resonance, due to their intrinsical and practical relations that come into register. This coming into register gives the sufficient coherence.

When looking at the critical data, you realize that this dynamical process of coming into synchrony is not a question of all or none. You can compare it to a group of people who all have to act together: it takes a while. They have to exchange signals, and after a while it gels into the current state, before it gets undone again. There is what is technically known as a relaxation time. The now is not just here; it is in the process of this slow arising of combinations which forms the complex assemblage. This allows

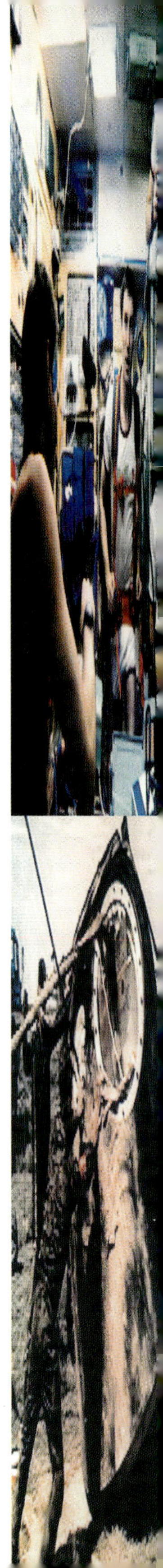

you to understand the moment, not in the trivial sense of tick-tick-tick, but as a process of very complex assemblaging that according to the watch takes a while. In fact it takes a fraction of a second. Which is a paradox: now lasts, now is a lasting time, one-third, one-fourth of a second. We know this from a number of experiments. And meditators also report this very clearly.

So we have an account from neuroscience that is purely objective, based on measurements, with a deep theory of dynamical systems behind it that explains why it's hard to assemble this synchronization in the brain. And we also have an account of the lived time that allows me to say: my experience of time is the way it is because of how I'm constitutionally made. Time happens as in the rising of a wave that then subsides, like a wave that comes from the sea. Time is a dynamical process. In every trajectory – and that is why the metaphor of the trajectory is such a beautiful one – you have a point that moves, and this moving point has a trail, which is the immediate past states of the trajectory. This trajectory is in a context, a landscape, and you know where it's heading. It's like seeing a ball rolling down a mountain: although it has many options, you can see that it is already geared to go this way and not that way. Now we can illuminate the first-person perspective. Husserl used to say: retention is a total paradox. How can you have a past that is in the present? From the standpoint of dynamical systems you get a much

of weightlessness we return to our state as embryos in the womb." The exploration of the most unknown terrain to us earthbound creatures – space – is simultaneously the exploration of the most familiar thing within us: our first consciousness. In this "high," there is no greater pleasure than staring out the window at Mother Earth. From the void, an empty universe, the cosmonauts look out at what makes this void endurable: their planet. Our planet.

deeper understanding: retention is a paradox only if you think of time as discrete units. It's not a paradox in this geometrical sense, of which Husserl or James had no idea – this is science of the last 50 years at the very most.

What have we accomplished with this exploration? First of all, we get an account of time that integrates the external and the internal, and both constrain and guide each other. We can discard scientific hypotheses and scientific results and illuminate that these are incomplete in their description. We get a three-dimensional perspective of what temporality is. In the end that's what interests me: the fact that the world phenomenon and the lived phenomenon are part of the same hybrid phenomenon. Why should I be biased toward one or the other? I don't want to be biased; I want to encompass the whole shebang. That's what's aesthetically pleasing about this kind of work.

In your article you use the term "transparency" to describe the expectation of the way things in general will show up. Transparency has everything to do with the habits we develop in learning processes. And transparency is also an important notion in art. As an artist you can use a medium in a transparent way, and pay no attention to the medium that is between you and the reality that is represented through the medium. But you can also go for hypermediation and force your audience to look at the medium instead of looking through it and denying its existence. Which is basically an artist's strategy of deregulating the transparency to create an awareness of not just the medium but also of the process of looking, of your own embodiment as a looking person. Somehow there seems to be a connection between these two approaches of the notion of transparency.

Maybe it's different, maybe it's the same. Let's have a look. In my article I'm trying to better understand the notion of protention, which is the least understood notion in this whole story. Protention is about the future. It is not about having a sense of what's happening in the now. In the now you always know that there is a content, a retention, something. What is interesting about the future is the lack of this sense, since it has not yet happened. Nevertheless, it's crucial, and we call it expectation. What is an expectation? That's not so obvious. What we're seeing in our expectations about the future are our preconceptual tendencies. They come from pre-noetic layers of our mind, and they almost set the stage for the future to show up. It's entirely based on a preconceptual way of thinking. Essentially it is the drives, the instincts, the emotions that will give you this protention, because that's the level of life that is preconceptual. Intrinsic to this level is the shift in emotional tone. See a shift in the emotional tone, and you see the protentions at work.

Take surprise. You're walking down the street, and you are in your now, now, now. The now when you take the first step on the street and the second now after that are pretty much in continuity. But all of sudden you hear: honk! It's a surprise, and an emotional shift precedes you. It's already there when you wake up in another future, in which the emotion is entirely different: you're scared, you're startled, whatever. That new now is of a completely different nature. There you have the protentive, affective intelligence at work. When there is no change in the affective tone, things are transparent. You walk down the street without any sense of the fact that you're walking down the street. But at the moment the car honks the transparency is lost. You have to reinvent your behavior. You can step back, run forward, scream at the car. The breakdown in transparency is an extremely interesting moment, because it's the moment the now reconfigures itself, the point at which we see the process of temporality at work. It allows us to see the work-

ing of the world. It's not that different from exploring the presence of the now in meditation. You were distracted, then you go through the meditation practices, and you come back to the now. Again, that's a break in the transparency. The moment the transparency breaks is the moment we realize that the now really exists.

One could call this breakdown of transparency awareness. This awareness seems to be different from consciousness, which is more like a general background.

Time is really a specious topic. We talked about the now and its protention and retention – which is a temporality or time that is always referring to the manifestation of some content. But there is also what Husserl calls the longitudinal intentionality. It provides you with the realization that in spite of the fact that the now is always different, there is a basic continuity, which Husserl also calls the absolute flow and is totally preconceptual. The longitudinal intentionality gives you a continuity from one moment to another, but it's not a continuity of "yes, I know what is happening," it is a basic layer of what might be called primary consciousness, a prenoetical, prego consciousness, that belongs to me, to the basic emotional and affective level, which has to do among other things with the fact that we're constantly in a body that lives regularly, that has a continuity of systems and aliveness. And that basic aliveness is manifested in the longitudinal continuity. It also has to do with the protention, because it will show up in this affective manner, but at the same time it stands in contrast to the time that is more explicit and more conscious. The three-part time is a time that has broken through to come to awareness. But there is also a temporality which may not come through in the present and is pervasive.

How would you define an experience?

It's a funny question, almost redundant, because an experience is who you are now. You can say: I experience the now, but in fact experience is who you are, the who-you-are in its full volume. The problem with human beings, for evolutionary reasons or whatever, is that we're not always, as they say in California, in touch with our experiences. Our biological system is built to pay attention to the world, to objects, to what's outside, and our experience recedes in the background. In that way it's exactly like the body. You walk around, and your body is transparent to you. But when you step on something and you feel a little pain, your body immediately rises up, and you realize that's who you are. Your lived body is who

Claudia Kölgen

Meditation, according to Francisco Varela, "is the stopping of the hurriedness and the tick-tick-tick of the clock, to reassess the now." Meditation is not closing yourself off to the outside world to experience timelessness within yourself. On the contrary, it is a technique that enables you to concentrate in such a way that you learn to experience the present, within yourself, within the workings of your own consciousness. Meditation is a return to what Varela calls the "deep now." A "now" which the person meditating discovers is an individual entrance into an impersonal level of consciousness that spans the centuries and that develops with each new generation.

Photography is a similar technique, not for individualizing fragments from time and thus placing them within an ahistorical timelessness, but precisely for concentrating the present in the "now" of photography – for the one-hundredth or even one-thousandth of a second that the camera shutter is open. Photography's method for doing this is completely the opposite of that of meditation technique. Photography opens itself up completely to the outside world it records. It removes subjective hurriedness from the world in order to make the present visible in all of its objective glory and detail. And in doing so, it delivers a no longer personalized "now" that remains accessible for generations to come.

The photographs Claudia Kölgen shot of people meditating in their everyday surroundings form a subtle confrontation of the techniques available to us to experience and explore "the now."

Sitting

THE DEEP NOW

Francisco Varela

you are, not something where you live, not something you can put away.

In that sense the word "experience" is not redundant, because in the natural life we lose contact with our experience and put it in the background. And there's some truth in saying our experience has to be explored, studied or brought to the fore. That is, again, why the Buddhists use the technique of meditation. You stop what you're doing and turn inward instead of constantly flashing outward. So experience is the ground moment in which you are who you are. It's a very intimate moment because it's at the core of being alive, of who you are. But at the same time it's not really individual, it's very much decentered, because you wouldn't be alive without the lives of others. It's very artistic in fact. I'm convinced that the aesthetic experience is related to coming back to one's own. Maybe one could say

Sitting "Leslie"

Sitting "Stephen"

that beauty is letting experience come to the fore. Often that is what is artists do: they shake you sufficiently to break your transparency, and let you come back to who you are.

In your description, perception is not just sitting down and looking, as in the third-person approach. Perception always needs a sensorimotor activity – the whole body is involved in perception, which is the first-person approach. I'm wondering about photographic images or film or video, which form a strong argument for the objectivist view of the world. You can prove that the world exists independently of yourself, because you can make a picture of it, even without a human being making the picture. Another thing is, you can look at photos without hardly any sensorimotor activity. Cinemas are designed to make you forget that you are a body. Is this, in your approach, wrong, or a mistake?

It's neither wrong nor a mistake, but it's an extreme case. From the beginning of one's life, embodiment first and foremost means this active handling of and coping with the world. Without that there is no world altogether. There are no objects, there is no sensation of objects, no quality of objects, and no vision. Scientifically that is already proven. Active coping is basic, but once you've acquired that, you can do things like watching a picture, which requires only eye movement and not the entire body.

In a visually oriented society like the one we live in, photographic or technical images are very ...

Central. You're absolutely right. Unfortunately there are cultures where people, out of poverty or boredom, watch television all the time and in that sense are not embodied. You get a kind of disembodiment. When you do that kind of watching too much, it's pathological. That's a mistake. It's the same with people who sit before computer screens for eighteen hours a day. That is completely contrary to who they are and to their bodies, and that creates all kinds of problem.

At the beginning of cyberspace, in the 1980s, there was this whole mythology of disembodiment, of leaving the body behind and migrating into the computer. You relate this to the lack of sensorimotor activity?

When you put it like that, the sensorimotor activity doesn't seem to be a big thing.

What I mean with embodiment is the fact that what you experience in conceptual thoughts and imaginary perceptions and images is nevertheless based and grounded in your body. That, again, is good science. Even language is grounded in your body. When you completely immobilize the body, you'll move more and more into the dream life, the imaginary life. Sleeping and dreaming is exactly that: you stop. Evolution has invented sleep to rehearse the images and go around them in dreams. Which is very good and creative, provided that you wake up and put them into action. Otherwise you get totally disconnected lives. Maybe I'm very traditional, but I don't see that as healthy. Because again, it puts your experience in the background. Whenever you bring your experience back, the depth of your being a human being, the body comes with it. That's why people say: yes, I feel myself again.

But you're saying that embodiment is not just the natural condition, it's also an ethics of health.

Well, it's definitely not healthy not to bring along your heritage. Who knows what can happen in disembodied societies? We have no idea. Evolution certainly hasn't experimented with that. So at least I say we should be very prudent and go very slowly. A disembodied society or sub-society would be extremely pathological.

There is another aspect of time to art. Art always dreams of creating timelessness, eternal beauty, duration: to make an object and remove it out of time. One finds this sense of timelessness not just in art but also in religion. How do you see this?

I must say it's not something I have reflected on for a very long time. My spontaneous reaction is: I'm too much of a Buddhist to give too much credence to that idea. Beauty is in the fleetingness, beauty is in the open and the impermanent, in the constant renewal of the movement of life creating life. I don't have a particularly strong feeling for permanence and an aspiration for eternity. That's a very Christian idea, and after all these years of trying to deconstruct my Christianity, I've come to adopt an openness or emptiness that comes from the Buddhist tradition. That seems much more accurate and true.

It's not just the Christian tradition, it's also the tradition of modernism in the arts to create an object that has duration – "Gib den Dingen Dauer," as Gottfried Benn put it. But if it's done properly, it creates the experience of nowness. Modernism is not just about duration, but always also about the notion that only the now is real, the "continuous present." The rest of time is imaginary. That's somehow always in the back of the mind of an artist.

It's in the back of mind of every scientist, too.

But it's part of science not to go for the absolute truth, but only for temporarily proven theories. But this doesn't seem to interest you.

I'd say it doesn't particularly move me. I don't relate strongly to that. My search has been to get more and more embedded into the view of life which is about change, and giving up and letting go, rather than holding up.

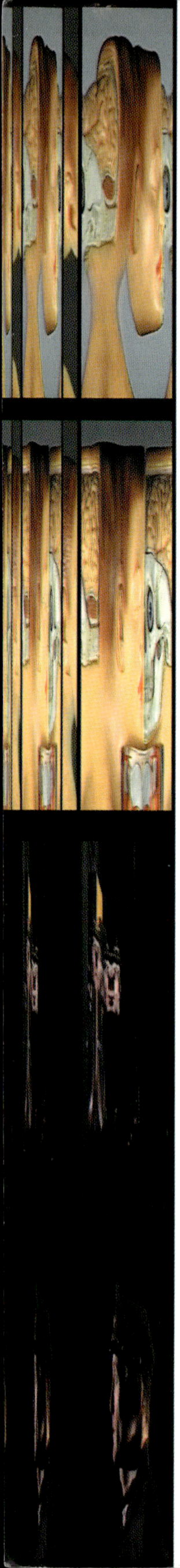

Maybe I should put the question differently. What is your view on death as the end of all change?

If you ask me like that, death is clearly not the end. Death is the wave that subsides back into the ocean, but the flow of life and mind continues. When Francisco dies, it's just Francisco who dies; big deal. But the flow of life continues. Not that I believe in reincarnation of people as single individuals. But I strongly believe or feel or understand that there are streams of consciousness, and that consciousness has a certain continuity somewhat as it happens in evolutionary genetics. When you see an apple that grows onto an apple tree year after year, you don't say the apple is reincarnated. Nevertheless, you could say that, because year after year you have an apple, that is the same as and different from the one of last year. Underlying this is the understanding from bio-integration and biology of the stream of life, which integrates the tree and the seed and the nutrients and the water, and then you can envision the process that makes the apple. It's not the same apple, it's not on the same branch, but there is a continuity of life. About the mind we know much less than about genetics and ecology, but I represent it in pretty much the same way. Consciousness has trends, tendencies, and death is like the end of one cycle, but the flow continues.

You suggest that there is a genetics of consciousness, in the sense that there's an underlying pattern moving on?

Yes. I'm using the analogy of what we know for certain of the flow of life, because that also seems to be true for the flow of consciousness. This is yet another example of the first- and third-person points of view relating to each other.

To me this sounds a bit as if there's a world spirit, as a disembodied entity moving through time.

No, that's a view that takes on from the idea of souls. I think it's a entirely nonindividual process. There's no "me" that comes by; there are tendencies, like the tendency of an apple tree to grow an apple. This particular flow of mind will have tendencies or proclivities in this or that direction. All I'm saying now is, of course, entirely from the first-person point of view. But there is a merit to that. In the first-person point of view the depth of consciousness is something to be reckoned with. As much as the present has depth, so does consciousness have a depth. How are we going to account for that? I take the Buddhist tradition very seriously that states that there is a continuity of consciousness – it's exactly the same idea. When you die, you die. Francisco is no more, but the underlying stream of consciousness continues. It's not personal, but it does contain and accumulate the tendencies that I have put into action in my life. If I have behaved vilely, those tendencies continue, but if I have behaved compassionately toward other forms of life, these tendencies continue.

So you believe in an evolution of mind?

Yes, absolutely. That's why I take the ethics of actions so seriously. If it was a fact that life could end and that's all there is to it, then I shouldn't be too concerned about ethics. For the consciousness, ethics is interesting and important only because of its long-term effects. The little things I do here have repercussions everywhere. I would love to see this researched. And I don't think it's beyond the scope of science. Because it's phenomenal, it's a phenomenon and you can observe it. But science only works within the boundaries

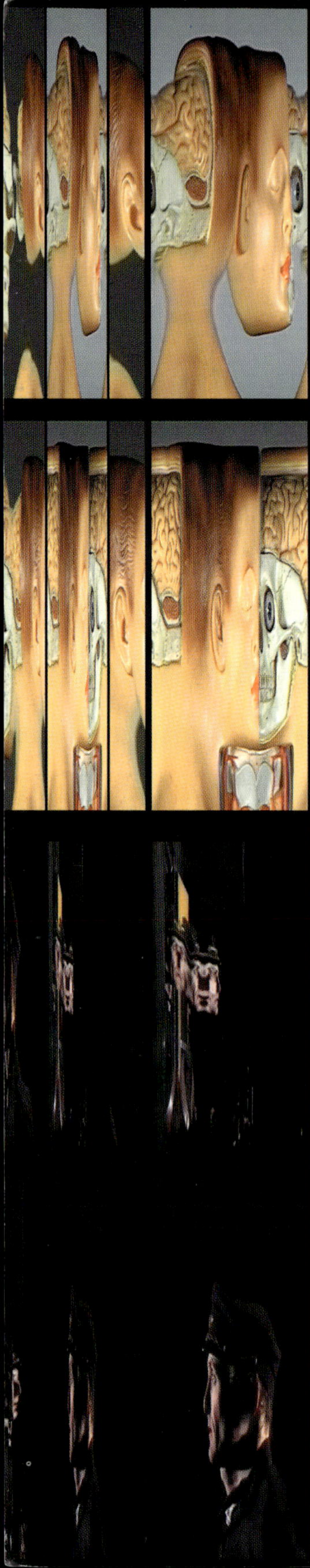

of what it considers possible. It has been so influenced by the fact that it had to fight against the church to survive that it had to reduce everything to a very simple materialistic basis. But I don't see science as intrinsically and necessarily materialistic. Science is based on phenomena, so when there are phenomena, you can work on them. We really have to extend the notion of the material basis beyond the present scientific scope.

I read The Embodied Mind *as a completely materialistic book, philosophically speaking. All spiritual processes are embodied and, in that sense, material.*

Oh yes, they are embodied, and that's an important thing. But that's not to deny that when you go deeper into it from a first-person point of view – which we don't do in the book – there's a depth to attentiveness. I've written another book on this subject which consists of a series of dialogues with the Dalai Lama, *Sleeping, Dreaming, and Dying* (1997), in which we explore precisely all these different, subtle levels of consciousness. It's true that science apparently can only work with levels of consciousness that can be described as embodied, and that's what we do in *The Embodied Mind*. That's already a big step. You can't do everything at the same time, otherwise people think

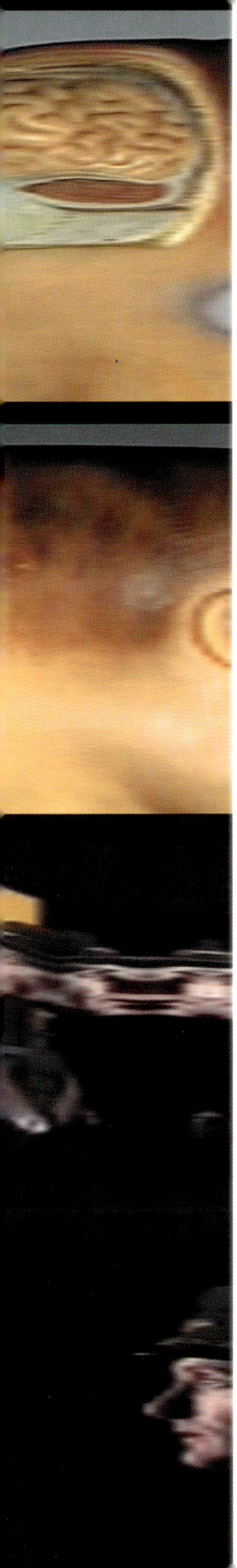

you're not just half crazy, but completely crazy. But I think there is more to consciousness then we describe in that book. In other words, there are more subtle levels of consciousness. And it's yet to be seen how these subtle levels can be related to science as we know it. Are these phenomena just imaginary, or is science limited? I honestly don't know, but I think the research of the future, of the next century, is going to be about just that.

(Paris, July 4, 2000)

Francisco J. Varela Ph.D. is Director of Research at CNRS (National Institute for Scientific Research) at the laboratory of Cognitive Neurosciences and Brain Imaging (LENA) located at the Salpêtrière University Hospital in Paris, where he is the head of the Neurodynamics Group. He is also Senior Faculty at CREA, Ecole Polytechnique. His publications include: J. Petitot, F. Varela, B. Pachoud and J.M. Roy (Eds.), ***Naturalizing Phenomenology: Contemporary Issues in Phenomenology and Cognitive Science*** (1999); F. Varela and J. Shear (Eds.), ***The View from Within: First-Person Methodologies*** (1999); F. Varela, ***Ethical Know-How*** (1999).

Arjen Mulder is writer and translator. His most recent publications include: ***Het fotografisch genoegen*** (The Photographic Enjoyment, Amsterdam 2000) and ***Book for the Electronic Arts*** (Amsterdam 2000, with Maaike Post).

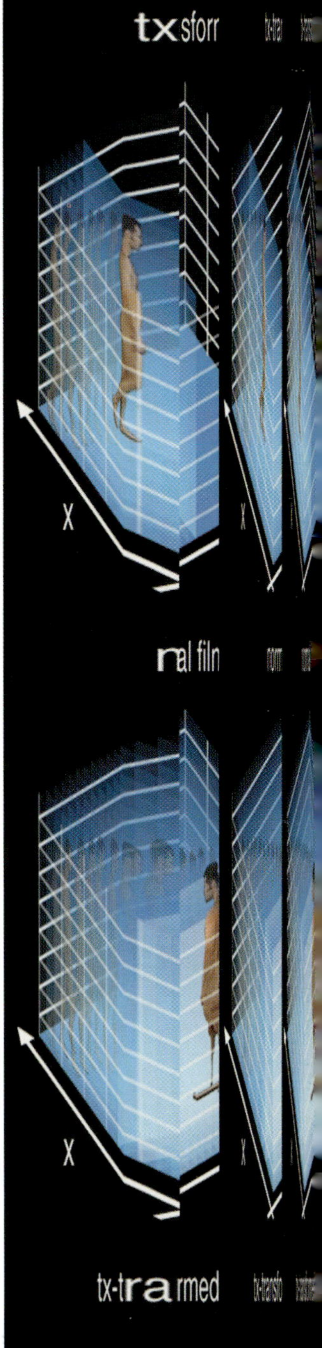

tx-transform

Martin Reinhard & Virgil Widrich

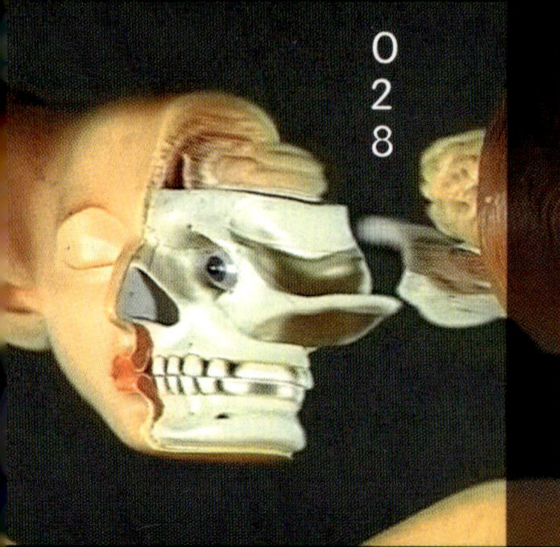

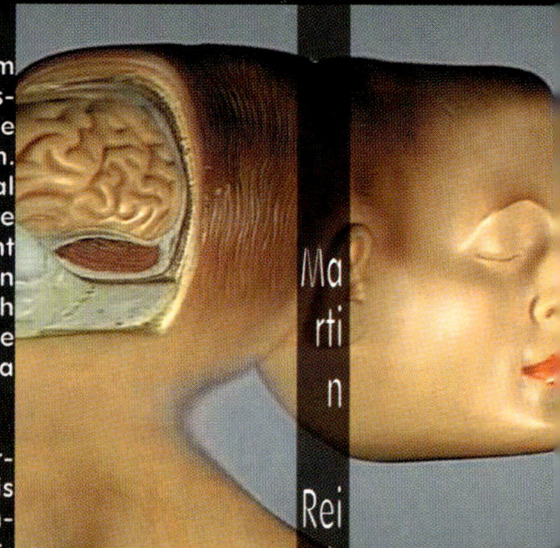

tx-transform is a new film technique which transposes the time axis (t) and the space axis (x) in film. Normally, each individual frame depicts the entire space but only a moment in time. This is reversed in tx-transformed films: Each frame shows the entire period of time but only a tiny portion of the space.

A simple way to understand tx-transformation is to imagine a flipbook containing a sequence of pictures. When rapidly riffled with the tip of the thumb, an illusion of motion is produced. Like a reel of film, this toy contains all the spatial aspects of motion and can be understood as an "information block." Normally, this block is riffled from front to back along the time axis to create the illusion of a moving image. *tx-transform* riffles through this "information block" in quite a different way by cutting through the space axis instead of the time axis. These "space cuts" through the "information block" produce a series of astounding visual effects: houses start to move, heads grow out of themselves, moving trains become shorter and shorter as their speed increases, and much more.

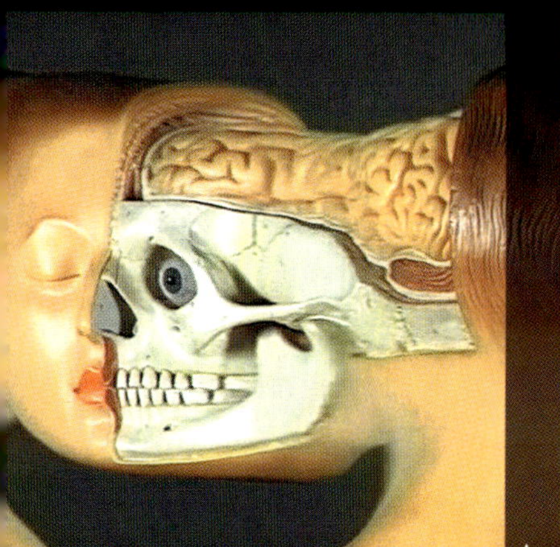

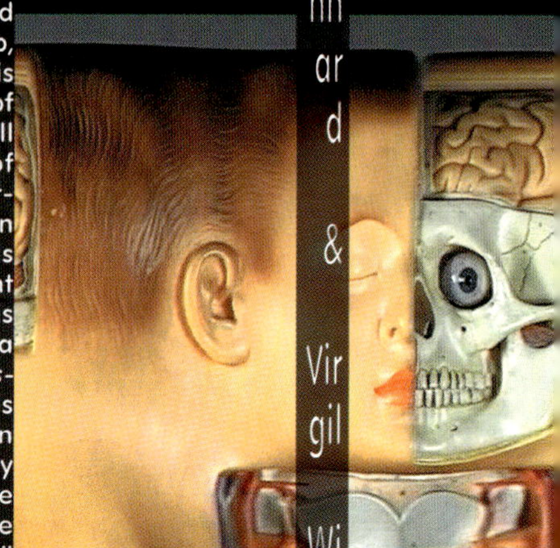

The "tx-transformator" that is shown for the first time at DEAF00 in Rotterdam is an interactive installation in a way similar to a photo booth. Consisting of a camera and a computer, the visitors can produce "space cut" films almost in realtime. Different shooting angles and speed of the automatic camera's pan can be chosen and the results of these self-made transformations can be seen immediately on a monitor.

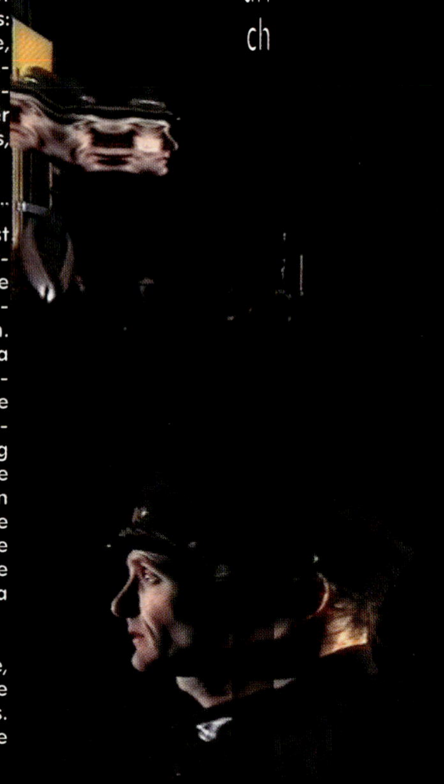

"By movement in space, the objects of a set change their respective positions. But, through relations, the

THE RHYTHMS OF HAPPINESS

An interview with Detlef Linke

by Arjen Mulder

Detlef Linke

THE RHYTHMS OF HAPPINESS

Which rhythms are the important ones in the body and the brain?

Apart from the longer circadian rhythms, there are shorter rhythms connected with sensomotor responses. Sensomotor actions all have their proper times, which are a function of their regular cycles. You might say that the body runs on a kind of pacemaker of its own. If you move over to the cognitive plane, however, this is not the case. Event-related cognitive potentials have no fixed relationship to the EEG rhythm. It has proved impossible to pinpoint a pacemaker for the basic rhythms of the cerebral

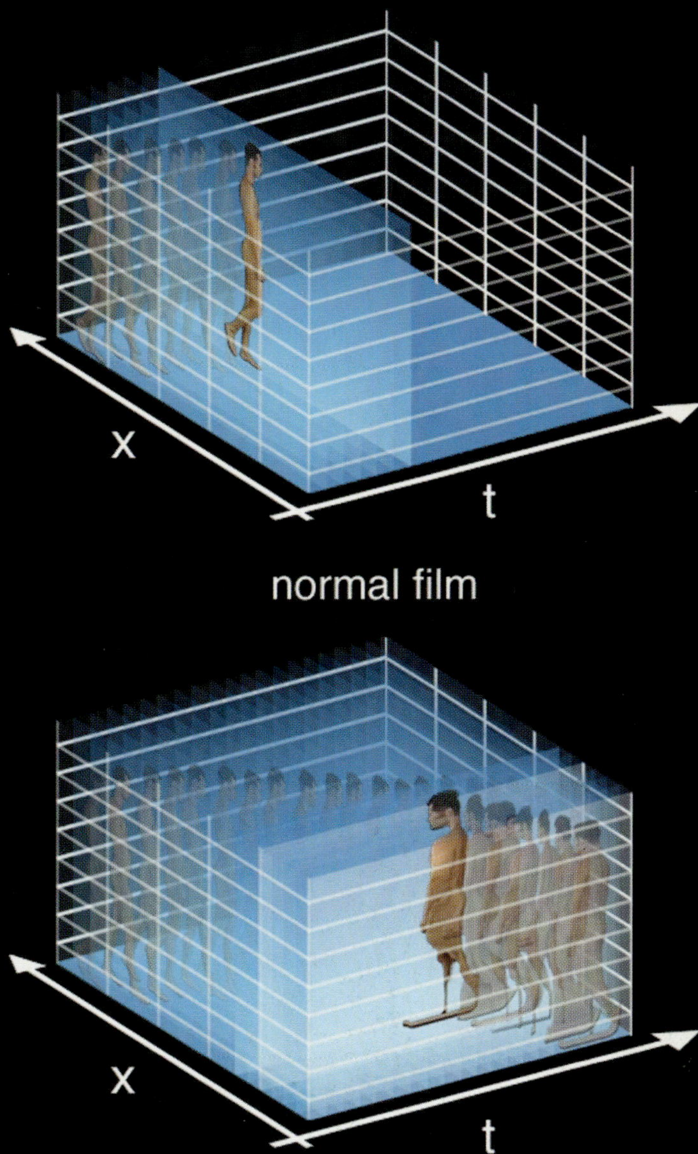

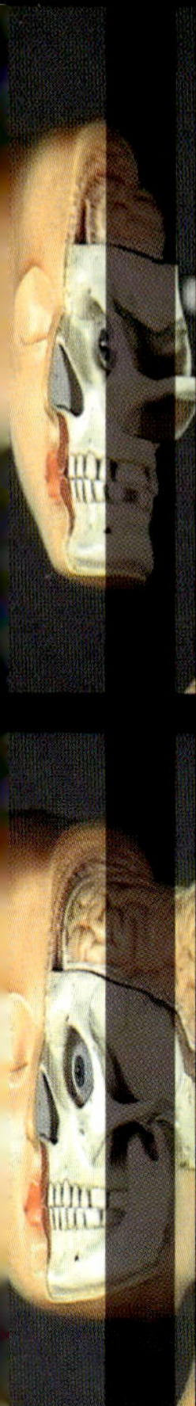

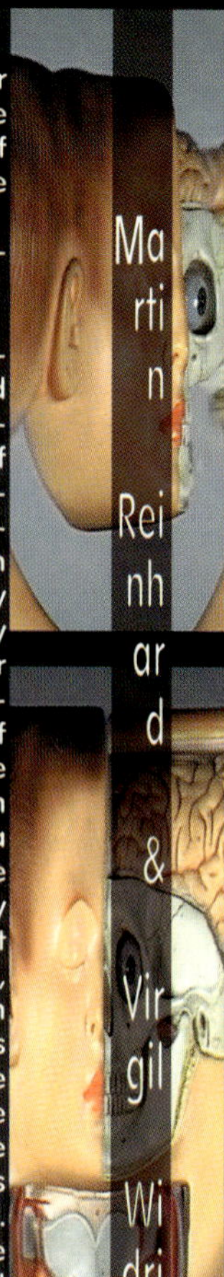

Martin Reinhard & Virgil Widrich

whole is transformed or changes qualitatively. We can say of duration itself or of time, that it is the whole of the relations." (Gilles Deleuze, "The Movement-Image")

Film involves the relationship between time and space and can be understood as a linear system of order, which assigns a certain spatial or visual configuration to a certain point in time. In everyday life, time is normally understood as a linear dimension of an unequivocal quantity. This view of reality corresponds to the progression of time in film. A strip of film has a beginning and an end; the direction is determined by the direction in which it runs through the projector, and the relative duration of the projected events can be calculated on the basis of the length of the film material and the speed at which it moves through the projector. What we perceive as time is for the film a spatial dimension, which expands in a certain direction.

tx-transform

With *tx-transform,* objects depicted in a film are no longer defined as images of something that exists concretely; they become conditions in time. The digital realization of this technique in no way influences film's special character as a fundamental model of order and perception.

http://www.tx-transform.com

Credits:
Concept and idea: Virgil Widrich, Martin Reinhart
Software: Georg Dorffner
Hardware: Georg Hirzinger, Martin Reinhart

THE RHYTHMS OF HAPPINESS

currents, so we must assume that they originate in a complex interaction of different regular cycles which are capable of producing highly variable accelerations of the EEG frequencies. The cerebroelectrical correlates of cognitive processes prove to be largely independent of the phases of the basic rhythm of the cerebral currents. Thus, in contrast to the motor reaction times of the body, we cannot assume a completely defined time pattern for them. The cognitive potentials are capable of freedom of movement, which applies also to their relations to lower regular cycles in the bottom layers of the brain – the sensomotor cycles, for instance – which have their own peculiar temporal characteristics. The brain does not come equipped with an original metronomic default setting: the rhythms of cognitive events are situationally determined. They adapt themselves to external stimuli. The problem with any attempt to codify the information in the nervous system is precisely this absence of any indication of a proper beat. The various pieces of information reach the brain in a state of almost chaotic muddle, so that they have to receive their rhythm inside the brain before they can be processed further at one of the cognitive levels. The problem of finding the information beat – the beat, that is, alongside which information may be codified – is much more acute in the case of patients who have suffered injury to the brain. I have thought of providing brain-damaged patients with a tactile clock to help them to orient themselves towards this external time. We are, all of us, always looking for rhythms in the external world, because we

possess too much information that simply cannot be accommodated to a time that is proper to the organism. The organism does not and cannot possess such a time, because the information it was receiving could not them be decoded correctly in accordance with external reality. We have different intervals for different actions. In cases where we have to perform motor movements and cognitive actions simultaneously – let's say we are in a conversation with someone while out on a walk and are suddenly confronted with a difficult problem – we generally cancel one of the actions. We stand still, and only after we have solved the problem do we continue our walk. If thoughts ran metronomically, we would never be able to focus on them. We would be unable to switch off a thought in the way we can switch off our walk. Our ability to engage the proper time of a thought and to gear the codification, the information and the content of the thought itself to the nuanced structure of the brain's information assimilation is very crucial to us. Which is why the rhythm of this information processing needs also to be an open one, and it is also the reason why our thoughts are sometimes so chaotic.

What happens if there are no external rhythms?

The information processing then gets more chaotic, and in the attempt to acquire a proper time in order to establish a coherence of thought, the circle closes more

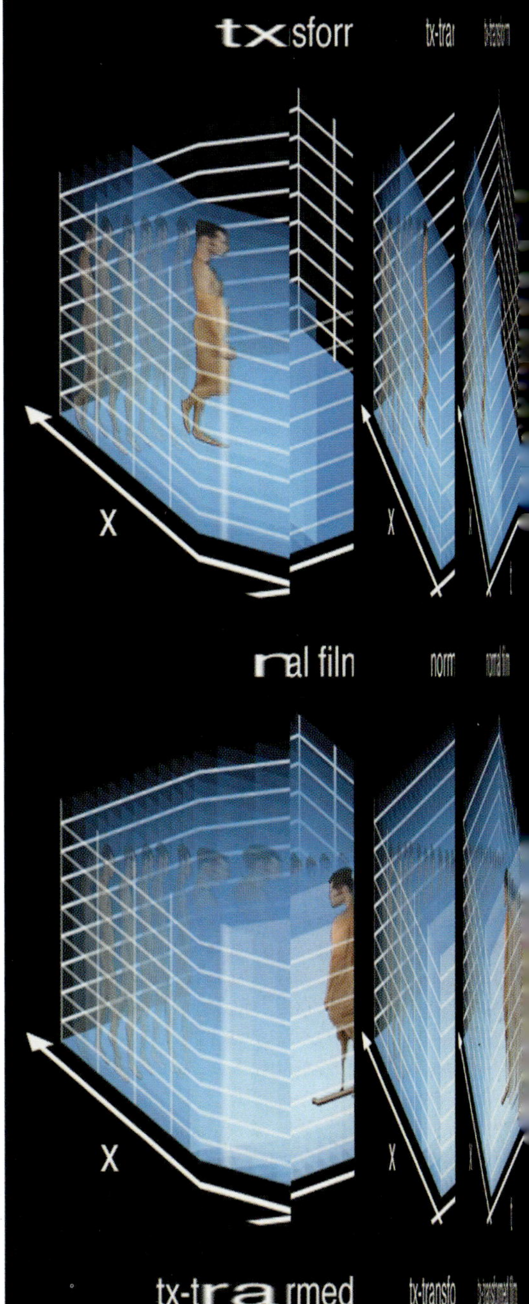

tightly now and then, and the coherence of various areas of the brain becomes more problematic. You are then no longer able to integrate your brain functions, and this can lead in the end to psychotic reactions. You see, it is not as though we have a subject-point in this network from which everything is controlled. Normal cognition moves in such a way that impulses from different areas of the brain, which are either synchronous or in some form of temporal correlation, come together, giving rise to a succession of thoughts. That is to say that we actually need a different way of putting this question of how it comes about that two impulses manage to meet. It is not as though there were two pre-established impulses whose coincidence is certain. The coherence and temporal synchronization of two different points is not absolutely predictable, and the flow of thoughts in a particular direction differs from one moment to the next. The establishment of a contact between distinct points is artificial. What normally happens is that the topic changes as a train of thought develops and another idea is introduced, and so on. We can try to impose a certain coherence on this and to train ourselves to avoid digression, and it's then fairly probable that certain impulses will meet and that certain meanings will come into being just as we planned them.

So it's possible to learn these brain rhythms?

We learn all our brain rhythms unconsciously, but learning to control them consciously is a different matter. You can observe your EEG, for example, and then train yourself to regulate these brain rhythms. The self is then in a certain sense an objective observer of its own brain rhythms, striving to bring them under its control. If we really were to reach a point of being able to control our brain rhythms to the extent that nothing unexpected could happen inside our brain any more, we would actually have produced an android. We have to bear in mind that because of its adherence to neurophilosophy, contemporary research into the

brain is working with an android model of the human being. The self is construed as a neuronally engineered supervisor, positioned like a spider in a web and capable of surveying everything with perfect precision. But were it the case that everything could be directed and controlled from this self, we would possess an algorithm for a human being. Or rather, not for a human being, but for the android we had reconstructed. We must therefore be careful not to bring in too much of this self as though it were some sort of center. The human individual is always capable of self-reference, and that is possibly a loop via which we are able to withdraw from all the various layers of the brain's activities. But if we take our stand on this self, this set point or assembly, which would be firmly fixed and from which everything else would be controlled, then we end up as appalling monstrosities, consciously designed androids. We have to be careful not to build something like that, and also not to fashion humanity in the image of a conscious android.

Turning ourselves into androids in the process.

Yes. In both neurophilosophy and neuroscience there is a tendency to reduce the human individual to the instinct of self-preservation and ego control. But I don't think that this is enough. The extreme example of the kamikaze pilot demonstrates that in given circumstances the survival instinct can be made quite subordinate.

How can brain rhythms be influenced? There are, after all, many social activities based on rhythm, from music to military organization.

People are certainly always in search of synchrony and rhythmicity, particularly when their own emotional states are chaotic. Rhythmicity has something sustaining, but also

something orienting. Rhythmicity has something that produces pleasure. But a state of total rhythmicity would be an epileptic fit. If one had turned oneself into pure rhythm or beat, so that everything was being discharged synchronously, one would be unconscious, and that would be the end of that clarity of consciousness in which the matrix of functional changes is located in the first place. Unless there is some disorder among the nerves, the brain is not functioning properly.

> *In today's techno music the rhythms are often very complicated. There's a beat, but there are all these other extremely complicated rhythms as well.*

Part of this is that the brain, including the emotions, never relies solely on currently prevailing external conditions, but is constantly setting up expectations, expectations which include certain anticipations of rhythm. If I really desire something to delight my entire brain, it must always contain the odd syncopation or occasional diversion. Consciousness is always concentrated on identifying regularities, and it is only when these tonal regularies suddenly cease that the stream of sounds can, properly speaking, enter consciousness. The brain would quickly stop registering pure rhythm, because the mechanisms of expectation and evaluation of regularities would no longer be active, and the brain would cease to derive enjoyment from them.

But doesn't this kind of music aim at the inducement of a trance? And isn't that also the idea behind military marching?

Well, again, we have this sensomotor level – the lowest stratum of the brain, that is – and if the sound out in the world happens to be exactly matching it, the brain does become so synchronized that there is no room left for thought. These synchronizations create pleasurable feelings. The sexual act is another example. In sexuality, is it not the sense organs or sensuality that is decisive. The sensations on the skin during the sexual act are only a means of synchronization, of falling into a common rhythm. The wonder of sex lies in the anticipation of achieving oneness through empathy with the motions of the other – or by varying one's own movements syncopatically in relation to the other's. One might describe sensuality as such as a particular way of relating to time. Sexual intercourse is actually pure time – time as the sole content of experience, the experience of the rhythms in the brain. There's a poem by Bertolt Brecht in which he recalls a love affair in his youth, and it consists of nothing more than the memory of a white cloud which actually has nothing to do with the affair. In other words, the state of arousal cannot be remembered: only the hotel room is recalled, or the place on the beach and the white cloud that hung there in the sky. The convergence of arousal itself eludes memory. If we were able to recall it completely the nervous system would no

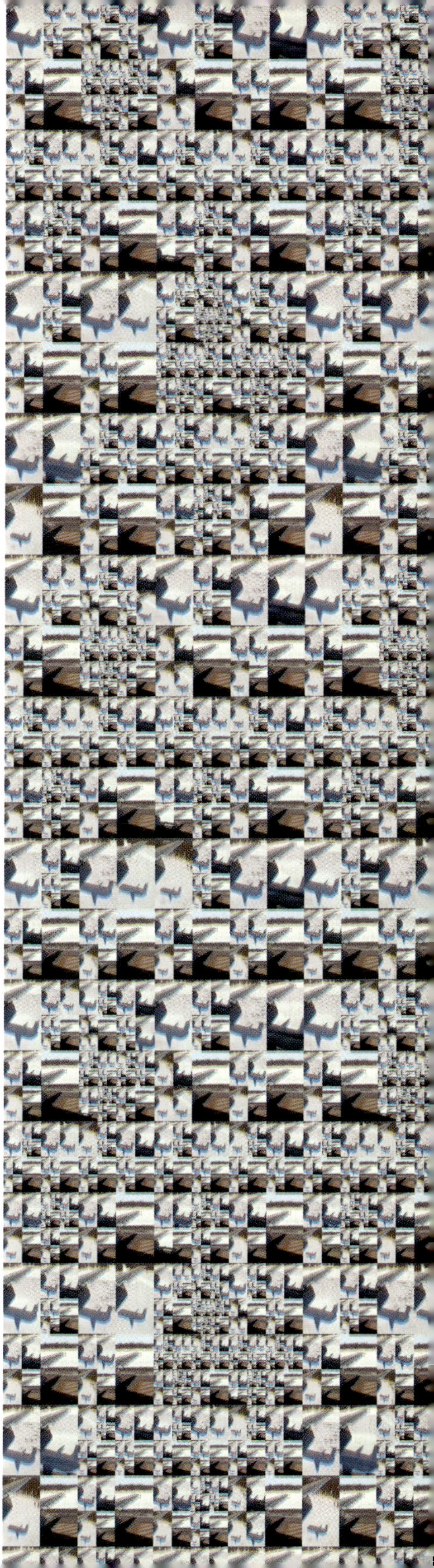

longer be able to find its way around in its own home. The memory of the arousal would cause total confusion, for the arousal can only take place on the level on which the memory itself ensues. In order to represent the state of arousal we are compelled to add something extra, like Brecht's white cloud. I cannot properly recall arousal, or only with difficulty and with the aid of metaphors. If it could be remembered perfectly, the state of arousal would confuse the representation of arousal or, more precisely, the representation of the system, since the system itself would need to be recodified. That is to say that the time at which something is represented cannot itself be represented; otherwise the two codifications would overlap and nothing would be represented at all. This is also another reason why sexuality is something that our systems of representation can never quite control. Non-recall is a way in which the organism protects its own nervous system. The theory of sensu-

Mari Soppela

Heimola

Reindeer in the snow. On a computer screen. In four rows of four, sixteen different images next to and under each other. Fifteen of the deer are standing still, while one is moving frantically. You approach the screen: the moving reindeer freezes, the other fifteen go wild. The effect: emotion, bewilderment. A primeval experience surfaces as soon as the reindeer start trotting. You take one step back and the animals freeze again, except for the one that stood motionless, which now bursts into frantic movement. The effect this time: being touched by timelessness, dismay, sadness at purity. The idea that the world could be stopped is existential poison; the Fates lay down their spools and sing; the song of the Sirens resounds. Leo Anemaet's music, which accompanies the piece, reinforces the effect of the change.

Heimola is an interactive installation of hypnotizing simplicity and beauty. It is nothing but an interface between the machine times of photo and film. A photograph is the technical bearer of an illusion of immortality: our capacity to step out of the pace of time through an image and to preserve "the now" for once and forever. Our consciousness does not know its own death. But as soon as the photograph turns out to be a part of a film, this consciousness is reversed: time progresses inescapably, lightning-fast even. Film is the technological bearer of our illusion of transitoriness. Everything is headed for death.

In the installation we, the spectators, are the ones who put time in motion or make it stop. We are the ones responsible for the death of the reindeer. Mari Soppela tells us that every year in her native Finland, the free-roaming

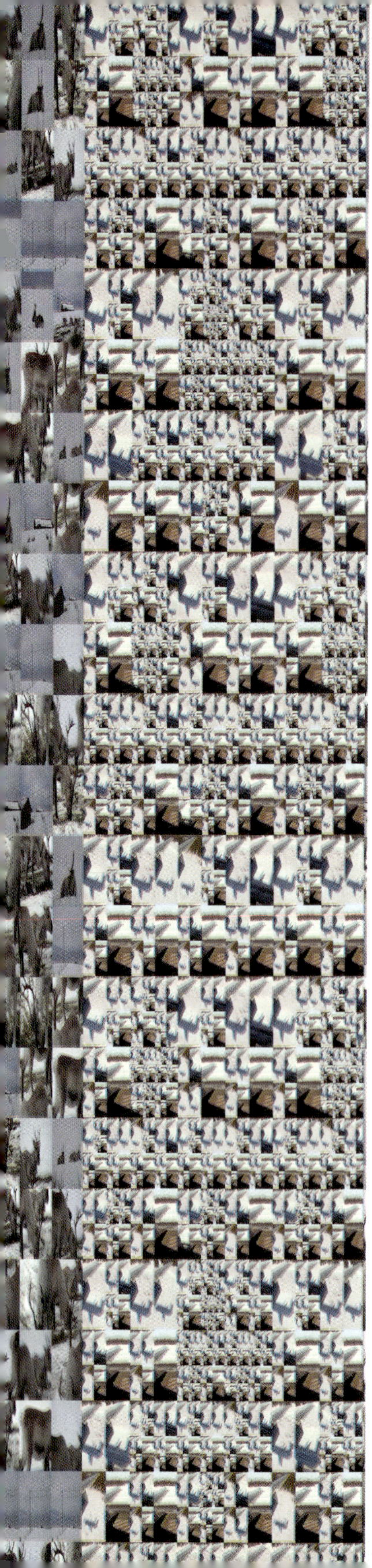

ality supported by philosophers and aestheticians is certainly also an attempt to think sensuality out of the nervous system and to posit it as representable. In reality, all that remains is this cloud of Brecht's. The synchronization of time is something in the nervous system itself, and it is inaccessible to one's personal sense organs. For the senses, on the skin for example, the preeminent experiences are differences of intensity. Even sexuality needs to generate difference through motion.

Lost times really are lost, then? There's no return?

What's left's just the madeleine in the tea, no more. That's regrettable, but it's one of the reasons why we devote so much time to the future.

But surely we can go on wanting exact memories, even though we can't have them?

Yes, of course. We try. Moreover, we continue to be energetically charged with images, which become symbols capable of bearing the weight of time lost. Everything is then concentrated on these images.

Why is it that these rhythms produce happiness?

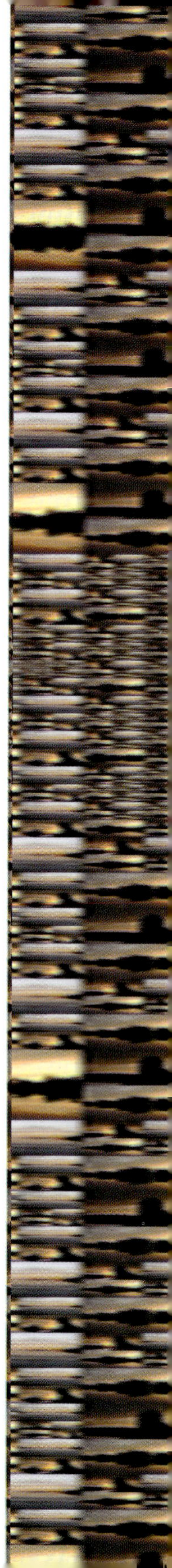

Detlef Linke

That's a difficult question. Freud took the view that we cannot achieve happiness if we are charged up with too much energy. Happiness is a matter of having as little energy as possible in the system. The energetic charge leads to hysteria. In his model, sexuality is a sort of energy disposal service. What Freud's model actually amounts to is that we have to strive for a state in which there is little energy in the nervous system, so that everything reacts exactly as required. Physiologically, however, the system is such that it requires a reserve of energy in order to act at all. The problem, then, is that these reserves constitute an energetic charge, so that action becomes problematic all over again. If there is too much reserve energy with no possibility of relief through activity, it must somehow be disposed of or deployed in other places, which leads to hysteria and so on. In fact, however, energy is never just completely disposed of. In physical actions energy is consumed by muscles, which receive the energy from the circulation of the blood, but there's almost nothing coming from the brain. The brain enters another state, but you can't simply describe that as energy disposal. But the Freudian model was one of the attempts to explain why we are happy, with sexuality as a key example. However, if we look at the matter informationally and on the basis of the codification – and this approach was not yet available to Freud – then I think one must think more in terms of the establishment of an order. And this leads us to the strange idea of sex as something concerned with order. People normally think of sex in terms of chaos, but

Mari Soppela

Heimola

herds of reindeer in the north are rounded up in a corral, or "heimola," as the Laplanders call it. Here, the ones that will be slaughtered are selected. The reindeer know this: for them the heimola is the place of death. To us westerners, Soppela's installation is that place. By killing the reindeer, we become aware of what awaits us when our film becomes a photograph, our photograph a film. Human consciousness is being aware of our own mortality, of the mortality of everything on this earth. Including the most beautiful thing of all: reindeer in the snow.

synchronization would be something that can reestablish a certain order of difference which could be used for information processing. When one achieves synchronization with someone, one is bonded with that person at a very deep level, and one can share the structure of time with him or her. In this sense of time structure, one can say that the two truly become one flesh. This is actually a dimension of which we hardly ever catch a glimpse in the course of our normal information processing. But I regard this dimension of the temporal structure as the basis of the sexual act, which is thus a means whereby temporal differences are reestablished after synchronization and which enables me to process items of information from which I can shape my world physically.

Another way might be through violence. The energy model fits in with the idea that youth always has too much energy and will look for ways of expending it.

That would be the worst scenario. One might also ask oneself this: we have so much information, how are we supposed to unify it? There are, after all, certain traditions which are bent upon bringing everything together into a unity, on the grounds that we would otherwise become enslaved to heterogeneity. The attempt to establish unity is paradoxical, however, in that it creates an image of unity, whereas life itself might have a quite different structure. Philosophical treatments of this topic do not lead to the establishment of unity, but rather to the articulation of a self-image that one could call a Doppelgänger. I just need to imagine myself as a unity and I can think I am master of the entire situation, but this is just a construction – it has nothing to do with reality. It's a false solution. But it is clear that we will continue to try to cope with heterogeneity and multiplicity, simply for the sake of our nerves. This can mean, maybe, that one says: I'll just stick to multiplicity and see if it works. Variety is increasing all the time and has become virtually the dominant characteristic of a world devoted to the ceaseless production of novelty, and this could lead to an overtaxation of the nervous system. Paradoxically, however, this overtaxation is actually sought. The bombardment of the nervous system with too many impulses is perhaps even pleasant, for it stimulates me to look for a rhythm. The pursuit of highly rhythmical music could well be connected to this, and if I have been nicely massaged with rhythms, in a boutique perhaps, I may be more disposed to buy something – to allow myself to a little heterogeneity.

But it is said that with music such as hip hop, there's so much information on offer at once that it is like an exercise in dealing with huge amounts of information at a physical level, of which one can longer be conscious.

When you're dancing, you're not shopping.

I'd like to return for a moment to the first rhythms that we learn, to our time as a fetus in the womb. The fetus adapts itself to its mother's pulse in developing its brain activities or consciousness.

This is an interesting phase during which we are absorbing external rhythms, primarily the pulsations of our mother's aorta, but even after birth we may have preferences for music heard by our mother during the time she was carrying us. Naturally, however, it is the aorta that is the most obvious source of rhythm, as the child is lying with its ear practically right up against it. This is an interesting phase, because here the subject-object model of perception has still to develop. At this stage the nervous system lacks rhythm, for it must first develop its time, but there are already certain notchings in this growth which in other respects may be

regarded as continuous. Next there comes a phase in which something can actually be perceived, but the fetus is not yet properly able to situate its perceptions in relation to each other. There's a highly interesting dynamic process here affecting perception itself, including the perception of rhythms. This is an extremely exciting area of study which has not yet properly been explored. An increase in functions has been observed in this phase, but at the same time there is also a loss of neurons. You find the same thing in the development of the child in its fourth year, when neurons are again lost. Development is not continuous in the sense that the neurons simply go on increasing until a point is reached at which only the neuronal axes and synapses increase. In the fourth year of life certain connections are discontinued and certain neurons die. This has to do with the fact that the structure of the nervous system is altered by the growth of perception, and with it the structure of cognition. The speech faculty improves dramatically as well during this phase. Our exploration of the neurobiology of the young human being is in a certain sense still only beginning, but it could become important for educational theory, which should be able to find points of contact with the cognitive level and with neurological development. The phase at which neurons are being lost, and when certain structures are taking shape in the nervous system, is precisely the phase within the family structure during which the law of the father can be imposed upon the child. The unpleasant aspect of having to reorient oneself to society has entered the myth of Oedipus, which is perhaps the symbolic representation of a deeper neuronal event: castration at a deep neuronal level. Not everything Freud tells us is wrong, but it refers to only one cultural situation in which the overlapping of particular family structures conceals the neuronal process of civilization. This opens up a very interesting dimension: the process of self-orientation in society ought to be described quite differently, because the nervous system itself is interested in acquiring a structure. This is what makes it what it is. It creates for itself a legitimate guarantee of order, otherwise the chaos becomes too great. We cannot survive without a law or a

structure. Today there's a tendency to say – in theories of self-organization for example – that things just organize themselves automatically. But it is wrong to say that the law is something alien, something notched onto the nervous system from outside. If we know that this notching process is something actually in ourselves, we may perhaps understand more readily what our nervous systems need to enable us to orient ourselves satisfactorily in society. The neurobiology of human development is in need of a few minima moralia.

Detlef B. Linke is a neurologist at the University Hospital of Bonn and teaches clinical neurophysiology and neurosurgical rehabilitation at the University of Bonn. In his research he focuses on the correlation between brain functions, perception and notions of reality. His work poses important questions about the origin and distortion of self images. Linke has published texts on ethics, coma, brain death, personality and brain chips, including: ***In Würde Altern und Sterben*** (growing old and dying dignified, 1991); ***Das Gehirn*** (The Brain, 2000); ***Einsteins Doppelgänger, Das Gehirn und sein Ich*** (2000).

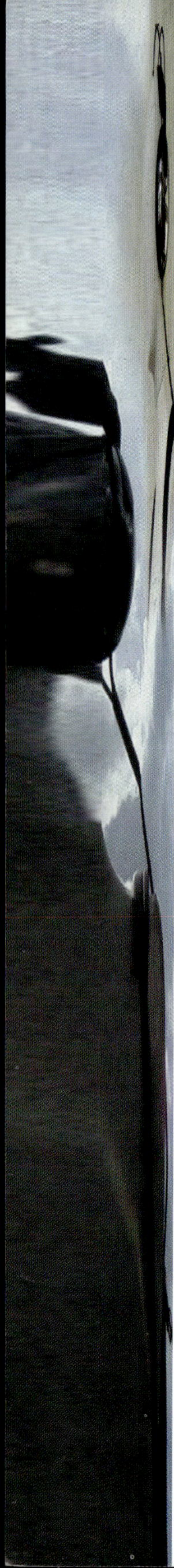

An interview with Mark C. Taylor

by Arjen Mulder

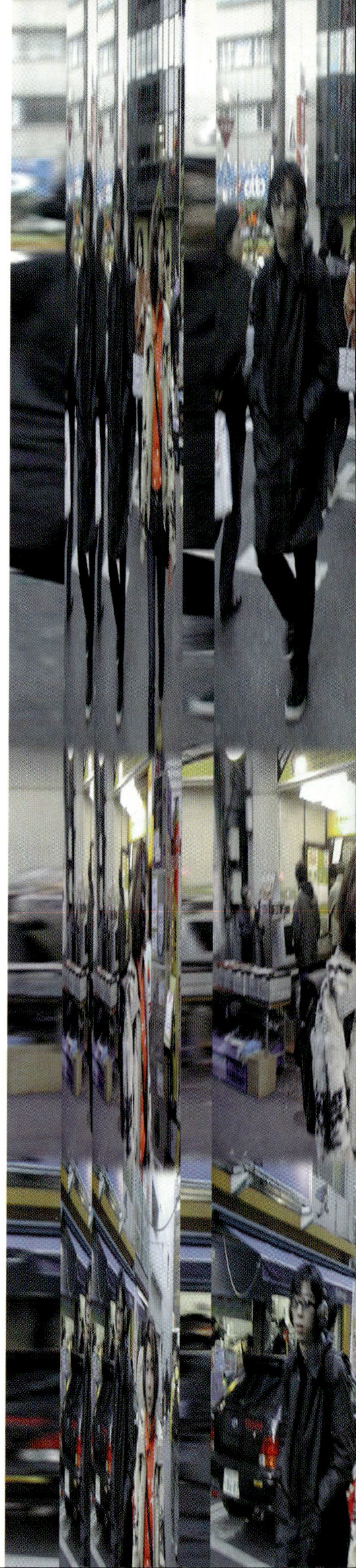

WE ARE THE INCARNATION OF COMPLEX WORLDWIDE WEBS

In your essay The Betrayal of the Body, *you reject the traditional idea that health is the primary condition of the body, and disease a secondary condition that befalls the body as if from outside – a fall from grace, with medicine as the savior that redeems us from this fall. Instead you describe how the autoimmune system is in fact always attacking its own body which it is supposed to protect against "alien intruders," and how health is basically the suppression of this autoimmune response. The developing fetus in the womb is attacked by the immune system of the mother, which considers the fetus as a foreign body. This is what you call the betrayal of the body. But why blame the body? Why not blame the philosophical, cultural, religious, social tradition that denied the body its right to disease?*

It is not a question of blame – be it of the body or of philosophy. In the essay to which you refer, I use the word "betrayal" in two senses. In English, betray most often means

to be disloyal, but it can also mean to reveal or to show – as when I betray a secret. So the betrayal of the body can be understood as both the body's disloyalty, as it were, and as the body's disclosure. What does disease reveal about the body? The point of departure for these reflections was my own wrestling with disease. When disease strikes – and it will strike – it is virtually impossible not to feel a sense of betrayal. We seem to take it for granted that our "original" condition is one of health and, thus, disease is an aberration – even a failure. As I pondered this experience, the issues deepened.

Two points are relevant in this context. The disease I was considering – diabetes – is an autoimmune disease. As I studied the biochemistry of this disease, it became clear that the body is an information system and the disease is a function of something like interference in this system. This interference disrupts the system and makes transparent communication impossible. But the model of transparent communication and systems that are in equilibrium is problematic. If one studies information theory and biological systems, it becomes clear that no system can function without interference. Moreover, equilibrium models are abstractions that do not reflect life. Living systems are complex and always operate far from equilibrium. This line of analysis suggests the necessity of recasting the health/disease binary.

When you describe the body as an information system, you use a metaphor that was elaborated by

the cyberneticists in the 1940s and 1950s. It is not a philosophical metaphor or model but a military one developed during World War II and only later described in terms of mathematics and physics. Descriptions of the immune system are also always full of militaristic metaphors, as you note in your essay. This is just one example of the fact that when we talk about the health/disease binary today, we are outside of the realm of philosophy and religion and in the domain of hard science: physics, tactics, mathematics, optics, medicine ... Did your diabetes push you out of the philosophical and theological domain into the scientific worldview?

Mark C. Taylor

Let me begin by responding to your last point, in which you indicate that

Akitsugu Maebayashi

Sonic Interface

Our experience of reality is strongly dependent on the synchronicity of our senses. We must, for instance, hear or touch what we see while we see it in order to be able to determine reality and in order to decide what to do or how to react. The decoupling in time of sight and sound – as when we first see the lightning and then hear the thunder – can create a disturbing irritation when it affects our immediate surroundings: imagine that you only heard the cars passing you on the street after they had already passed, or that you could hear conversations which had been held minutes before in a different location from where you were.

Sonic Interface experiments with human perception by amplifying and manipulating the synchronicity of the auditory environment. Equipped with a portable hearing device made from a computer and headphones, the user is invited to walk around the city's public spaces, such as squares, shopping malls and underground stations. The random urban sounds the user hears are first transmitted to the headphones without modification, but then the computer program begins to create an artificial sonic environment from the sounds it picks up.

Three different types of software feed the headphones with digitally manipulated sounds. In one instance, the ambient sounds are delayed to different degrees, decoupling visual and auditory perception of the surrounding space. Then the sounds are cut up and recomposed into a mosaic in a new chronological order. Finally, the sounds are made to repeat themselves and overlap with each other. In each case,

today when we talk about health/disease we are outside the realm of philosophy and religion and in the domain of hard science. This is another binary opposition that needs to be undone. The metaphors of hard/soft are, of course, highly charged. I think science is softer than it often appears. Furthermore, I believe it is impossible to escape philosophy and religion. There are philosophical and religious dimensions to contemporary science. Needless to say, these are often overlooked, but they can be teased out if one knows intellectual and cultural history.

The diagnosis of diabetes came totally out of the blue. I had always been very healthy, and there was no history of the disease in my family. Wrestling with a chronic disease forces one to confront the fragility of life in a very concrete way. One of the most difficult things about diabetes is its relentlessness: it never takes a holiday. Indeed, one must deal with it hour by hour, day in and day out. As I attempted to come to terms with the disease, I tried to learn as much about it as possible. The more I discovered about the biochemistry of the disease, the more intrigued I became. As you suggest, diabetes is an autoimmune disease that is the result of a breakdown in the body's communication system. The body, in effect, misreads itself as other and proceeds to destroy a part of itself, thereby making it impossible to maintain the proper balance in glucose metabolism. Again, as you note, much of the rhetoric of the disease is militaristic – agents and counteragents, etc. This is partly the result of the early formulations of information theory. As is well known, in their early versions, infor-

the sonic ambience and the space in which the sounds were formed in the past are being remixed in the present.

According to Jacques Lacan, the defenseless ear is the "only orifice which the field of consciousness cannot shut off." As an organ closely related to the brain, it not only perceives ambient sounds but also influences the spatiotemporal perceptions which control our sense of equilibrium. It is obvious that the interposition of technology with such a vital organ will permit an expansion of senses, but might also trigger an sense of destabilization and confusion. As Friedrich Kittler has noted, "In our times, when it is technically possible to explode the ear, the story of the ear more and more becomes a story of madness."

(Yukiko Shikata, exh. cat. Montreal 1999).

Akitsugu Maebayashi

Sonic Interface

mation theory and cybernetics were developed for wartime communications technologies and servomechanisms that could be used for military purposes.
However, this was not what impressed me.

Throughout the 1980s and early 1990s, I was deeply immersed in deconstruction. It seemed clear to me that diabetes is, in a certain sense, the embodiment of deconstruction. Again, the body becomes the other of itself and thus cannot establish harmony, balance, or equilibrium. For this reason, alterity is not outward but is "within" as an exteriority that cannot be inwardized. In recent years, I have continued to explore information theory and have expanded my understanding of the implications of diabetes. In so doing, I've moved beyond the perspective of people like Shannon and Wiener and have drawn on recent complexity theory and theoretical biology. Part of this analysis involves the development of a notion of distributed information.

Information is not merely what is in the computer and transmitted over various networks; it is distributed through all biological, chemical, and physical processes. The body is, in effect, an information-processing machine. From this point of view, disease is something like noise. But noise is not merely the opposite of information; rather it is the condition of the possibility of information. Furthermore, noise in one context or at one level is information in another context or at another level. Noise, if you will, is always information. There can no more be life without disease than there can be information without noise. The human dilemma, therefore, is not to find a

cure (there is none) but to learn to live with the impossibility of a cure.

WE ARE THE INCARNATION OF COMPLEX WORLDWIDE WEBS

But from Descartes and Newton onwards the project of science was to get rid of the metaphysical aspects of knowledge by reducing every phenomenon to the material level, et cetera. But modern sciences, like cybernetics, complexity theory and theoretical biology, seem for you to have, yet again, philosophical and religious dimensions.

It is far too simple to suggest that from Descartes to Newton and onward the project of science is to get rid of metaphysics. Few people realize that Newton wrote more theological treatises than scientific treatises. Even when he turns to science he does not leave theology behind. Newton's world is the clockwork world of the deists. God is the transcendent creator who establishes the laws by which the world operates and then withdraws to let it run. In addition to this, Newton's vision is guided by a model of equilibrium systems in which time is linear and causes are proportional to effects. One of the most important points in this cosmology is that order is imposed from without.

Let us contrast this model to the current analysis of complex adaptive systems. Complex Adaptive Systems (CASs) operate far from equilibrium. Moreover, they are nonlinear and have effects disproportionate to their causes. Unlike classical systems, which tend to be closed, CASs are open. Rather than imposed from without or programmed at the beginning, order in complex adaptive systems is emergent. Such systems can be biological, chemical, political, economic, and neural.

While it is not difficult to detect theological traces in Newton's classical system, CASs might appear to be antitheological. Once again, this point of view is too simple. It is possible to follow a certain trajectory from classical to complex systems. The gods don't simply disappear, they gradually go underground. The source of order descends, as it

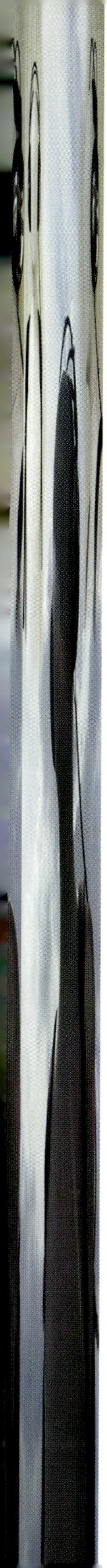

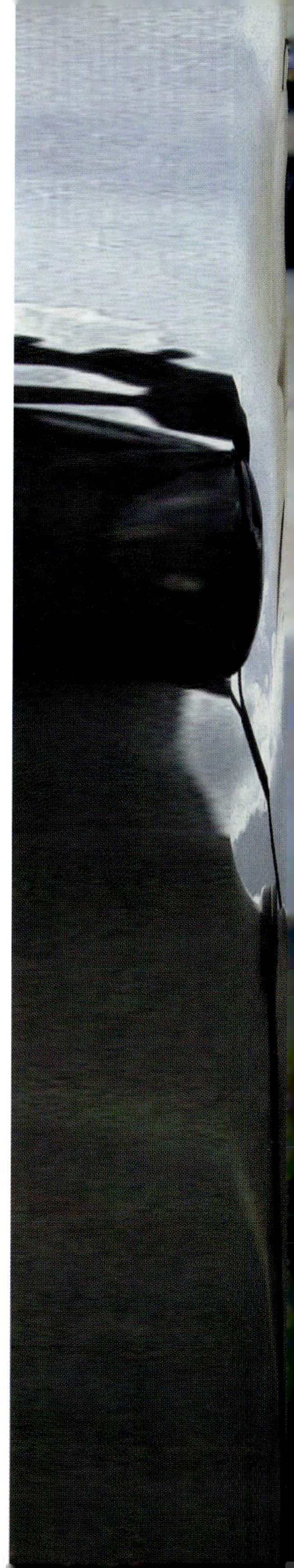

were, from transcendent Platonic forms to the mind of God, which is reflected in the human mind as the structures of consciousness and self-consciousness (e.g. Kant's categories of understanding), and then go underground as the infrastructures that are the foundation of reality (e.g. Marx's economic infrastructures, Freud's instincts, Jung's archetypes, Levi-Strauss's structures, Chomsky's generative grammar, Dawkin's genotype, etc.). Such infrastructures are, of course, merely the inversion of theological suprastructures. Part of what postmodern criticism shows is that the infrastructures are of the same order as the suprastructures; neither is the foundation of the other.

This does not mean that there is no order but that order is neither foundational nor prescribed. Parts create the whole, which, in turn, creates the parts. This process has an order, which is emergent and, thus, aleatory. The structure of this complex whole approximates the structure of Hegelian Geist. For Hegel, of course, Geist or spirit is both objective (i.e. the structure of nature) and subjective (i.e. the structure of history and subjectivity). This structure is articulated in his Science of Logic, which he understands as the mind of God. Nature and history then, are the embodiment or incarnation of the logos. If Hegel's argument is rethought through the theory of complex adaptive systems, it becomes possible to understand objective spirit as distributed information and subjective spirit as information processing necessary for consciousness and self-consciousness. The logos becomes the complex networks of relations in and through which we are created and sustained. We are, in other words, the incarnation of complex worldwide webs.

If there is no foundational or prescribed order, then disease of course is not a disturbance of some natural order but a different kind of order, as necessary to life as noise is to information. This sounds reassuring enough. But where do panic, guilt, despair fit into these philosophical schemes? The idea that we are not an island but a worldwide web seems to deny the legitimacy of such highly personal emotional reac-

tions to the realization that disease has finally hit you.

You raise two important questions. First, you correctly stress that disease is as necessary to life as noise is to information. This implies that disease is not the disturbance of a natural order or a disruption of some kind of a balance. Everything is, I think, always out of balance. Perfect balance would be death rather than life. I would like to distinguish the emotions of panic and despair from guilt for a moment. Panic and despair are perfectly understandable responses to the actuality of disease. To be in despair is to be without hope. Such hopelessness is unavoidable when dealing with a chronic disease. But the acceptance of hopelessness can be liberating. As I have noted above, the recognition that there is no cure harbors an unexpected freedom. In contrast to despair, which comes with the recognition of hopelessness, panic is experience when disease is suspected but not confirmed. Panic is what we experience when we are waiting for the phone to ring with the test results we already know without knowing.

Guilt is a different matter altogether – and this is a very important issue. To experience disease as guilt is to experience it as one's own fault. The assumption is that our so-called natural condition is health and disease is a result of what we do or don't do – smoke, drink too much, don't eat right, too much stress, not enough exercise, etc. Often people who are trying to be helpful insist that if only you change your lifestyle, your condition will improve.

But nothing will make my pancreas produce insulin. And as long as I do not accept that condition, I must live with the tyranny of hope.

The second question you raise concerns the status of the subject in worldwide webs. A point of clarification: I did not say that we are "islands" in these webs, but nodes. "Node" derives from a word suggesting knots. A node is constituted by the intersection of various forces and vectors. To be is to be related. Relations to others are constitutive of the individual identity of everyone. Thus, inscription within worldwide webs does not erase or repress the personal and the individual but constitutes it. This way of understanding our condition reverses the common understanding of subjectivity as individual and relation as secondary. There are not subjects without relations and no relations without subjects. Neither comes first or second because you cannot have one without the other.

There is a creative side to disease as well. This ranges from the shamans of old, who all had to go through a dangerous period of disease before they could become real healers, to the TB-suffering artists of the nineteenth and early twentieth century, up till now. It is as if the disease pulls the individual out of normality, out of the comfortable social context, and places him/her in the spiritual realm where art or wisdom or healing, et cetera, become possible. It is as if the disease is an individualizing power that drops the individual out

of his/her social, cultural network, into a solitude that makes life, or the world, extremely real – so real that one has to go and create works of art, et cetera. I tend to think that disease is a counterforce to the node of the worldwide webs that every person is, as you put it.

Mark C. Taylor

I agree that there is a creative dimension to disease. Furthermore, I think you are right when you suggest that disease resituates one in relation to normal routines and familiar patterns. If there is a spiritual dimension to this process, it is the result of marginalization, which is not quite the same as individualization or even solitude. Relationships are always dialectical; thus, distinction or difference from is also relation to something. The condition of marginality is always relational. The margin, in fact, is nothing other than the play of differences. Since individuality, as I have suggested, is

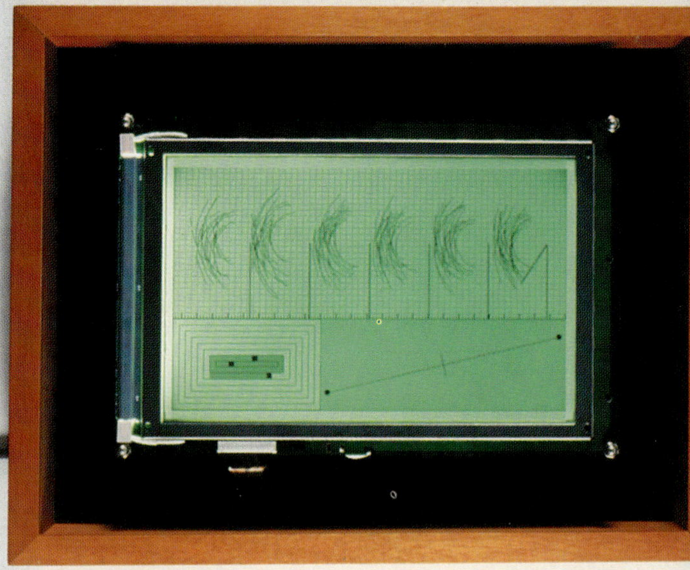

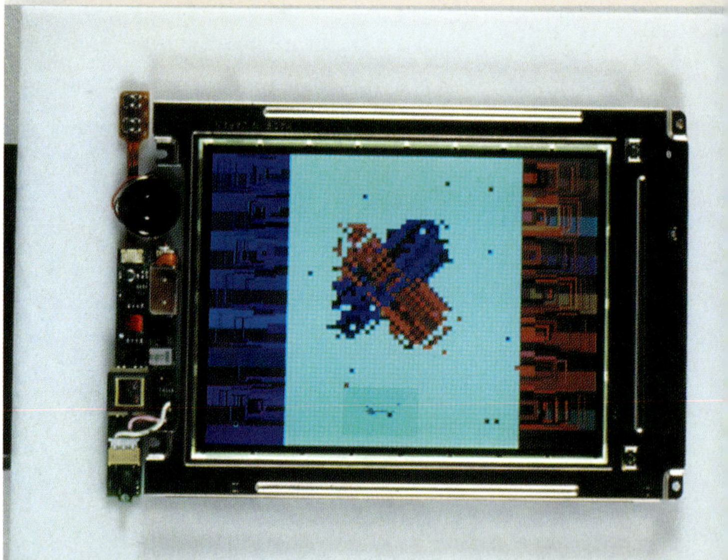

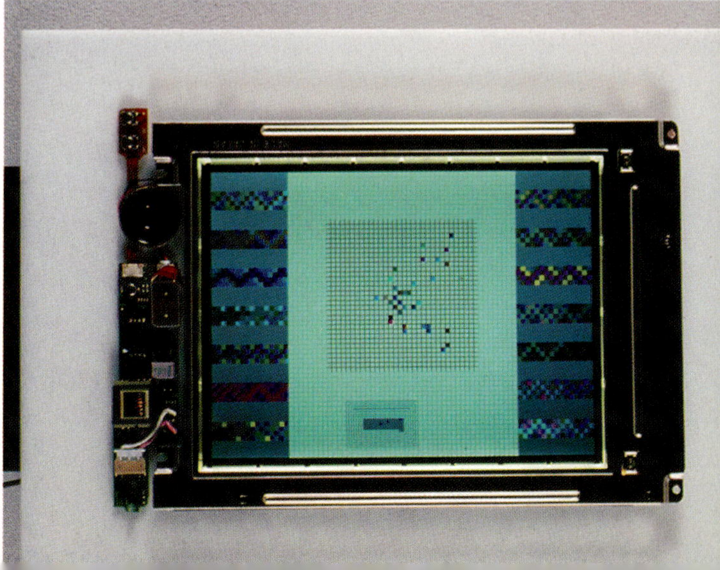

John F. Simon Jr.

Every Icon

Given: A 32 x 32 grid

Allowed: Any element of the grid to be black or white

Shown: Every Icon

Can a machine produce every possible image? What are the limits of this kind of automation? Is it possible to practice image-making by exploring all of image-space using a computer rather than by recording from the world around us? What does it mean that one may discover visual imagery so detached from "nature"?

Every Icon progresses by counting. Starting with an image where every grid element is white, the software displays combinations of black and white elements, proceeding toward an image where every element is black. In contrast to presenting a single image as an intentional sign, *Every Icon* presents all possibilities.

The grid contains all possible images. Any change in the starting conditions, such as the size of the grid or the color of the element, determines an entirely different set of possible images. When *Every Icon* begins, the image changes rapidly. Yet the progression of the elements across the grid seems to take longer and longer. How long until recognizable images appear? Try several hundred trillion years. The total number of black and white icons in a 32 x 32 grid is:

1.8 x 10308 (a billion is 109).

Though, for example, at a rate of 100 icons per second (on a typical desktop computer), it will take only 1.36 years to display all variations of the first line of the grid, the second line takes an expo-

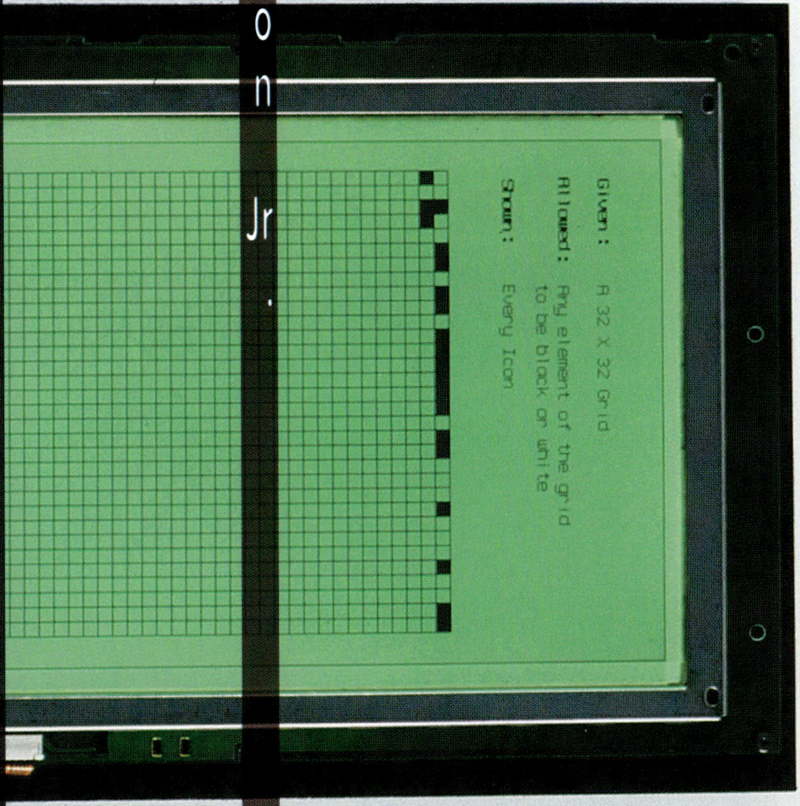

constituted by intersecting sectors or forces, nodular subjectivity is inescapably marginal. The relationships constituting, deconstituting and reconstituting the subject are always in flux. As one moves from the ordinary and familiar routines of life to the margin, the familiar becomes strange. This does not mean that one is driven into solitude. Rather, one becomes involved and entangled in other communities and relations. There is a community of the diseased, which is in some sense a community of outcasts. One of the strategies by which those who believe themselves healthy deal with those who are sick is by marginalizing them. But the outcast does not disappear; to the contrary, the outcast haunts the community from which it is excluded as disease inhabits the body.

I wasn't thinking about strategies of marginalizing when I mentioned the individualizing power of disease. I remember a quote from one of my favorite authors, Denton Welch, who describes in his masterpiece A Voice Through a Cloud *(1950) how he has a bicycle accident and ends up in a hospital with the agony of a broken spine (that would eventually kill him). In his first night in the hospital he has a vision: "In the middle of the furnace inside me there was a clear thought like a text in cross-stitch. I wanted to warn the nurses, to tell them that nothing was real but torture. Nobody seemed to realize that this was the only thing on earth. People didn't know that it was wait-*

Mark C. Taylor

ing for them quietly, patiently." This horrible accident and insight made Welch into a great writer instead of the not-so-good painter he was until then. His view is, to me, the absolute opposite of the technological optimism and conformism of today, which seems to be more in line with your way of thinking. How would you respond to Welch's challenge?

I completely reject the claim that what I'm talking about is technological conformism or optimism. Technological pragmatism, yes, but not conformism or optimism. I also reject the claim that something like torture or disease are real in any kind of a foundational way. You cite Welch as asserting: "Nothing is real but torture." I would counter: "Nothing is real" (in all senses of that phrase). The way in which you take Welch's assertion seems to me to suggest a form of nostalgia for the real that is no longer possible. As with disease, the problem is not to find or recover the real but to learn to live with its absence.

I would, of course, agree that there is a great deal of technological optimism and conformism around today. What I'm talking about is the way in which emerging technologies can be deployed for novel creative processes. My primary concern is how to use these technologies for new forms of pedagogy. Am I optimistic? Not necessarily – as is evident from every page I have ever written. Am I hopeful? In this case, yes – but hope is in no way the same as optimism. I would argue that the tendency of so many educators, artists, and critics to reject the

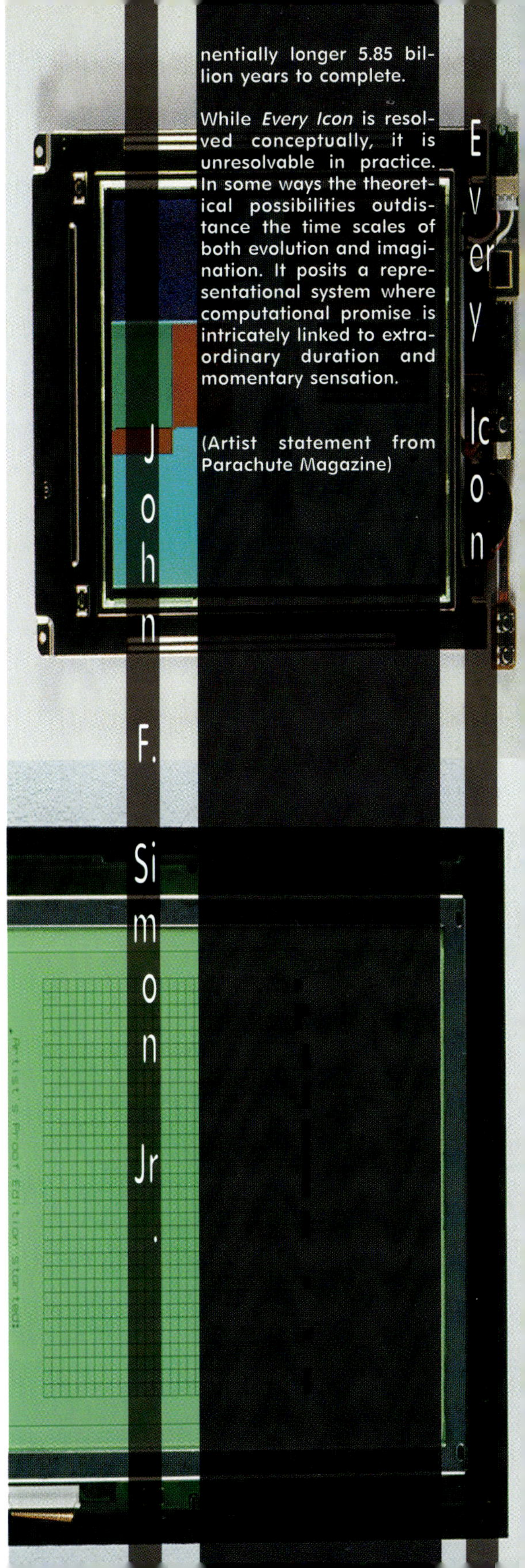

John F. Simon Jr.

Every Icon

nentially longer 5.85 billion years to complete.

While *Every Icon* is resolved conceptually, it is unresolvable in practice. In some ways the theoretical possibilities outdistance the time scales of both evolution and imagination. It posits a representational system where computational promise is intricately linked to extraordinary duration and momentary sensation.

(Artist statement from Parachute Magazine)

creative possibilities of these technologies is the worst form of defeatism and is, in the final analysis, socially irresponsible.

What I mean by technological optimism is that nowadays all problems – human, economical, ecological et cetera – are considered to be technical problems, and in that sense they're all solvable with technological means. And if it can't be done now, it will be done in the (near) future. But what I miss in this technological approach to the future is the tragic notion that whatever problems we can solve, each one of us will die eventually. That's how I understand the quote by Denton Welch. I don't think I'm nostalgic about death as the final truth or reality. I prefer to live.

When understood in this way, I am in substantial agreement with you. Every day we read in the paper the promise of curing new diseases, finding the gene for a particular problem that will enable us to solve it, etc., etc., etc. Nor are such claims limited to journalism. Serious thinkers like Ray Kurzweil and Hans Moravec make outlandish claims for technology by suggesting that in the near future we will be able to download consciousness and create "brains in a vat." This represents what I call "cybergnosticism" and revives ancient dreams of escaping the body. But the body cannot be escaped. Though the body is an information-processing system, information is always incarnate. While it is undeniable that technology sometimes leads to progress in treating disease – and here diabetes is exemplary – a complete cure is never possible. I am not sure I would describe this impossibility of cure as "tragic." That suggests that it should be otherwise. Rather, disease and death are part of the human condition and must be embraced as such.

How did your own disease change your ideas about the future, about the depth of time, the end of time?

Temporality, I believe, is inseparable from contingency. One of the most profound aspects of my own experience of disease was the encounter with the completely unexpected. I had none of the traits that usually go with a disease like diabetes. When I came down with the disease, it was a complete surprise. All too often we think of the future as the outgrowth of the past and the present – and to a certain extent it is. But the future also invades the present as a beyond that can be neither anticipated nor controlled. This is what disease teaches. Now it is, of course, possible to argue that even this future grows out of the past because disease must be written in the genes and therefore must have been programmed. But I do not believe in simple genetic determinism. Rather, I think the biological organism and the environment interact in unpredictable ways. And this unpredictability is what time is all about.

(August 1-10, 2000)

Mark C. Taylor is Cluett Professor of Humanities at Williams College and the founder of the Global Education Network. His books include ***Nots*** (1993), ***Imagologies: Media Philosophy*** (with Esa Saarinen, 1994), ***Hiding*** (1996), ***About Religion: Economies of Faith in Virtual Culture*** (1999), ***The Picture in Question: Mark Tansey and the Ends of Representation*** (1999), and ***The Moment of Complexity: Emerging Network Culture*** (2000).

REGENERATIVE MEDICINE: WE CAN REGROW IT FOR YOU WHOLESALE

Eugene Thacker

REGENERATIVE MEDICINE:
WE CAN REGROW IT FOR YOU WHOLESALE

"Ten millennia ago the development of agriculture freed humanity from a reliance on whatever sustenance nature was kind enough to provide. The development of tissue engineering should provide an analogous freedom from the limitations of the human body." Drs. David Mooney and Antonios Mikos

" ... Perhaps the entire evolution of the spirit is a question of the body; it is the history of development of a higher body ... The organic is rising to yet higher levels. Our lust for knowledge of nature is a means through which the body desires to perfect itself." Friedrich Nietzsche

Biologies Without Technologies

The recent science-fiction film *The X-Men* provides us with two examples of "regenerative medicine." The first is the character of Wolverine, who, aside from having surgically-grafted, extractable metal blades, also has the ability to rapidly recover from any injury through tissue regeneration. As the *X-Men* mythos goes, Wolverine is thought to be the product of military experimentation on humans using biotechnologies to craft the perfect human fighting machine, with an anatomical structure fortified by a near-indestructible

metal and an internal biology designed to efficiently regenerate and repair itself in response to injury. Wolverine bears the signs of both industrial technology (his cyborg-like metallic claws) as well as contemporary biotechnology (the flesh wounds that we see healing right before our eyes).

In contrast to the militaristic robustness of Wolverine, there is also the character of Mystique, who is defined by a single ability: molecular bio-morphing. Though the computer graphics artists working on the *X-Men* film did, of course, use graphical morphing software for Mystique, within the narrative of the film Mystique actually morphs her body at the cellular level. We usually think of morphing as two-dimensional, image-based process in which an animation is created by extrapolating between two different images. Mystique does not use morphing as an illusion, but, we might guess, she actually controls her body on the cellular and molecular level. This is the capacity to shape-shift on a biological, three-dimensional level – something which makes the issue of her identity a very slippery matter.

Between these two characters – the fortified, regenerative body of Wolverine and the flexible, bio-morphic body of Mystique – are two slightly different versions of the field known as "regenerative medicine." Put simply, regenerative medicine is a field within biotechnology which harnesses the power of the body's own healing and regenerative properties towards medical or healing ends. Imagine that your entire body could heal itself in the same way that a paper cut on your finger heals by the next day. The basic idea of regenerative medicine is to take a biological process such as cellular regeneration and technically redirect that process towards a more "natural" approach to healing the body. The incentive for regenerative medicine is both medical and economic. According to a 1993 survey conducted by two leading researchers, over $400 billion is spent in the U.S. alone on

patients suffering from organ failure or tissue loss, amounting to some eight million surgical procedures involving organ or tissue transplantation. But the real problem, aside from numbers, is the shortage of organ donors for such procedures. It is estimated that over 100,000 people die in the U.S. from organ or tissue failures, many while they are on an organ donation waiting list. Regenerative medicine claims to be a response to such medical problems. The term itself has been heavily promoted by William Haseltine, CEO of Human Genome Sciences, and the field combines the practices of gene therapy, tissue engineering, stem cell research, biomaterials, and bioengineering. Already researchers in different labs have shown that many body parts – skin, cartilage, bone, kidneys, heart valves, and bladders – can be grown in the lab, prompting some researchers to envision a future of “off-the-shelf organs.”

The most common procedure thus far – pioneered by Joseph Vacanti and Robert Langer – involves the treatment of a biopsy or cell sample taken from the patient. Take the case of a patient with a diseased kidney. Those cells are then replicated in culture and infused with growth medium to prompt cellular division. The skin cells are then seeded into a lattice structure made of biodegradable polymers that help guide the growing cells, making sure they grow in the proper shape of a

kidney. The whole complex is then surgically placed back into the patient, whose body takes up the new cell/organ structure, allowing vascularization (the growth of a network of blood vessels) to occur. In contrast to other biomedical approaches – whether the use of drugs or the use of mechanical devices – regenerative medicine uses the body's own biological processes of cellular growth, replication and regeneration. This is, of course, aided by an array of techniques, including cell delivery techniques, isolation of cell lines of stem cells, development of biochemical growth factors for cells, and the construction of biodegradable lattice structures for the seeding of cells.

Biotech companies such as Geron, Advanced Tissue Sciences and Genzyme Tissue Repair have been specializing in areas of regenerative medicine, hoping to land key patents and develop key services or techniques that will transform medical approaches to healing the body. In 1998, the U.S. FDA (Food and Drug Administration) granted approval for a tissue-engineered, bioartificial skin product called *Apligraf* made by Organogenesis. Around the same time, Joseph Vacanti's lab at the University of Massachusetts shocked the public by growing a tissue-engineered human ear on the back of a mouse. And in February 2000, three biotech companies merged to form Curis, in one of the first col-

Panoramic Acceleration

Marnix de Nijs

Panoramic Acceleration is an interactive experience machine which works with extreme rotational movement upon the physical body and visual perception.

The visitor sits in a racing seat on a motorized rotating arm and looks at a video projection on a screen which turns with him. The seat is fixed above the axis of the rotating arm, always pointing the view to the screen which circles around the axis.

Two identical video loops are mixed and projected onto the screen. The speed of one of these loops is determined in advance, while the speed of the other is controlled by a joystick in the hands of the viewer. The viewer-driver's attempt to gain control over the situation and to see a stable image requires him to synchronize the speed of his own rotation with the speed of the first video loop, determined by the machine. A sensation of relative visual stasis arises only when the position and the speeds of the two loops coincide.

Panoramic Acceleration radicalizes the relationship between the perceiving body and the image machine. While the normal setup for viewing video images depends on stable and mostly fixed positions of viewer and screen, de Nijs' installation creates an image structure which forces the viewer into an extreme rotational movement – on the verge of nausea. The exaggerated physicality of the setup emphasizes the precarious synchronicity of machine, image and body time.

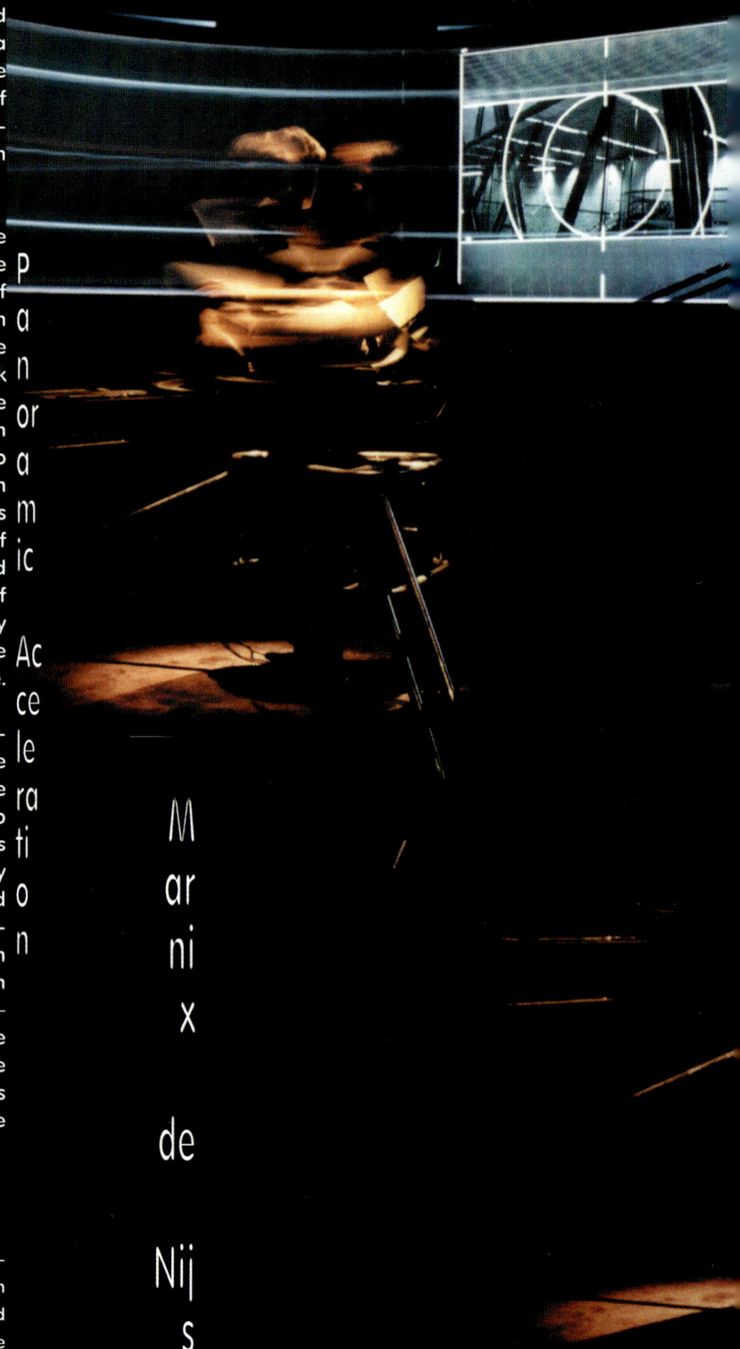

Panoramic Acceleration was produced in cooperation with MonteVideo/TBA (Amsterdam) and presented for the first time at the World Wide Video Festival '99 in Amsterdam. Panoramic Acceleration is based on experiences during the CTL '98 experiments in Linz, Austria.

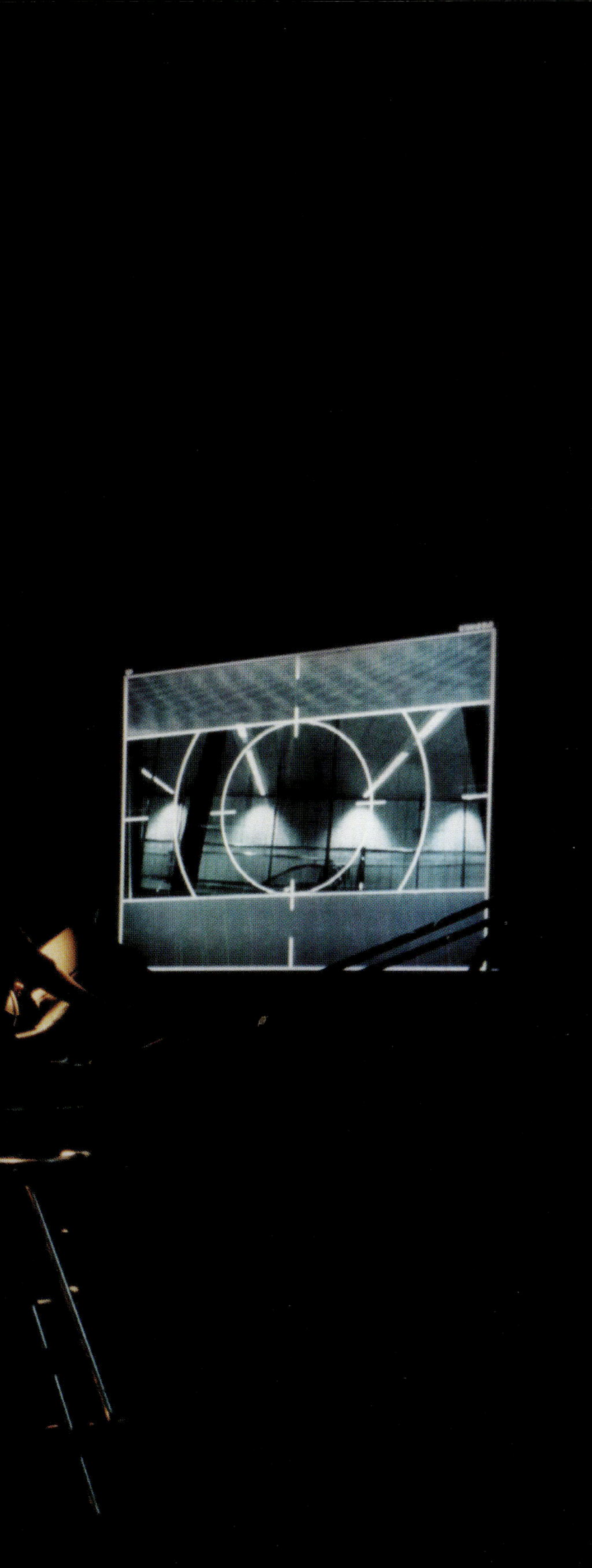

laborative mergers to cover all the major research areas in regenerative medicine.

Regenerative medicine is one of the paradigmatic examples of contemporary biotechnology. This is not the domain of hardware cyborgs, but rather of pure wetware, organs grown on demand, tissues regenerated through tweaked immune systems. Regenerative medicine is unique because it sidesteps the biology-technology, human-machine divide altogether. In doing so it raises some important philosophical and social questions about how our notions of our bodies within medicine and health care will be transformed in the future.

Ready to Wear

In order to understand the kinds of questions regenerative medicine is raising, it will first be helpful to understand the actual techniques

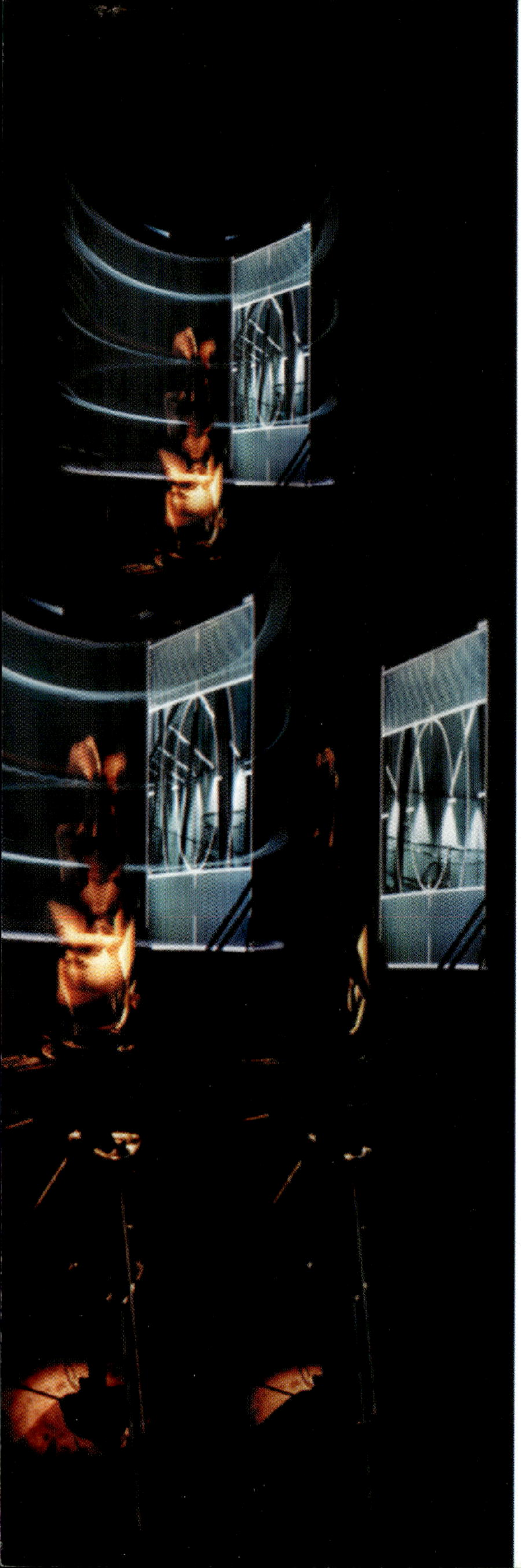

involved in its research and practices. Within each practice, each technique, there is embedded a "technical paradigm" that tells us something about the implicit assumptions between medicine and the body.

A good way to talk about the techniques of regenerative medicine is to differentiate it from current biomedical approaches that similarly address the body's incapacitation through organ and tissue damage. Currently, there are two basic approaches within medical practice to organ and tissue failure. The first involves the use of hardware to take the place of the malfunctioning organ. Bionic devices, artificial organs and prosthetics are examples. The paradigm here is that of displacement. The mechanical organ – be it a pacemaker or a dialysis machine – functions in place of the biological organ, but because such hardware is often not physically amenable to the body's daily functioning, it also often requires a radical change in the physiology and lifestyle of the patient. The drawback of medical hardware approaches is that, by imperfectly miming biology, such devices can require extensive maintenance, even when surgically implanted. Thus their longevity is put into question, as they function mostly as short-term solutions.

A second biomedical approach involves organ and tissue transplantation.

This can be from one human donor to another; it can involve biomaterials donated from tissue banks (blood being the most common example); or it can be an animal-to-human organ transplant (xenotransplantation). Transplantation requires a view of the body as modular – like a set of automobiles with equally interchangeable parts. This is a paradigm of replacement, which takes one kidney to be like another, simply necessitating an exchange. Unfortunately, two major problems have been with transplantation since its beginnings in the 1960s: organ donor shortages and immuno-compatibility. First, demand simply far exceeds supply (despite stories of organ black markets in Singapore). And even when organ donors are available, the problem of immune system rejection can often negate all possibilities except a donor that is a blood relative.

In contrast to these two approaches – that of displacement (medical hardware) and replacement (transplantation) – regenerative medicine takes the patient's body itself as its resource. Though this approach is more sophisticated, it is certainly not without its own set of problems.

Briefly, there are several techniques used by regenerative medicine researchers, and one primary biological resource. That resource is the stem cell, discovered in humans in 1998 by Geron Corporation and named the "discovery of

the year" by Science magazine in 1999. Stem cells are cells that contain the capacity for specialization within the body. They are extremely rare and are found in an undifferentiated state in bone marrow and the brain. At the very first stages of embryonic development just after fertilization, the embryo in its single-cell state can be described as "totipotent": that is, it contains the potential to turn into any type of cell – its potential is total. Just after this, the embryo undergoes a series of cellular divisions, and as it does this, the cells gradually begin to specialize – a process known as cellular differentiation. The cells at this early stage are known as "pluripotent" – their potential is now limited by the range of cells they may turn into. The human body is composed of some 60 trillion cells, and there are 200 different kinds of cells in the body, ranging from bone to muscle to skin to blood cells. Each cell, though it contains the same genetic information as the others, performs a specific set of functions in the body, and each cell type responds differently to the onset of disease or injury. For instance, the cells lining the stomach regenerate on a daily basis in order to handle the effects of acidity during digestion. In a different vein, skin cells regenerate on a weekly cycle in response to the effects of the environment. And finally, the cells of major organs such as the heart have very little regenerative capacity – damage to them will elicit a response of shutting down the organ.

All of this immense regenerative potential of the body has been directed into different types of regenerative medicine techniques. This is a markedly different paradigm from the displacement or replacement of malfunctioning organs mentioned previously. The paradigm of regeneration has to do with a complex balancing act between a technical approach to the body and an emphasis on its natural biological processes. To regenerate something is not to try to

find an adequate substitute, but rather to use the very processes of development to let an organ exist again – a kind of biotechnical reiteration within the body.

Generally speaking, there are three techniques that regenerative medicine research is currently exploring. The first borrows techniques from gene therapy and involves the site-specific transplantation of prepared stem cells into the region in which regeneration is to take place. As with gene therapy, the challenge is effective delivery, and researchers often use a viral vector (a virus whose genetic material has been replaced with the genes that prompt cells in the body to regenerate). The idea here is to prompt the cells to replicate, either through the isolation of the genes or genetic triggers in adult somatic cells, or through the culturing of embryonic stem cells that would then be injected into the patient's body. This approach is both the most promising and the most difficult. Finding the genetic triggers which take a cell down one line of specialization or another is an extremely ambitious task, given that in all probability there are multiple genes and signal pathways involved. However, researchers do know that certain stem cells can be directed along certain developmental paths: hematopoietic stem cells can develop into blood and neural cells; neuronal stem cells can develop into neurons, bone marrow, and blood cells; and mesenchymal stem cells can develop into bone, muscle, cartilage, and tendon cells.

Two other approaches have focused less on stem cells and more on the ways in which organs, tissues, and limbs form during embryonic development. The field of "tissue engineering" is geared towards creating the conditions where biological regeneration can be facilitated with a minimum of technical intervention. Tissue engineering proposes to make use of the body's own cells for the regeneration of tissues and entire organs, with the assistance of biochemical

growth factors, bioreactor technology and biomaterials science. In animal experiments and human clinical trials, tissue engineering researchers have demonstrated that it is possible to grow and re-implant entire organs into the organism. To date, bone and cartilage structures, skin, livers, pancreases, kidneys, bladders, and neural cells have all been grown using this approach. Tissue engineering can take place through two techniques. The most common approach is the in vitro technique, in which a cell sample is taken from a patient, grown in the lab and then surgically implanted into the patient. A second approach is in vivo tissue regeneration, which is both more difficult but also more desirable. Here, instead of growing the organ or tissues outside of the patient in the lab, regeneration is triggered within the patient's own body, using a complex set of biomolecular signals and the necessary biomaterials for structural cohesion. So little is known about the genetic basis of cellular regeneration and differentiation, however, that this remains the least explored avenue of regenerative medicine approaches.

Biotechnical Speed

As we've seen, the approach of regenerative medicine is different from current bio-

medical approaches to tissue and organ failure, in that it uses the body's own cellular processes towards novel ends. The very techniques these approaches use also show us the extent to which this means that the body itself comes to inhabit a unique type of temporality, partially defined by the biological processes of growth, development and decay and partially defined by the technical enhancements of a punctuated, triggered regeneration.

Between what Paul Virilio calls the "metabolic speed" of the body's biological processes (digestion, respiration, growth, excretion, etc.) and the informatic speed of current computer technologies, we might locate a "biotechnical speed" in which biotechnology makes a technology of the biological body itself. In relation to regenerative medicine, this biotechnical speed is certainly geared towards increased efficiency and production, but more than that, it is centrally defined by the way in which the body seeks to optimize itself independent of its context or environment. This means that the body is not just responsive to an array of environmental signals, but is rather contextualized by the punctuated regeneration of technique.

What kinds of bodies might regenerative medicine produce through biotechnical speed? Thinking about the body on a philosophical and political level, we can outline three possibilities, based on current

INCREmental

Eugene Thacker

REGENERATIVE MEDICINE: WE CAN REGROW IT FOR YOU WHOLESALE

research:

Immune System 2.0: While regenerative medicine research has been able to stimulate singular instances of cellular regeneration, its dream is to be able to reprogram the body on the cellu-lar-molecular level to accomplish this on its own. This necessitates thinking of the body's immunity operations as not only offensive (attacking designated molecules) but also defensive (capable of triggering regeneration at diseased, weakened sites). The goal of regenerative medicine research into diseases such as Parkinson's or Alzheimer's is not just the replenishment of neural cells, but the programming of the body's immunity networks to respond to congenital disease by triggering targeted regeneration. If we extend this basic process – not just the replacement of cells, but the design of a biological replacement system in the body – then regenerative medicine would seem to become a kind of directed metastasis.

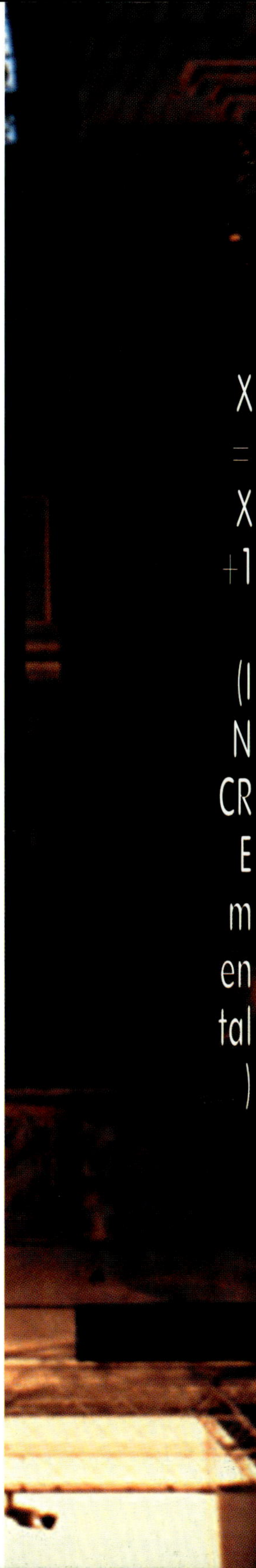

X=X+1 (INCREmental)

X=X+1 (INCREmental) is both an endless film and a computer-based, continuously evolving installation. It shows a screen with a human head that is counting to infinity.

INCREmental is a metaphor for computer art, because the piece could not have been realized in any other medium. At the same time, the installation reflects on the infinite progression of time: "In 1994, I produced my first computer piece, *Landing Place*. With this first work, the possibilities for "endlessness" that the computer possesses and the notion that it can harbor an art piece that transforms itself constantly came to fascinate me. I think about virtual space in the same way I think about real space. I'm interested in the properties, the parameters, the structure and how virtual space influences the viewer's perception. The term "virtual space" is actually nothing new. It has always existed in the arts, in other forms, of course. An example would be the "space" in which a fairy tale takes place: this is a space that we cannot enter because of the physical nature of our bodies, but which we can create and influence, in terms of what happens there, and into which we can look" (Eike in conversation with Zsolt Kozma, April 2000).

INCREmental constructs the passing of time as such a virtual space. The virtual character in the installation counts on and on, without ever stopping, without hesitating and without making a mistake. From one exhibition to the next, the work accumulates the figures that have been counted and vocalizes continuously growing numbers. Using a human head and a

Ei
k
e

Gero-tech: As with all biomedical innovations, the bioethical line between necessity and vanity, between disease and design, is ever-present in regenerative medicine. Biotech companies focusing on cellular aging (in particular, the telomeres, or the protective caps of chromosomes, which get progressively shorter each time a cell divides) are pointing to telomere research as a fountain of youth. If regenerative technologies can be utilized to counteract the telomere-shortening process, then cellular aging would turn into cellular longevity and biological aging would turn into biological immortality. The age-old concept of defeating the aging process and cheating death has found its newest exemplar in the very idea of regeneration. Once cells, tissues, and organs can be grown on demand, outside or inside the body, then the line dividing medical necessity and metaphysical vanity becomes more ambiguous.

Off-the-shelf organs: We should never forget that biotechnology is, first and foremost, an industry. Although medical application provides an impetus for the research, its true test will be whether viable products and services can emerge out of this research. The existence of bioartificial skin products on the market is testimony to this bio-economic drive. For regenerative medicine, this means patenting and marketing techniques used to trigger cellular regeneration for medical purposes. The development of novel, genetically designed drugs aimed to biochemically trigger regeneration or stem cell development is another area of focus. What regenerative medicine shows us is that the body can be approached as a biological storehouse, a cell bank that is constantly being replenished. This is a body that defines itself not according to cycles of growth and decay, but according to biological surplus, encouraging the view of a biological time that is defined by disposability.

Biotechnical speed transforms the biological time of the body into something that is by turns fractionated, disjunctive, and repetitive. As the above examples indicate, biotechnical speed transforms the biological body into a technology, whose product is the constant regeneration of the biological body itself, mediated by the network of biotech products and services. These bodies of biotechnical speed are hyper-responsive (immune system 2.0), biologically immortal (gero-tech), and disposable bio-economies (off-the-shelf organs).

"It satisfies me on a molecular level"

We need to be aware of the fundamental changes biotechnology approaches like regenerative medicine are having on the

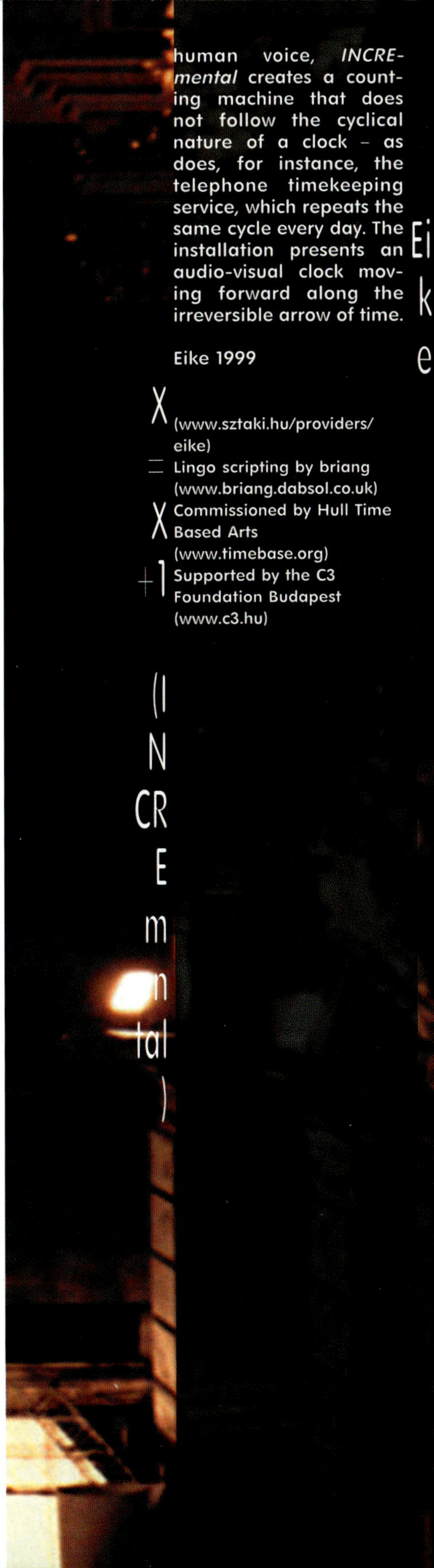

human voice, *INCREmental* creates a counting machine that does not follow the cyclical nature of a clock – as does, for instance, the telephone timekeeping service, which repeats the same cycle every day. The installation presents an audio-visual clock moving forward along the irreversible arrow of time.

Eike 1999

Eike

X = X+1 (INCREmental)

(www.sztaki.hu/providers/eike)
Lingo scripting by briang (www.briang.dabsol.co.uk)
Commissioned by Hull Time Based Arts (www.timebase.org)
Supported by the C3 Foundation Budapest (www.c3.hu)

way we view ourselves as biological organisms living in time. When tissues and organs can be grown on demand, our views of health and disease are bound to be affected. Similarly, when programmed stem cells can be transplanted into our bodies to facilitate tissual recovery, our relationships to our bodies are bound to be altered. There are certainly positive and negative aspects to regenerative medicine, but there are also many confusions present in its approach to the biological body and biotechnical speed.

To begin with, there is in regenerative medicine a general non-distinction between healing and augmentation, recovery and improvement. While we may view research directed towards Parkinson's disease as a positive thing, the research into the cellular origins of aging seems to be both problematic and vain. But suppose that neurodegenerative diseases such as Parkinson's could be effectively treated through regenerative medicine. Wouldn't the next step be the augmentation of neural cells or the immune system itself with the capacity to counteract abnormal cellular degeneration? In such an instance, would the immune system simply be improved, or would it be fundamentally modified? There are virtually no nonorganic materials used, no mechanical prosthetics or surgical implants, no materials that the body doesn't already contain. Where exactly do we locate the technology in fields like regenerative medicine? Technology intersects with biology to such an extent that the body becomes a tool and biological processes become congruent with technological processes.

This leads to a particular kind of technical objectification of the body through the filters of science research and medical practice. Medical science has had a long history of treating the body as a mechanical object, and Western philosophy has given us a Cartesian ontology to go along with it. However, regenerative medicine shows us that you don't

necessarily need metaphors of machines to approach the body as a machine. Instead, through a highly technical practice, regenerative medicine suggests that the body – as fully biological, fully "natural" – can be turned into a technology, a producer of stem cells, a regenerative biological technology and a producer of value for recombinant capital.

The body of regenerative medicine is disposable ("I can always grow it back"), modular (in the interchangeability of off-the-shelf organs) and compartmentalized (in the biotech industry's bio-economy of products), and the body is transformed into a biological database, a wet storehouse of valuable cells, tissues and organs.

Science fiction has always had much to say about such scenarios, allowing us to imagine a combination of fears and anxieties, as well as the potential fissures which may lead in more positive directions. And indeed, we can imagine a dark postgenomic dystopia in which regenerative medicine has a place. Imagine a near-future Bangladesh or Seoul, in which street-level black market dealers, as well as technocratic telemed intelligent agents both participate in a fluctuating bio-economy of resources for regenerative bodies. Regenerative medicine has become a hot topic, not only for medical practice but for real-TV horror shows, S&M clubs, MP3 porn and high fashion. Stem cells are few and far between, and only the best technicians know how to grow sustainable organs or intelligent immune systems. A unique underground community of "Regens" circulates, trained in biomedicine, nanotech and computer programming, using their own bodies to slowly, gradually modify the body into a posthuman form that is based on the principles of flexibility and adaptation ...

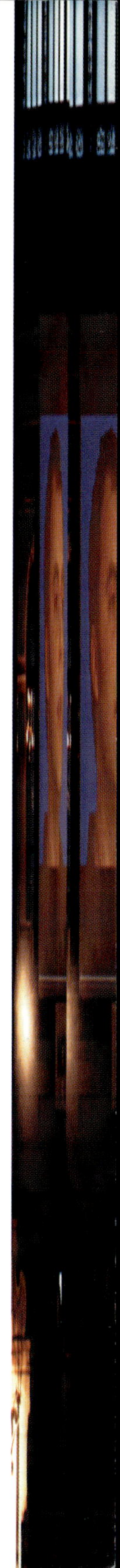

References

Catherine Arnst and John Carey, *Biotech Bodies* (BusinessWeek, July 27, 1998), 56-63.

Lawrence Bonassar and Joseph Vacanti, *Tissue Engineering: The First Decade and Beyond* (Journal of Cellular Biochemistry 30/31, 1998), 297-303.

Stephen Hall, *The Recycled Generation* (New York Times Magazine, 30 January 2000), 28-35.

Andrew Kimbrell, *The Human Body Shop: The Cloning, Engineering and Marketing of Life* (Washington D.C.: Regnery, 1997).

David Mooney and Antonios Mikos, *Growing New Organs* (Scientific American, April 1999), 60-67.

Roger Pedersen, *Embryonic Stem Cells for Medicine* (Scientific American, April 1999), 68-75.

Roy Porter, *The Greatest Benefit to Mankind: A Medical History of Humanity* (New York: W.W. Norton & Company, 1997).

Paul Virilio, *The Art of the Motor* (Minneapolis: University of Minnesota Press, 1995).

Gretchen Vogel, *Harnessing the Power of Stem Cells* (Science 283, 5 March 1999), 1432-34.

Eugene Thacker teaches technology & culture at Rutgers University, where he directs [techne] New Media. Much of his theoretical work has to do with the relationships between the body and technology, especially in contemporary biotech and biomedicine. His work has appeared in Alt-X, Ars Electronica '99: ***Life Science, Body Modification*** (ed. Mike Featherstone, Sage, 2000), CTHEORY, ***Flesh-Eating Technologies*** (ed. Sylvere Lotringer, Semiotext(e), 2001), Leonardo, Mute, Switch and Theory & Event. He is a contributing editor at The Thing and a member of Fakeshop.

Some of his recent essays are: ***The Post-Genomic Era Has Already Happened*** at The Thing Reviews http://bbs.thing.net, ***Point-and-Click Biology: Why Programming is the Future of Biotech*** at MUTE (Issue 17), ***Database/Body: Bioinformatics, Biopolitics, and Totally Connected Media Systems*** at Switch, http://switch.sjsu.edu.

079

Eugene Thacker

Douwe Draaisma

THE CLOCKWORK OF THE MIND

THE CLOCKWORK OF THE MIND

Here's a scene from *A Predicament*, one of Edgar Allan Poe's lesser-known stories. The main character, one Signora Psyche Zenobia, is taking a stroll through the streets of Edinburgh. For reasons she doesn't understand herself, she obeys an impulse to enter a Gothic cathedral and to climb the tower. After climbing a seemingly endless staircase, she arrives at the chamber of the belfry. From floor to ceiling, the gloomy room is filled with "cabalistic looking machinery": wheels, axles, pinions, bars, chains and pulleys. She faces the seemingly motionless cogwheels of the cathedral's clock. The only window in the room is a square opening about a foot in diameter with a thick iron bar in it. Zenobia squeezes herself into the narrow space between the wall and the man-sized wheels and pokes her head through the hole. The view is magnificent. Below her, the church square bathes in the late afternoon sunlight, and in the distance she can see the fields on the outskirts of the town. The aperture through which she sticks her head appears to be an opening in the face of the cathedral clock. She observes the immense size of the hands, made of solid steel, with sharp edges. The minute hand is well over ten feet long. The hour hand points in the direction of the V.

Zenobia is absorbed in the glorious prospect below. She loses all sense of time. Suddenly she feels a cold pressure on the

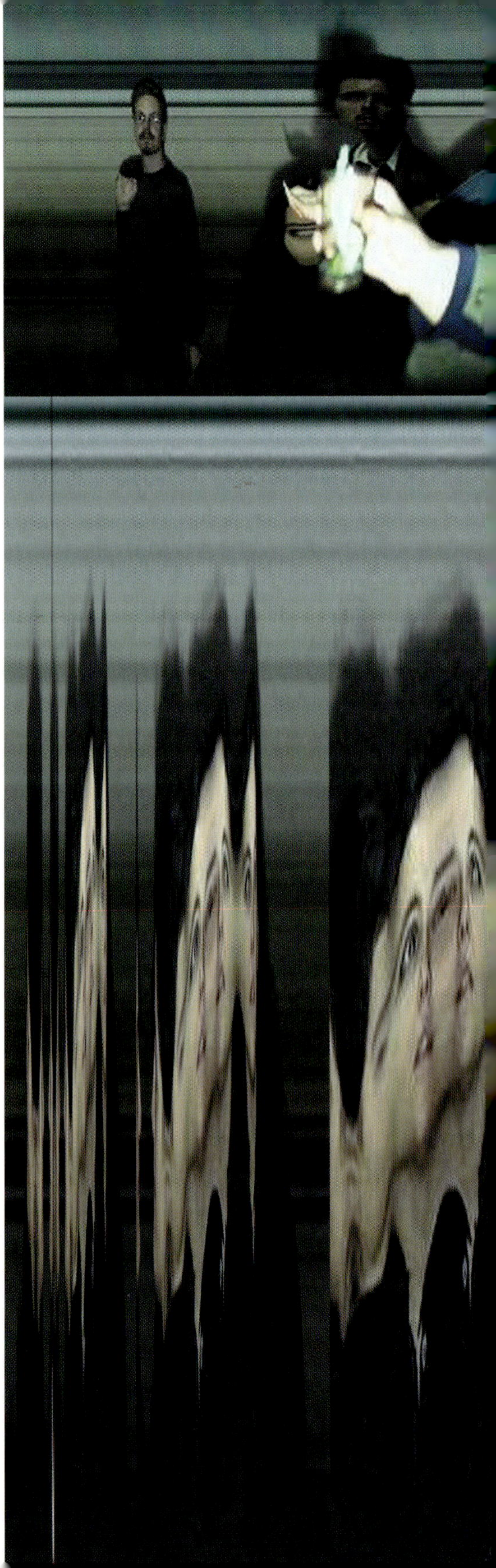

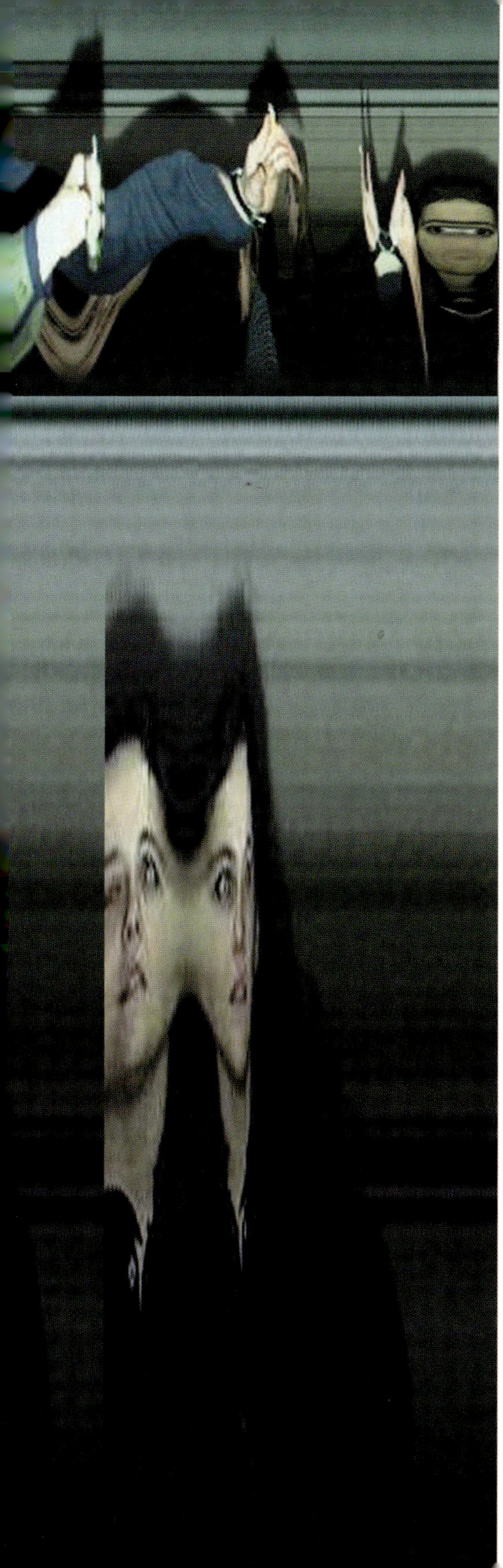

back of her neck. Alarmed, she carefully turns her head. To her horror, she sees that the minute hand has descended upon her neck. She tries to pull back at once, but it is too late: she is caught in the ever-narrowing angle between the two hands. Slowly the sharp edge of the minute hand buries itself in her flesh. It's a quarter past five.

The pain soon becomes unbearable. Her mind starts to ramble. The steel figures on the clock face seem to dance before her eyes. The pressure of the bar makes her eyes begin to protrude. The tick-tock, tick-tock of the clock behind her beats ever louder. A little later, one of her eyes tumbles from its socket. It rolls down the steeple into the rain gutter and stares up at her with contempt. At twenty five minutes past five ("precisely"), the inevitable happens. Like a huge pair of scissors halfway between heaven and earth, the hands sever Zenobia's head from her body. A few moments later, her head plunges into the middle of the street.

In Poe's stories, clocks spell death and disaster. In *The Tell-Tale Heart*, perhaps his most famous, the murderer hears the heart of his victim, dead and buried under the floor of the room he's in, as it continues to beat – "a low, dull, quick sound – much such a sound as a watch makes when enveloped in cotton." In *The Masque of the Red Death*, a giant clock of ebony produced from its brass lungs a sound so peculiar and sinister that when its chimes rang, "it was observed that the giddiest grew pale, and the more aged and sedate passed their hands over their brows as if in confused revery or meditation."

In Poe's writing, clockworks tick, strike and chime – like the day's residue in

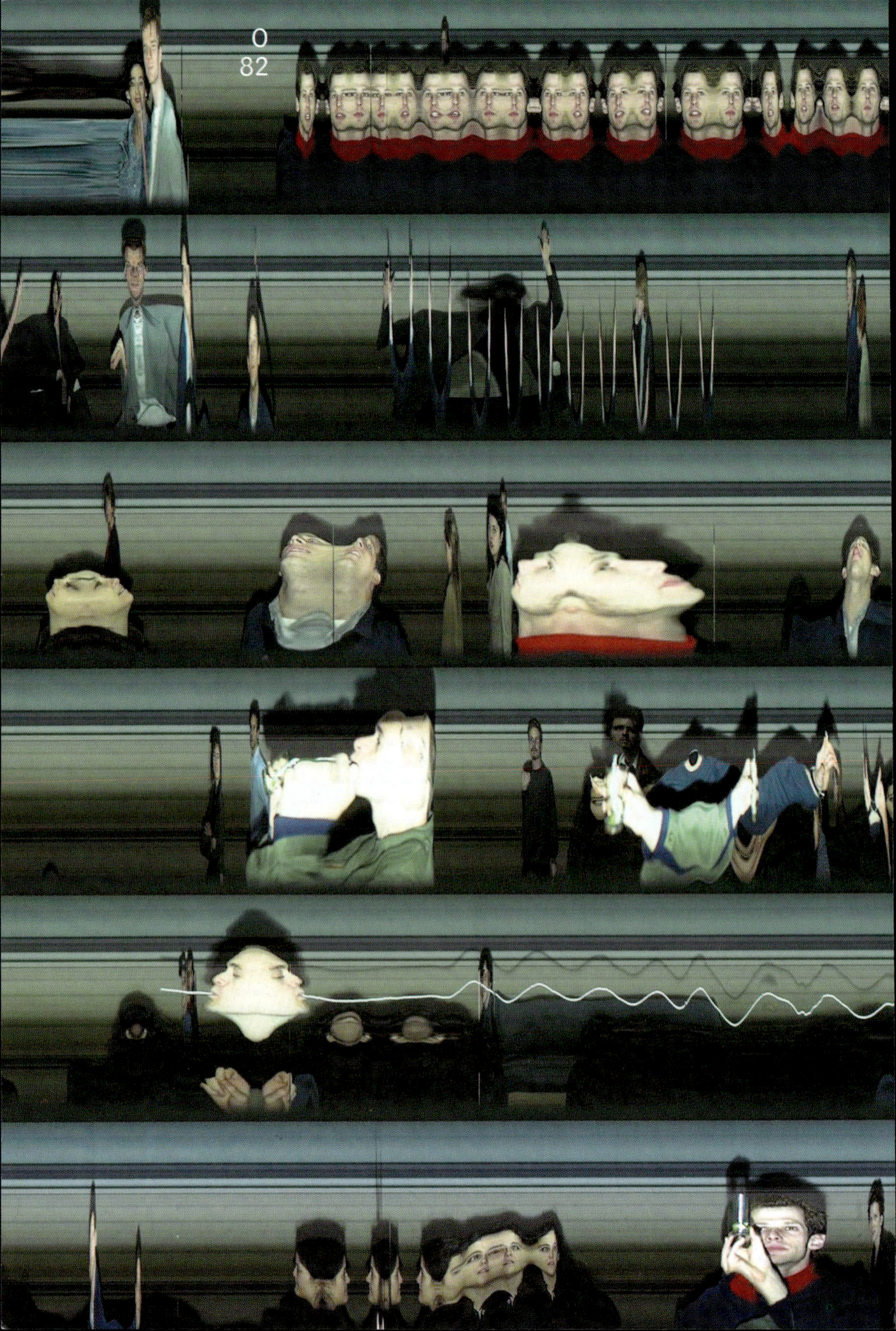

THE CLOCKWORK OF THE MIND

Douwe Draaisma

a dream – and they sounded increasingly louder in everyday life as well. He wrote his stories in the mid-nineteenth century, at a time when an essential quality of clocks was becoming increasingly obvious: clocks create the conditions of their own proliferation. Every punch clock that was installed, whether at a factory or an office, forced laborers and clerks to buy clocks or pocket watches so they wouldn't be late at the punch clock. From the moment that the railway companies implemented a strict timetable, punctual to the minute, travelers were obliged to keep an eye on the clock if they wanted to catch their trains. This miraculous self-proliferating mechanism ensured the establishment in the nineteenth century of the chronocracy we now live in. In Poe's day, time discipline, the natural obedience to clocks, now second nature to us, still had to be forced upon people.

Time and surveillance

It is easy to understand why punch clocks in particular,

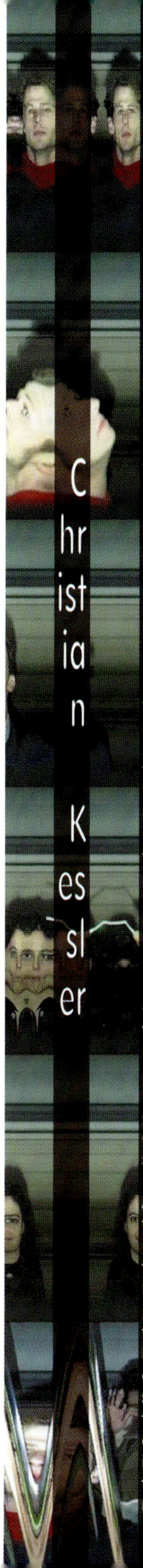

Christian Kessler

Transverser

The interactive computer-video installation *Transverser* acts as an apparatus rearranging the temporal and spatial structure of vision. It reflects the presence of the viewers by transforming their movements into a continuous stream of image and sound. As the visitor steps into the light rays marking the camera eye's range of vision, he leaves trails on the installation's projection screen. The results are time-space-distorted reflections of the viewers themselves, varying according to their movements in front of the installation, from an empty landscape through regular camera and mirror images to surreally morphed forms.

Transverser, or "Querläufer," is based on the principle of chronophotography. Movements are recorded in a way that makes their course in time visible in space. Unlike classical, photomechanic chronophotography, *Transverser* uses a video camera and a computer to generate the image of time, so the development of the images can be followed in real-time. Images are recorded by a stationary camera pointed at the visitors, continuously fed into the computer and processed; a strip of time becomes visible, ever growing and stretching across the projection screen.

A slide projector focused to a narrow, tall line of light from the direction of the camera provides the lighting. It also marks the position of the viewers in the installation, as they have to stand in the slice of space lit up by the source in order to affect the resulting image. In addition, each movement in the light causes sounds to be played by a connected Midi device.

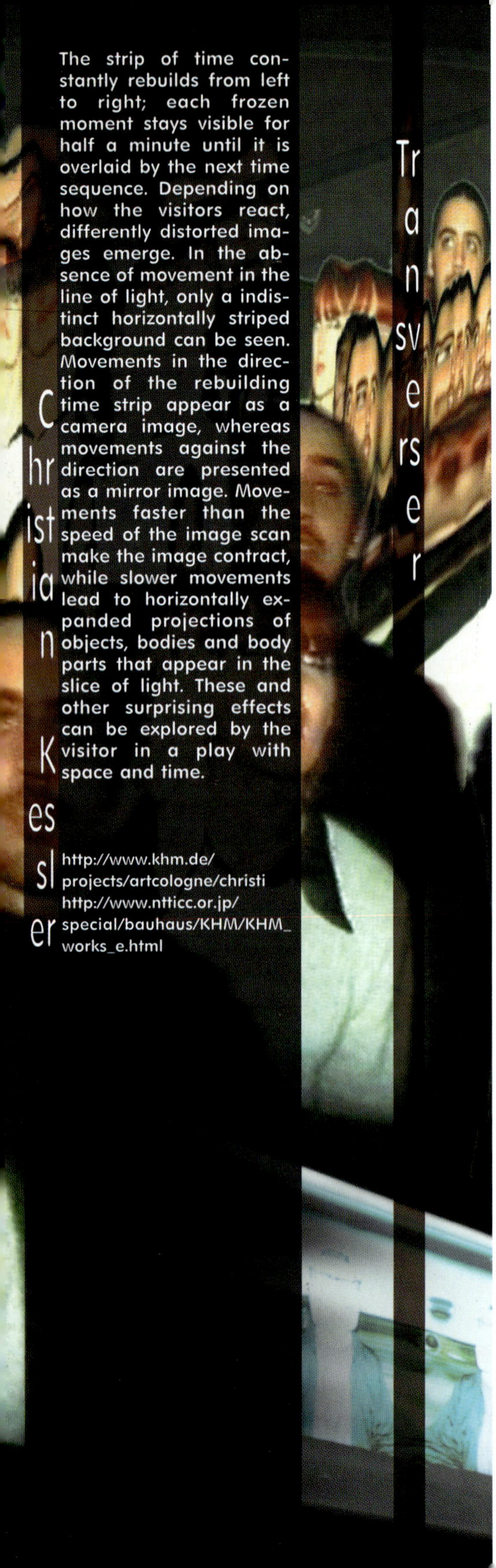

Christian Kessler

Transverser

The strip of time constantly rebuilds from left to right; each frozen moment stays visible for half a minute until it is overlaid by the next time sequence. Depending on how the visitors react, differently distorted images emerge. In the absence of movement in the line of light, only a indistinct horizontally striped background can be seen. Movements in the direction of the rebuilding time strip appear as a camera image, whereas movements against the direction are presented as a mirror image. Movements faster than the speed of the image scan make the image contract, while slower movements lead to horizontally expanded projections of objects, bodies and body parts that appear in the slice of light. These and other surprising effects can be explored by the visitor in a play with space and time.

http://www.khm.de/projects/artcologne/christi
http://www.ntticc.or.jp/special/bauhaus/KHM/KHM_works_e.html

nicknamed Tell-Tales, found their way into the literature of those days as a sinister metaphor for an inescapable coercion: punch clocks were both the symbol and the executive power of this new regime. Punch clocks have always been associated with discipline, supervision and inspection. The first punch clocks were designed to check on watch guards. In order to prove that they had made their rounds, the guards had to push down pins at clocks located at various places in the factory. They could only do so if at that specific time – say 2 a.m. – they were at the clock. If they let the hour pass, the 2:00 pin remained as it was and their negligence would be discovered the next day. Such clocks were often referred to as "Tell-Tales." And though later registration clocks usually time-stamped cards, the term punch clock stuck.

By the end of the 1880s, several types of punch clocks were being mass-produced, and within a few years "punching" became un unquestioned routine for factory workers and office clerks. This is not to say that the introduction of punch clocks didn't meet with opposition. The punch clock's disciplinary nature was resented, and not everyone wished to resign themselves to its authority. The introduction of punch clocks is also the story of how a central and hierarchical authority managed to establish itself. The fact that a popular punch clock model was called *The Autocrat* illustrates this nicely: clocks had become self-willed machines.

The proliferation of registration clocks was connected to technological inventions like master and slave clocks, telegraphic time signals and the distribution of standard time, but also with processes like industrial-

ization and urbanization. All these inventions and social processes meshed like so many cogwheels – the end result was a smoothly operating control system that forced every citizen to be punctual. Advertising campaigns for punch clocks pointed out that accurate time registration was beneficial to both employers and employees.

A 1911 advertisement by the International Time Recording Company (later IBM) claims its machine treats workers fairly because it makes them master of their own time – they can always use the card with their data on it to prove their presence. Whether the average employee was very appreciative of these benefits is doubtful, to say the least. Most punch clocks were used to punish latecomers, for instance by withholding one hour of pay for being five minutes late. Punch clocks were seen as instruments that reinforced the powers of company management, and this was in fact their intend-

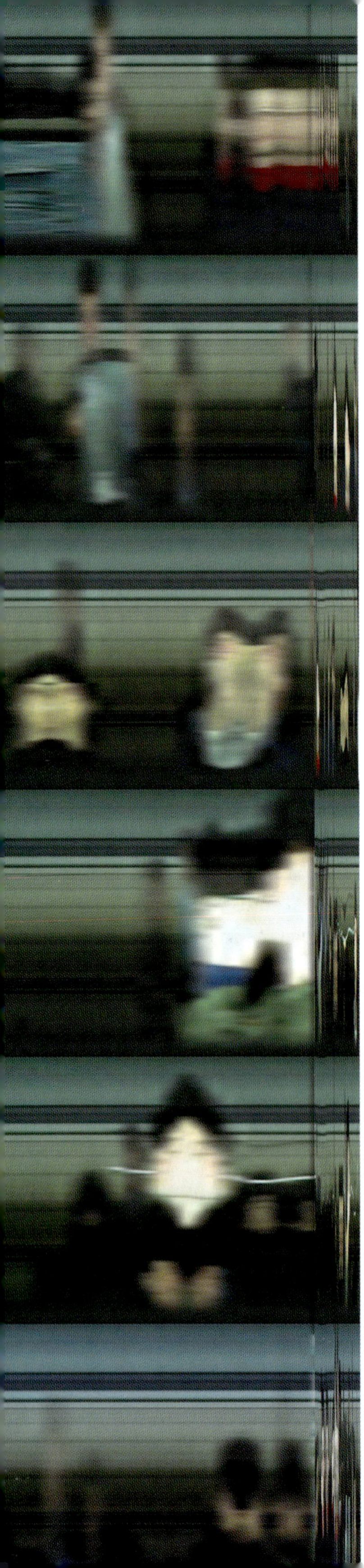

ed use. The same advertisement, published in a magazine for managers, features a long row of employees with a couple of figures in black: the "unprofitable employees," who set out to be on time every morning but are always late. "The only way to make employees appreciate the value of lost time," the ad explains, "is to let them pay for it themselves." This will also serve efficiency, for "late-coming and early leaving are twin-brothers to inefficiency." The machine featured a two-colored ink ribbon device: green for "punctuals" and red for "irregulars."

The time the punch clock indicated was the standard time. This time was centrally imposed and distributed to clients via a hierarchy of instruments. The punch clock was one of the contacts between this central time and those that had to comply with it. The fact that the punch clock developed into an unquestioned part of a normal working day is the best proof of how the time regime, which at first had to be forcibly imposed, gradually became internalized. Nowadays we are automatically punctual, seemingly of our own volition. We have become model citizens of the chronocracy we live in.

The Greenwich Bomb Outrage

Artists sometimes show a seismic sensitivity to latent fears in society. Their stories, paintings, novels and poems may reflect some of the secret changes at deeper layers of social life that are imperceptible to most of us. Half a century after Poe wrote his ominous stories on the deadly machinery of clocks, two employees of the Royal Observatory in Greenwich witnessed a scene involving timekeeping that ended equally fatally. In the late afternoon of 15 February 1894, two staff members were working in the Lower Computing Room of the observatory when suddenly there was a loud explosion. Both men ran outside to find a badly wounded man lying some 50 meters from the observatory. His left hand had been ripped off and there was a gaping hole in his stomach. Although still conscious, he refused to state his identity or explain what had happened. He died half an hour later. That

same day he was identified by police as 26-year-old Martial Bourdin, a French anarchist. According to the police, he had been on his way to the observatory, armed with a bomb. What happened next remains a matter of speculation: maybe he tripped and fell, or maybe the time mechanism wasn't set properly. But in any case, the bomb went off prematurely. The funeral was attended by a crowd of anarchist sympathizers.

But why Greenwich? Ten years earlier, in 1884, an international geodetic conference in Washington had accepted the Greenwich meridian as the prime meridian, designating Greenwich as the center of the irrefutable grid of time and space that formed the basis of all commerce, communication and industry. Standard time, derived from the eternal cycle of the stars by precise time measurement, was distributed by the Astronomer Royal, Sir George Airy, throughout British society – and from there all over the world – via an ingenious system of telegraphically synchronized master and slave clocks. Standard time was both condition and effect: nineteenth-century social order depended on a strict time regime and in turn was reinforced by it. Joseph Conrad seems to have sensed that anarchists could hardly have selected a more convincing and forceful symbol than Greenwich. He based his novel *The Secret Agent* (1907) on what came to be known as the "Greenwich bomb outrage." One of Conrad's anarchistically minded characters says: "The whole civilized world has heard of Greenwich. The very bootblacks in the basement of Charing Cross Station know something of it. See?" Conrad was right: at the end of the nineteenth century every man or woman knew that the rhythm and pace of social life was determined, ultimately, by the chronometers of Greenwich. In 1894, after the young Frenchman who fell victim to his own unfortunate timing had been carried off and employees of the observatory assessed the damage, they happily concluded that there was "not so much as a crack in the outside wall." In the Chronometer Room, deep within the observatory, all the clocks were ticking on imperturbably. And the explosion, by the way, still echoes on over a century later: an article about the assault on Greenwich's website (www.rog.nmm.ac.uk) mentions the fact that Theodore Kaczynski, better known as the

Unabomber, used the alias Conrad in his eighteen-year campaign against scientific institutions.

Organic clockwork

Signora Zenobia, Martial Bourdin – we've been discussing nineteenth-century timekeeping for only a few pages and we already have two casualties on our hands. This in itself sharply contrasts with how clocks and the measurement of time were appreciated before the nineteenth century. It would be unthinkable for an author from the Middle Ages, the Golden Age or the Enlightenment to present a clock as a demonic machine. Far into the eighteenth century, clocks were associated with positive values. They brought harmony and regularity to human existence. They were the symbols of precision and predictability. In allegories clocks stood for temperance, control, wisdom. Those who wished to show off their wealth had themselves officially portrayed holding open pocket watches or sitting next to richly ornamented table clocks. Clockwork represented the pinnacle of human ingenuity, and the order they brought was most welcome.

The way in which people dealt with time in the nineteenth century is the endpoint in a process that gradually removed nature from the way society kept time. Until the end of the Middle Ages the day was divided into twelve sun hours – "hours" which varied with the seasons and which, at European latitude, were twice as long on the longest day as they were on the shortest day. After "equal hours" were intro-

duced – constant 60-minute periods – the sun remained the standard of timekeeping until well into the nineteenth century: it was twelve noon when the sun reached its highest point.

Current timekeeping is no longer directly linked to the natural cycle of a rotating earth and its orbit around the sun. Our time is basically nothing but a collective agreement about what time clocks should display. This has had a paradoxical effect: it allows us to very simply adjust social time to nature. This is the idea behind daylight savings time: by moving the hands of the clock one hour forward in spring, we make the sun rise one hour later and shine one hour longer. The result of this is that the social day fits in better with the period of sunlight. If the conventions of time were not purely artificial we would never be able to take this liberty.

Every year, this manipulation of the hands of the clock – spring forward, fall backward – is again the cause of trouble and inconvenience, both emotional and physical, which reminds us of a different type of clock: the ones within our bodies. Dozens of clocks are ticking in our bodies, organic watch shops beating time in our systems. These clocks lend rhythm and cadence to our lives, and they are not as easily adjusted as the clocks we advance for daylight saving. Respiration, blood pressure, pulse, hormone discharge, cell division, sleep, metabolism, body temperature – all these processes have their own cycle and some of these biological clocks can take more than a week to settle into the new rhythm of social time.

Chronobiologists have so far discovered around a hundred biological clocks. This actually means nothing more than that all kinds of physiological processes are distinctively periodical. To call these processes "clocks" is offering a metaphor rather than an explanation, but this metaphor does raise some interesting questions. Can biological clocks be stopped? Can you make them gain or lose time? Can you reset a clock that is off its stroke? Are there master and slave clocks in nature? Is our body governed by a standard time, dictated by a central clockwork? Where are all of these clocks located, and who winds them? Here, then, is a brief tour of the watch shop of our internal cycles.

The fastest rhythms are to be found within the nervous system. Some neurons fire at a frequency of a thousand impulses per second. The cycles of brain activity, measured by an EEG, are less hectic: between eight and twelve cycles per second. This particular periodicity varies with the time of day and with the sleep-wake cycle: when night falls, brain waves come in more rapid succession, and during sleep the frequency is at its peak. Besides these fast

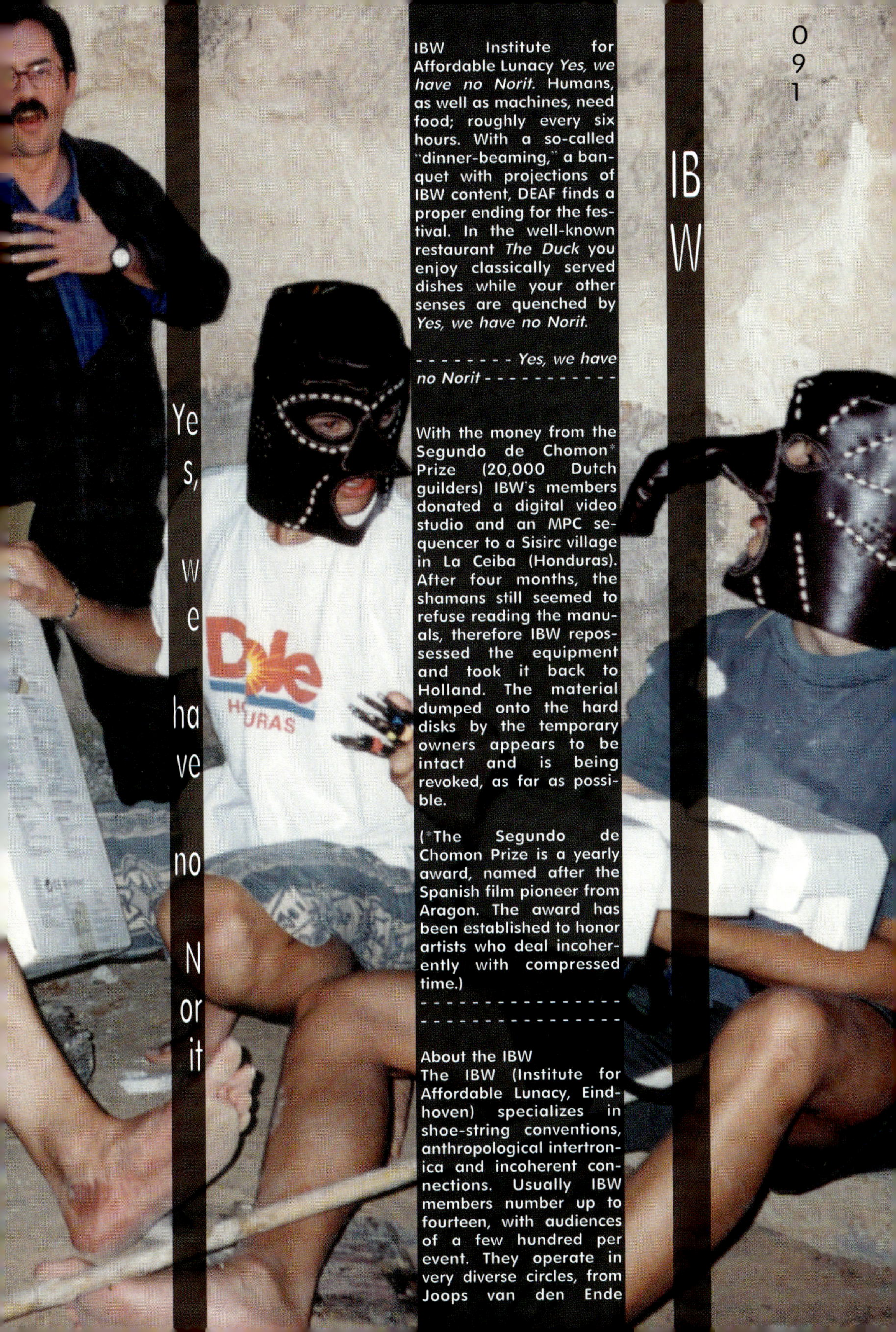

Yes, we have no Norit

IBW Institute for Affordable Lunacy *Yes, we have no Norit.* Humans, as well as machines, need food; roughly every six hours. With a so-called "dinner-beaming," a banquet with projections of IBW content, DEAF finds a proper ending for the festival. In the well-known restaurant *The Duck* you enjoy classically served dishes while your other senses are quenched by *Yes, we have no Norit.*

- - - - - - - - *Yes, we have no Norit* - - - - - - - - - -

With the money from the Segundo de Chomon* Prize (20,000 Dutch guilders) IBW's members donated a digital video studio and an MPC sequencer to a Sisirc village in La Ceiba (Honduras). After four months, the shamans still seemed to refuse reading the manuals, therefore IBW repossessed the equipment and took it back to Holland. The material dumped onto the hard disks by the temporary owners appears to be intact and is being revoked, as far as possible.

(*The Segundo de Chomon Prize is a yearly award, named after the Spanish film pioneer from Aragon. The award has been established to honor artists who deal incoherently with compressed time.)

- - - - - - - - - - - - - - - -
- - - - - - - - - - - - - - - -

About the IBW
The IBW (Institute for Affordable Lunacy, Eindhoven) specializes in shoe-string conventions, anthropological intertronica and incoherent connections. Usually IBW members number up to fourteen, with audiences of a few hundred per event. They operate in very diverse circles, from Joops van den Ende

IBW

rhythms, there are cycles that take four hours, such as the variations in body temperature and blood pressure. Of those cycles that take more than a day, menstruation is the most important one. The average menstrual cycle is one "moon month," or 29.5 days. Yearly cycles occur in weight gain and in the condition of our immune system. The immune system has a seven-day cycle as well, which is remarkable, because while day, month and year cycles are related to the orbits of the earth, the moon and the sun, the week is a social phenomenon.

Halfway between the fastest and the slowest cycles ticks the only clock we can actually hear and feel: the heart, a pumping muscle that tenses and relaxes under the control of a carefully tuned set of chronometers. Understanding the rhythms of these natural clocks enables us to design pacemakers, impulse generators that use electrical stimuli to beat time in an unsettled heart.

The heart itself is subjected to longer cycles. About half an hour before we get out of bed, our blood pressure rises and our blood clots more easily. The blood vessels of the heart are a little slow in adapting to this, which can result in less blood being supplied to vital organs and – with some heart patients – in pain in the chest. The chance of having a heart attack is twice as high between eight and ten in the morning as it is in the late afternoon or evening. The incidence of heart attacks has a marked yearly peak in January and February, regardless of climate. Of a more curious nature is this weekly cycle: there is a 40 percent higher chance of a heart attack on Mondays than on other days. This

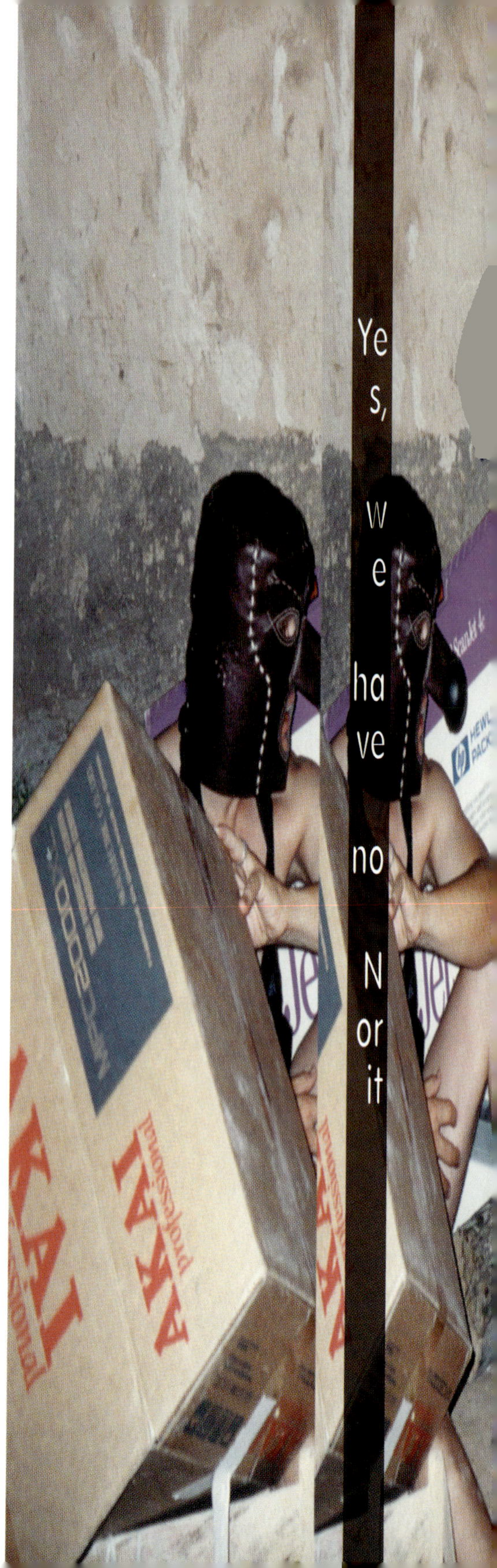

IBW

MetaTV to Catherine Davids MetaKassel, from pirate radio station Patapoe to pop culture TV in Costa Rica, from La Ceiba, Honduras to Krsko, Slovenia. Currently they have started up their own NGO, the Centro Periferico Internacional, operating from Calanda, Spain. Their sites are on hit lists all over. Their music is suspected everywhere. *ALL THIRTEEN GOLD*, the first anthropological CD-ROM, has just been published.

IBW (dutch)
http://www.dse.nl/ibw
IBW (spanish)
http://www.periferico.org

pattern cannot be sufficiently explained by relating it to the working week, since this Monday peak also occurs in homes for the elderly.

Day rhythms can define an individual as a typical night or morning person. A morning person's temperature begins to rise by the early hours of the morning, peaks around four in the afternoon and then slowly begins to go down again. When morning people have to work at night, their body secretes stress hormones. Their biological clocks are hours ahead of those of night people, who, with temperatures that peak later, remain alert and active at night and would actually prefer 26-hour days. As we grow older, these biological clocks tend to shift towards morning and these differences diminish. This old age synchronization, however, is accompanied by a considerable slowing down of the pace of life, which can sometimes make one wish there were separate windows for senior citizens at train stations and post offices.

The clock that times our clocks

Problems with the cycle of waking and sleeping that arise with age can be caused by a loss of cells in the supra-chiasmatic nucleus (SCN). This SCN – when intact – is as small as one mm^3, about the size of the head of a pin. It contains some 8,000 cells and is located just above the place where the optical nerves cross. The SCN functions as a master clock: when something goes wrong with this clock, a whole range of other clocks go off their stroke as well.

A master clock itself needs time

signals as well. Tests have shown that the SCN is regulated by light. This is why blind people often have difficulty staying in tune with cycles of light and darkness. Conversely, light can be used to manipulate the SCN. When experimental subjects were exposed to 30-hour light schedules in a laboratory setting, after a few days the slave clocks of the SCN also followed suit, as did the cycles of waking and sleeping and the secretion of hormones like melatonin and adrenaline.

Animal tests have shown that the hands of the SCN clock can be advanced or set back by using light, sometimes resulting in drastic behavioral changes. A Canadian researcher once locked up a group of juncos – songbirds that migrate south in autumn – in an outdoor aviary. When autumn came, he kept artificial lights burning longer each day, as if spring was on its way. By mid-December, the birds started singing mating songs, and when they were released in midwinter, they took wing and flew to the icy north. Apparently internal clocks can also be used to control navigation.

Manipulations with light can affect humans as well. Experiencing prolonged periods with only light or only uninterrupted darkness leads to time disorientation. During the winter of 1908-1909, polar explorer Cook tried to keep track of the days by checking the position of the moon, but he soon lost a couple of days. His diary entries show how the continuous darkness got on his and his crew members' nerves. "The veil of darkness that has descended upon the outside world and its icy desolation has also descended upon the inner world of our souls."

Nature's hours

Sometimes findings in chronobiology touch upon what one could call the sociology of time. One of the most fascinating interfaces between biology and sociology is the relationship between the natural rhythms of internal clocks and the somewhat arbitrary schedules of time management in society. After the French Revolution, attempts were made to

organize time according to the decimal system. Decimal time would have great arithmetical benefits, as does the decimal system of weights and spatial measurements. The Republican month was divided into three "decades" (the last day of each one being a holiday), the day into ten hours, the hour into one hundred minutes and the minute into one hundred seconds. This reform was not only an attempt at rationalization but also an illustration of the power of the new regime: via calendar and clock it now also controlled days of rest and working hours. The new time regime didn't last very long: in 1806 Napoleon restored the Gregorian calendar, and the faces of clocks once again showed their familiar duodecimal figures.

Of course Napoleon's decision can be interpreted as a manifestation of political power as well, but perhaps we mustn't rule out biological factors. The fact that internal clocks can adapt themselves doesn't mean they can be adjusted at will. Their cycles prefer certain lengths to others. The two most important ones are "hours" of 60 and 90 minutes. For some hormonal cycles the biological day contains 24 hours of 60 minutes. Sleep goes in relatively constant cycles of 90 minutes. During the day there are "hours" of 90 minutes when it comes to appetite, activity, level of concentration and sensitivity to pain. With other mammals these "hours" have different lengths, varying, or so it seems, with body size: for cats it's 30 minutes, for monkeys 45, for elephants 120. Each of these cycle lengths can easily add up to a 24 hour period. Decimal time, however efficient it may seem from an arithmetical point of view, is not very plausible in a biological sense. Biological clocks tick stubbornly on in the rhythms of six in which the Babylonians divided time.

When the rhythm of social life deviates from that of natural cycles, problems may occur. People who work night shifts, against the sun cycle, usually build up a sleep deficit. If these night shifts are frequent, both day and night rhythm can fall out of step; a condition of desynchronization that has been termed "industrial jet lag." Morning persons are afflicted the most: the ideal person to work in shifts is a night person of around 30 years of age. Employees of 40 or 50 often develop complaints, even after ten years or longer of working these shifts.

Another violation of natural cycles is the passing of time zones. Flying west makes the hands of the social clock move more slowly or even backwards, while one's internal clocks keep happily ticking along. Even worse – in terms of symptoms – is traveling east, as it involves the feeling of losing hours: it is later there, after all. If daylight savings time, with its one-hour difference, already causes mild disorientation, a jump of six hours or even more is very likely to cause some temporal harm to body and soul. Disturbances of digestion, sleep, concentration, immune system, mood and memory prove that we cannot live against the hands of the clock without suffering the consequences. There are hardly any remedies, although we can try to reap the benefits of the biological clock's natural "synchronizer": daylight. In the past few years the hormone melatonin has shown some promising results as well.

Poème symphonique

Again, sometimes artists seem to be able to find an expression for phenomena which are still hidden from view for most of us. Well before the discovery of all these biological clocks, tick-tocking away in our bodies, the Hungarian composer Ligeti wrote his *Poème symphonique,* informally known as "the concert for metronomes." On the stage are hundreds of metronomes, arranged like an orchestra. Each keeps its own time: some beat with short, fanatical ticks, while others' weights have been pushed up very high and their hands wave in a grand motion. At the beginning of the concert there is a hectic clicking and ticking, but gradually more and more metronomes stop and only the slower ones can be heard. The silence grows until, at the end, only one metronome is left, marking the rhythm of an inaudible melody. The end of this concert rhymes with what happens to our internal clocks at the end of our lives: just before we die – as doctors and nurses can tell you – the internal rhythms fail, beat and cadence disappear from our heartbeat and respiration, and an unmarked floating through time begins. Perhaps the occasionally still honored tradition

of stopping the clocks when someone has died is the finest expression of the idea that for them, time has ceased to exist.

Douwe Draaisma lectures on the principles and history of psychology at the University of Groningen. Together with psychologist Piet Vroon he wrote ***De mens als metafoor, over vergelijkingen van mens en machine in filosofie en psychologie*** (Mankind as Metaphor, on Comparisons of Man and Machines in Philosophy and Psychology, 1980) and ***Het verborgen raderwerk, over tijd, machines en bewustzijn*** (Hidden Wheels-On Time, Machines and Consciousness, 1990). The Dutch Institute of Psychologists awarded him the Heymans Prize for his research into the history of psychology.

Atau Tanaka

SPEED OF SOUND

SPEED OF SOUND

Music and sound are merging as art forms, with more shared concerns of material and structure than traits to distinguish one from the other. If music in the twentieth century was preoccupied with freeing itself from the limitations of tonal harmony,[1] indications are that in the 21st century the focus already lies in leaving pitched vocabulary behind altogether. If the art of sound arose in the early twentieth century as a vision to grasp, capture, and manipulate sonic phenomena,[2] we begin this new century extending and applying this vision to social domains.[3] In both cases, focus concentrates on the pure elements that constitute sound. The primary and fundamental component of music and sound is time, for sound is immaterial – it can only be described as a function of time and exists solely as perturbations of energy through a medium and across time. Time in sound operates on a multitude of levels – from the macro-level large-scale musical structures through the micro-level details inside the sonic event to nano-level temporal structures inside our physiology.

The speed of sound is not fixed but

changes as it traverses different media – air, water, electrical circuitry, digital logic, the human body. The speed of sound as we know it, approximately 340m/sec,[4] is the speed of transmission of sound as pulsations of air. This figure is not a constant but varies as a function of humidity and temperature.[5] In water, a medium with different transmission coefficients, sound travels at 1480m/sec. The speed of sound changes completely or becomes abstracted in the machine as acoustical energy is transformed into electrical signals. The existence of sound and audio signals across these different planes forcibly has an effect on the way aural phenomena are assimilated by human perceptive mechanisms.

Material

At the macro temporal level, sound exists to create an invisible architecture marking the rites of daily life. The Divine Office or Canonical Hours of the medieval church not only celebrated devotion but tied it to demarcation of time through the use of specific musical forms. In simplified form, church bells broadcast out to the populace to mark the hour. The Church thus consolidated power over its congregation, putting sound and music to use as keepers of time. In the secular realm, the rooster marked

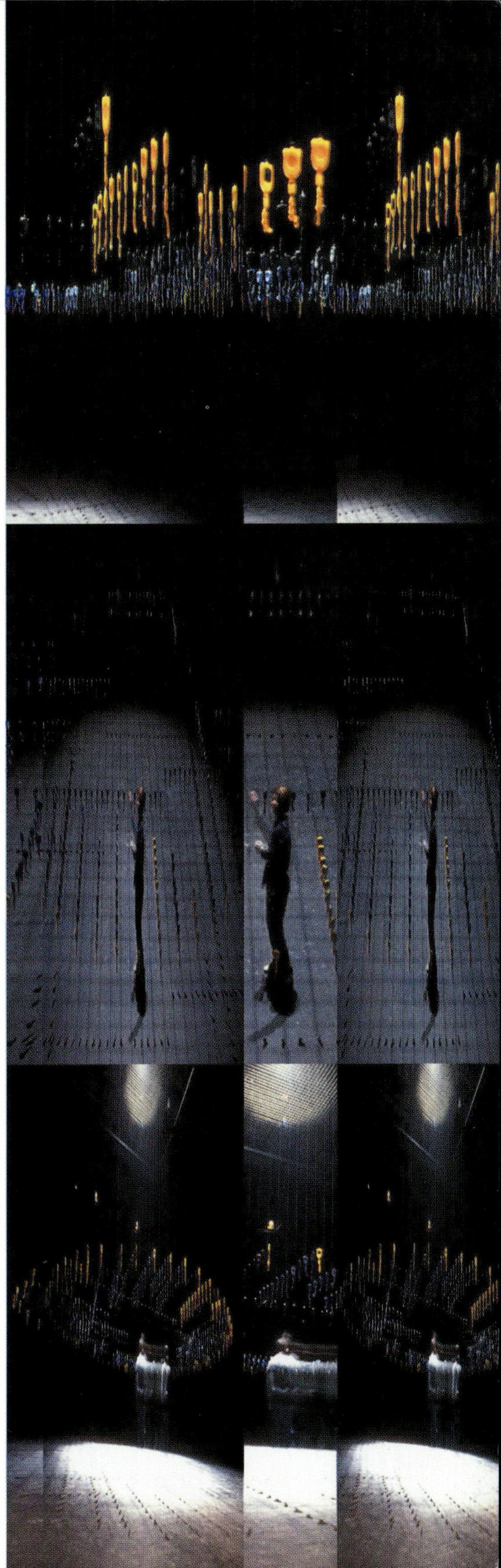

Making the World Safe for Piezo-Electricity, part 2

Technology aspires to banality. St. Exupery's visions of flight have long since given way to the mild boredom and slight dehydration of the airlines. The mechanical precision of a Rolex seems nostalgic and faintly irrelevant in a world where time is dear and timekeeping is cheap. As distance matters less, our postcolonial free ride is starting to end, and we are beginning to see the new disciplines to which we will be expected to submit.

Two years ago, I made *Making the World Safe for Piezo-electricity* as a portrait of these tendencies. The piece consisted of 720 watches set incorrectly so that their hourly chimes were heard all the time, and the alarms were clustered so that they went off every six minutes throughout the hours of exhibition. There were twelfe divisors of the 60 minutes in an hour (1, 2, 3, 4, 5, 6, 10, 12, 15, 20, 30, 60). These defined "meters" of one beat per hour, two beats per hour and so forth. Each of these "meters" was marked with 60 watches. (Since 720 = 12 X 60, there were precisely enough watches to mark the twelfe different meters.) The watches were evenly distributed across the pulses of each meter. The phase relationship of the "meters" were arranged to make the number of watches sounding per minute as uniform as possible. This still resulted in variations from a high of 61 watches sounding in one minute to a low of five watches sounding in another.

Today, the ring of the cell phone is more common than the beep of a watch, and setting a watch is becoming, er, anachronis-

the start of the day, and it remains a strong image describing time periodicity at the quotidian level. In machine times, these sonic elements begin to be manipulated – the mechanical cuckoo announces the hour, and the tick-tock marks the seconds – we begin to focus in on smaller units of time. The alarm clock indicates a desired time through sound, exercising a wish to control our relationship with time.

These examples demonstrate how time can be turned into a commodity and tool of power[6] through the service of sound. Occurrence and regular periodic repetition of sound ground our sensation of the passage of time. Once established, the converse becomes possible – the exploitation of time to commoditize sound in the form of music. It is through structures of time that musical forms are defined – be they religious masses, symphonies or pop songs.

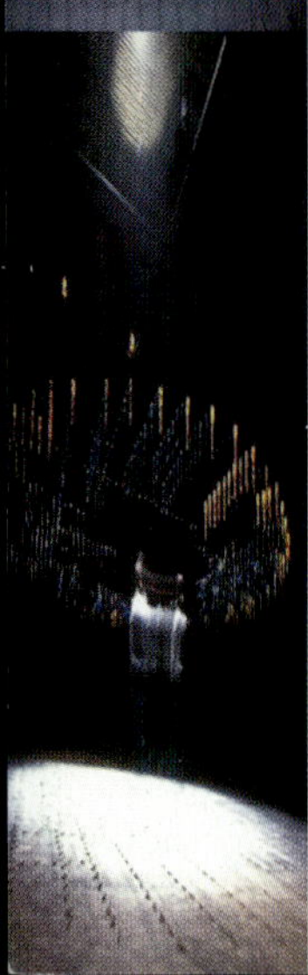

Formulas of time have been meticulously refined to stimulate the appreciation of music, often for the goal of capital gain. These have been closely tied to the media and materials of music delivery. Court-sponsored composers of the Enlightenment were careful in their symphonies not to push the patience of their audiences in the concert hall. The ideal length of a pop song is linked not just to attention span, but historically to the maximum time fitting on a 7-inch 45-rpm vinyl disc. The Beatles harnessed the longer time format of the 12-inch LP to create narrative structures of the "concept album." The even greater capacity of CDs has surpassed our effective attention span. Artists exploit this to create works shorter than the maximum time, then add bonus tracks or surprises after long durations of silence. Raves as all-night/all-day techno music events create a time continuum, expanding time to a state of near-suspension at the macro level, albeit propelled at the micro level by clocking the pulse to the human physiological rhythm.

Manipulation of time, then, is not just part of the technique of composing music but a tactical means for commercial entities to make a product out of music. The ultimate manipulation of time is to freeze the progress of time altogether. This can be in the form of fixed media such as scores or recordings, abstractions in the creation of a personality-driven star system, or documentation in the context of historical perspective. By removal or capture of the time element, these forces seek to establish an existence for music as a material commodity. Otherwise, time in its natural state, and thus music as a temporal form, leaves no trace.

As the church was resourceful in using sound to mark the passage of the day, it was equally clever in utilizing qualities of sound to demarcate space to assure a position of power. The reverberant acoustic quality inside a church is perceived by our modern consciousness as something beautiful, creating a sense of tranquility relative to the stressful bustle of the city. However, for the average human consciousness of 500 years ago, the effect must have been quite different.[7] The same reverberation was at once more contained than the open air of the field and more open than the narrow streets of the village. To the villager entering the church, the acoustic must have invoked an aura of scale, of otherworldly power. The sound reflections help to underscore the large cross-shaped architecture of the church. The church, it can be said, mastered subliminal special effects long before broadcast media. The use of temporal properties of sound was a key strategic element.

Ron Kuivila

Twilight of the Second Hand

tic. Timekeeping is no longer adequate; it is being replaced by networked synchronization of the human resources and the ever-finer subdivision of their time. It is your attention and your life that experience this ever-faster multiplexing.

Twilight of the Second Hand does the same. The hour is now divided into seconds rather than minutes – a 60-fold increase in resolution. The watches of the first piece reappear in a mazelike formation at eye level, but many are now dead – their batteries have expired. The few that still run beep, but rather timidly – they have been replaced. The primary sound of the piece is the same watch beep, but it is now synthetically reproduced by a single, central authority (a computer with twelfe channels of output audio) in a system of subdivisions based on the second rather than the minute.

There are 45 divisors of the 3600 seconds in an hour (1, 2, 3, 4, 5, 6, 8, 9, 10, 12, 15, 16, 18, 20, 24, 25, 30, 36, 40, 45, 48, 50, 60, 72, 75, 80, 90, 100, 120, 144, 150, 180, 200, 225, 240, 300, 360, 400, 450, 600, 720, 900, 1,200, 1,800, 3,600), defining 45 meters ranging from a familiar 60 beats per minute to a glacial one beat per hour. Each meter distributes 3,600 accents according to how frequently it occurs. One for one beat per second, two for one beat every two seconds, et cetera.

Ron Kuivila.

SPEED OF SOUND

If such use of sound diffusion was effective, it is because the human physiology is sensitive to, or in fact depends on, these cues. Reverberation is a cue that helps us to orient ourselves (or in the case of the church, disorient ourselves) in the space that surrounds us. Simple surfaces – a building across the street, a mountain cliff hundreds of meters across a valley – give us distinct echoes. Parallel surfaces – the walls of a staircase – give us repeating echoes that can merge into a pinging buzz. The complex dimensions of a church meld echoes together into smooth reverberation. The reflective acoustical properties of these surfaces and the dispersion time of sound between them govern these effects. Besides the readily demonstrated examples of mountain echoes and pinging staircases, the human perceptive systems are sensitive to far more subtle effects over shorter distances and lower amplitudes.[8] In the same way that echoes tell us how far away a mountain is, shorter echoes can help orient us in our immediate surroundings. The time that it takes a sound to come out of our mouths, reflect off the ground and come back up to our ears, remind us how tall we are. The modification of this effect as a function of the surface on which we are standing – an asphalt street, a grass field – change this, as absorptive materials dampen reflections. The acoustic of a snow-covered town gives us a "quiet" peaceful feeling, and perhaps even a floating feeling, as we have fewer cues indicating our height. Human aural perception is sensitive to these subtle changes not just at short distances but at larger distances as well. A clear sunny day feels more open than a cloudy day not just because we appreciate the sun, but because there are fewer reflections from above – clouds reflect sound, and lower clouds mean shorter reflection times than higher clouds. Without us being aware of it, the sounds of our environment are reverberated by the sky.

In discussing these subtleties of acoustics, we are dealing primarily with sensitivity to effects of low amplitude. Human auditory perception is equally sensitive to subtleties at the micro-level in time. The principal mechanism for distinguishing the location of sound in a horizontal plane is the difference of time of a sound's arrival in the two ears.[9] The width of our head is the extra distance that a sound on one side of the head must travel to reach the ear on the other side of the head. It is a distance small enough that the amplitude of the sound does not diminish so much, but is enough of a distance for the auditory perceptual system to distinguish time of arrival. At a speed of sound of 340m/sec, the difference in time of arrival over a distance of 20cm is 59ms.

Human auditory perception has its limits as well – the minimum time between sonic events that can be distinguished separately is on the order of 20 milliseconds.[10] Inside this limit, sounds begin to blur together to create first a buzzing, then a continuum. Although this may be the limit to distinguishing sounds as separate events, human hearing is extremely sensitive to the timing of events. Percussionists create musical sonic events that are distinct, typically separated by hundreds of milliseconds. The accuracy with which they articulate any given event, however, is on the order of a millisecond. Variations at this level create different musical feelings for the same notated rhythms, whether they be "pushing," "pulling" or "in the pocket." For continuous sounds, we are sensitive to differences within a single waveform. We are able to hear timing discrepancies between two identical sounds playing less than 1ms apart. This effect of comb filtering, whereby sound at multiples of a frequency are accentuated or attenuated, is called "flanging" and

comes from the analog era, when pressure was put on the flange of an open-reel tape recorder to desynchronize it with another.

We therefore have mechanisms for distinguishing relationships of time where we may lack ability to discern absolute time. Left in isolation, people tend to veer naturally towards a 25-hour day.[11] Indicators such as daylight cycles and church bells help to ground us in absolute time. Effects like the Doppler shift demonstrate that we are sensitive to changes – deltas – in the speed of sound. We know the effect of an ambulance racing by with its siren sounding – the sound itself is a constant melody, but it arrives at our ears at a higher pitch as the vehicle is approaching and shifts to a lower pitch as it drives away. The reason we perceive the sound as such is because the speed of the ambulance effectively adds to the speed of the sound emanating from it.[12] If the ambulance is traveling at 50km/hr, this is about 14m/s. As the ambulance approaches, then, the effective speed of sound of the siren is 340m/s + 14m/s = 354m/s, while as it departs, the effective speed of sound is 340m/s – 14m/s = 326m/s. This difference of 8 percent to the speed of sound is apparent to us as a musically significant pitch shift.[13] Time perturbations translating to pitch effects are a natural outcome of one of the fundamental principles of sound: that frequency is inversely proportional to time.

There are times when the combination of the speed of sound, human perceptive accuracy and performance medium create a situation requiring intervention by non-aural means. One example is the symphony orchestra and its conductor. The orchestra is a musical ensemble whose goal, more often than not, is to be perceived as playing together. The large number of personnel in an orchestra requires a large stage. This creates a situation where the speed of sound is insufficient to reconcile differences in timing resulting from the stage's dimensions. If a trumpet player in the rear of the orchestra were to follow by ear to play in ensemble with a violinist 10m downstage, the trumpeter would always be late. A distance of 10m at 340m/s creates a delay of 30ms – sufficient to be perceived by the listener in the audience as two separate events. This creates the need for the conductor who directs the orchestra through visual gestures. The musicians no longer depend on the speed of sound for synchronization, but on the speed of light, making a 10m difference in stage seating insignificant. Here is a case where our sensitivity to time in sound surpasses the speed of sound itself.

There are even cases where musical processing surpasses the theoretical limits of neural processing time. The speed with which an accomplished pianist can read and perform the score of a rapid pas-

sage is not only musically but physiologically impressive. If one takes the neural transmission time for a piece of visual information to be transmitted from the eyes to the brain, transformed into neural comands and sent down to the finger muscles, and then multiplies this by the number of notes on the page, a rapid passage can surpass the theoretical maximum tempo. There are direct eye-hand coordination as well as semantic phrase analysis processes taking place – the human being divides nano-time across different parallel processes to achieve an artistic feat of speed.

Our hearing mechanism uses time as a foundational basis. The inner ear is lined with hair cells in the cochlea. Movements of the hair cells trigger nerve firings. The arrangement of these hair cells allows us to distinguish different frequen-

Light Mills

Dieter Jung

Holography is a technological medium invented in the mid-twentieth century that presents images of three-dimensional objects and spaces, or rather, that produces visual perceptions of three-dimensionality. By means of lasers, objects are inscribed on a holographic plate and can be viewed as spatial objects again when the plate is lit appropriately.

In holography it has become possible to experiment not only with spatial structures but also with temporal structures, which means that it has become possible to represent movement in three-dimensional spaces. Using specific techniques, the holographic artist can inscribe moving objects onto the plate, a movement that can be revived when the viewer moves from one point of view to another in front of the hologram. The viewer thus becomes the projector of the holographic movement in space which is transmitted to the moving eye through refracted light passing through the hologram.

Dieter Jung's *Light Mills* are holograms which show abstract configurations of time, space, movement and color. They are based on abstract geometric shapes of different colors which seem to float in the three-dimensional holographic space. As a visitor moves in front of the hologram, each shape seems to turn at a different speed and a different angle, creating the perception of an effect that is physically "impossible." The Light Mills create the impression of a complex, polychronic and polychromatic space whose movement is generated by the perceptive "work" of the visitor.

cies.[14] This is in fact a temporal mapping – an imprint of time along the topology of the inner ear – that detects different frequencies along the length of the basilar membrane.

Media

To this point, we have considered the speed of sound as the speed of acoustic sound waves in air. Musical projects have been realized exploring the transmission of sound in other media such as liquid[15] and solids.[16] In the electrical domain, sound pressure waves are transduced to become voltage-based signals, changing the fundamental temporal nature of sound. Audio signals in electrical circuits travel essentially at the speed of light. Cable length becomes a question of signal strength, and less a problem of timing, for the same reasons given in the orchestra example above.

With digital systems, computation speed becomes the main concern with respect to time. The processing power of early systems was insufficient to treat audio as fast as it came in. The holy grail in that era was to achieve "real-time," and evaluation of a system was based on how many times "out of real-time" a process was. As processor power advanced, a one-on-one relationship with nature was no longer the

upper limit, and we began to see systems that could boast processing capabilities that were "faster than real-time".[17]

In the digital domain, analog audio signal voltages are encoded in a time-sampled linear binary form. Sound is thus quantified, both in amplitude and in time, 16-bit encoding 44,100 times per second in the case of the compact disc. Time in digital form, then, is frozen every $23\mu s$. Artifacts of this abstraction of time can be heard in frequency effects. The Nyquist theorem[18] states that the highest frequency that can be encoded is half the sampling rate. Signals exceeding the Nyquist frequency fold back and become audible in an effect called aliasing. By fixing an arbitrary minimum time slice, we in effect hear time wrapping around a boundary point.

Combining or mixing signals from multiple digital sources presents an interesting problem in time – that of synchronizing clocks. Even if time in the two sources is sliced evenly at the same sampling rate, the absolute occurrence of samples in time must coincide precisely for combinatorial data processing to take place. These are all problems inherent in a discrete time representation.[19]

Time latency is a characteristic inherent to real-time digital signal processing, and can be thought of as the "speed of sound" through computer algorithms. Signal processing inevitably makes use of

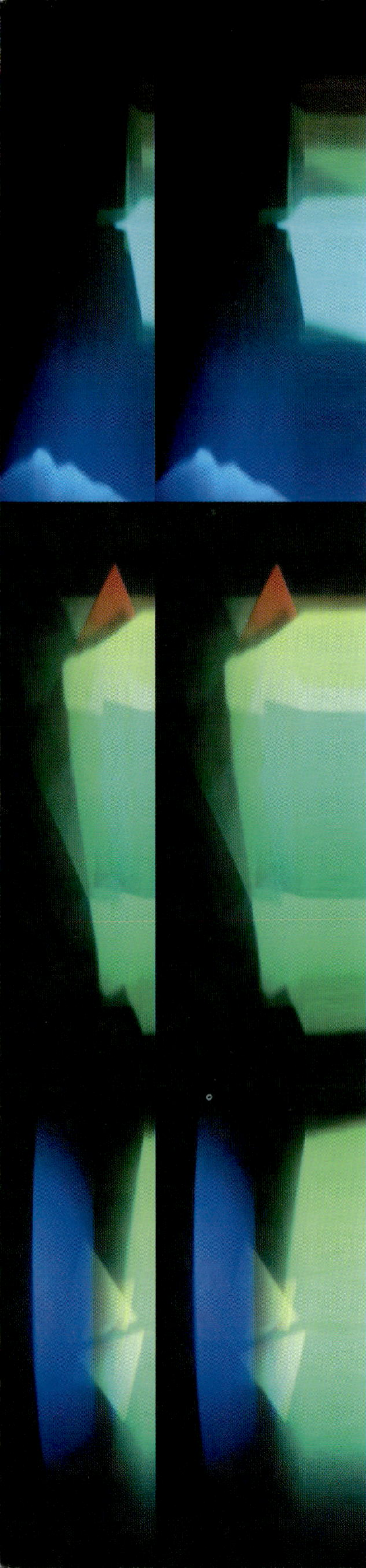

buffers – data caches that are units of temporary storage holding units of data to be processed. The classical way to depict a data buffer is to compare it to a bucket of water with a hole in the bottom. A faucet can feed the bucket, and the hole can empty it at desynchronized rates, as long as the outlet runs fast enough that the bucket does not overflow. Certain signal-processing algorithms require units of source data "looking back at the past" or "looking into the future" to be carried out, creating the need for memory in time. The buffer size defines the base input/output (i/o) latency of the system, and thus the characteristic time delay of the system. It is interesting to note that digital systems that are labeled "real-time" are in fact skewed by a constant delay with respect to absolute time.

Creation

The media-specific characteristics described above typically occur to the engineer as technical problems or system faults. Artists, on the other hand, can offer a vision of these temporal features not as technical shortcomings, but as characteristics defining the creative potential of a medium. There are tendencies, however, to try to force new time paradigms into old musical models. The worldwide millennium celebrations included a performance of Beethoven's Ninth over the network. The network's time latency was dealt with not in a creative way, but in a way consistent with the reallocation of time described above in the commodity industry. Adding a compensating delay to all parties created a situation that would normally be considered musically unsatisfactory.

Artists have instinctively adapted to and exploited physical phenomena and perceptive principles. Composers in the Middle Ages wrote music for the long reverberation times of the church by creating long and slow melodies. They even took advantage of this to sneak in melodies from popular songs into their cantus firmus. A tuba player naturally compensates for the slow articulation time of his instrument by playing in time with an orchestral tutti. J.S. Bach instinctively took advantage of human psychoacoustic stream segregation abilities in writing multivoice counterpoint interleaved into monophonic melody. Drum 'n' bass musicians push rhythm machine programming to our perceptual limits of discerning discrete events with their ultra-rapid snare drum fills. While Cage's *4'33"*, in its absence of sound and clear definition of time, heightens our sensitivity to our aural surroundings, the full frequency nature of Japanese noise music works to suspend our sense of time. Farmersmanual brings a parallel processing dynamic onstage to create non-event-like states in concert.[20] Transmission delays will be considered a hindrance as long as we try to superimpose old musical forms onto the network. But instead, a new musical language can be conceived that respects notable qualities of the medium like packet transmission and geography independent topology.[21] These features can be said to define the "acoustic" of the network, a sonic space that challenges existing musical notions of event, authorship and time.

Whether working in relation to or in the absence of structure, physical or formal, music and sound art take on architectural qualities. Composers create temporal forms often inspired by physical structures.[22] Improvisers depend on structures of time to free themselves from form. Artists place or displace sound in social and physical contexts. The human ear is a multichamber mechanism of sound detection, amplification, and sensation. The coordinate system characterizing sound is one of space and time – domains that, at base, we cannot touch. Music, sound art, and aural perception are

architectures along these axes, in realms that are intangible, that nonetheless shape and define a tangible universe. The speed of sound is the fundamental element, for velocity is a function of distance and time.

Paris, Tokyo, September 2000.

References

1. Pierre Boulez, *Orientations: Collected Writings* (Cambridge: Harvard University Press, reprint 1990). http://www.hup.harvard.edu
2. Luigi Russolo, *L'Arte di rumori* (New York: Pendragon Press, Monographs in Musicology, no. 6, 1986). http://www.pendragonpress.com;
   John Cage, *Silence: lectures and writings* (Middletown: Wesleyan University Press, 1961). http://www.wesleyan.edu/wespress/
3. Brandon LaBelle, *Sounding Out: Reverberations Across Social Space*, Just About Now (Rotterdam: V2_archief, 2000). http://www.v2.nl/archief
4. EnviroMeasure, *Speed of Sound Calculator* (1997) http://www.measure.demon.co.uk/Acoustics_Software/speed.html
5. O. Cramer, *The variation of the specific heat ratio and the speed of sound in air with temperature, pressure, humidity, and CO_2 concentration* (Journal of the Acoustical Society of America. 93(5), 1993), 2510-2616. http://asa.aip.org/jasa.html
6. Paul Virilio, *Speed & Politics* (New York: Autonomedia, transl. 1986). http://www.autonomedia.org
7. R. Murray Schafer, *The Tuning of the World* (New York: Knopf, 1977). http://www.randomhouse.com/knopf/
8. Hermann L. F. von Helmholtz, *On the Sensations of Tone as a physiologi cal basis for the theory of Music* (New York: Dover Publications Inc., 1954).
9. Jens Blauert, *Spatial Hearing: The Psychophysics of Human Sound Localization* (Cambridge: MIT Press, 1996). http://mitpress.mit.edu
10. Fritz Winckel, *Music, Sound and Sensation* (New York: Dover Publications Inc., 1967).
11. Stanley Coren, *Sleep Thieves* (New York: The Free Press, 1996). http://www.thefreepress.com
12. John R. Pierce, *The Science of Musical Sound* (New York: W.H. Freeman & Company, 1992). http://www.whfreeman.com
13. Harry Partch, *Genesis of a Music* (Cambridge: Da Capo Press, 1974). http://www.dacapopress.com
14. Juan G. Roederer, *The Physics and Psychophysics of Music* (New York: Springer-Verlag, 1995). http://www.springer.de/
15. Michel Redolfi, *Detours* (Nice: Mirage Musical, 1996).
16. Toshiya Tsunoda, *Monitor Units for Solid Vibration* (Sound Art – Sound as Media, Tokyo: NTT InterCommunicationsCenter, 2000). http://www.ntticc.or.jp
17. Miller Puckette, *FTS: A Real-time Monitor for Multiprocessor Music Synthesis* (Computer Music Journal. 15(3), 1991), 58-67. http://mitpress.mit.edu
18. H. Nyquist, *Thermal Agitation of Electric Charge in Conductors* (Phys. Rev. 32, 1928), 110-113.
19. Ken C. Pohlmann, *Principles of Digital Audio* (New York: McGraw-Hill, 1995). http://www.mcgraw-hill.com
20. Farmersmanual, *off-ICMC* (Berlin: Podewil, 2000). http://www.podewil.de

21. Atau Tanaka, *Netmusic – a Perspective* ("Festival du Web," Paris: Webart, 1999). http://www.webbar.fr; Atau Tanaka, *Network Audio Performance and Installation* (Proc. Intnl Computer Music Conf., San Francisco: ICMA, 1999). http://www.computermusic.org
22. Marc Treib, *Space Calculated in Seconds: The Philips Pavilion, Le Corbusier, Edgard Varèse* (Princeton: Princeton University Press, 1996). http://pup.princeton.edu; Iannes Xenakis, *Formalized Music-Thought and Mathematics in Composition* (Hillsdale: Pendragon Press, 1971). http://www.pendragonpress.com; E. L. Lowman, *Some Striking Proportions in the Music of Bela Bartok* (Fibonacci Quarterly 9(5), 1971), 527-528. http://www.sdstate.edu/~wcsc/http/fibhome.html

Atau Tanaka is an artist-developer who creates interactive music pieces for concert performance, fixed interactive media, and network. He lives in the U.S.A, France, and Japan. This transcultural perspective is reflected as his artistic activities move from concert to installation to recorded media, from acoustic to electronic to experimental. Physical interfaces are his instruments, and the network is a natural space for this music. His performances use corporeal gesture to articulate music and sound synthesis and real-time image transformation. He has published interactive media works, created installations, and has performed in Europe, North America, and Japan. Apple Computer France sponsers Tanaka as Artistic Ambassador for new technology.

Kodwo Eshun

VISIONS OF RHYTHM IN THE KINEMATIC PNEUMACOSM OF HYPE WILLIAMS

VISIONS OF RHYTHM IN THE KINEMATIC PNEUMACOSM OF HYPE WILLIAMS

Today, the music video, as the digital theorist Lev Manovich persuasively argues, functions as "a laboratory for exploring the new possibilities" of digital cinema.[1] New slownesses, new speeds, new fermatas, new polyrhythms, new dynamic events emerge from the elastic reality and softimages of broadcast entertainment culture.

Back in 1979, the Parliament-Funkadelic producer George Clinton linked audio, vision and movement, the components of entertainment culture, together into a single sleek equation – the rhythm of *vision is a dancer.*[2] This proposition allows us to analyze the post-1994 music video as the digital convergence of these intensities.

More precisely, we can hear and see how the processes of choreography and editing, effect processing and digital music fuse in the modern hip-hop and R&B video to become a new "animatography" – film director Dario Argento's 1971 term for a future cinema of animated photography.[3]

The music video is to the musical as the break is to the funk track: the concentrated essence of the digital image. It's all effect, nothing but special efx double plus. A slice

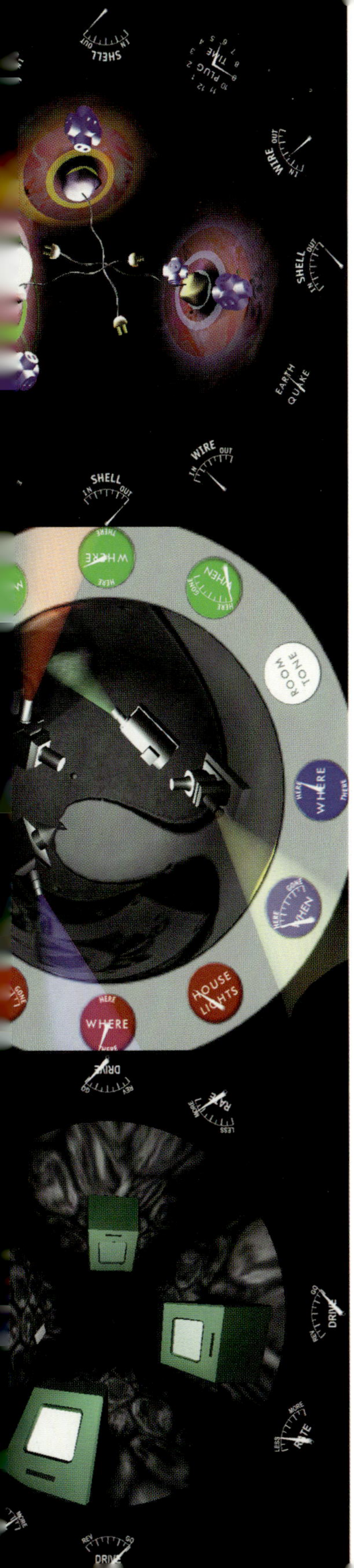

of time that enthralls and appalls in rapid succession. Nothing dates faster than the music video – and this is its value – to time-code the present as cultural fantasy.

We know that all digital music is out of date because today's music is partly made from samples constructed on the spot, partly from samples snatched from their dates, effects separated from their causes, sound-events looped from phonographic pasts which they drag along nonetheless. Times are sliced from their calendars, scrambling the inherited calendar of musical history, anachronizing traditions, rearranging legacies.

Since 1994, the video director Hype Williams has drastically reinvented the look of hip hop and R&B. In grandiose presidential epics (Puff Daddy's *Victory*), Messiah identifying playa fantasies (Nas' *Hate Me Now*), Buddhamorphic Mariko Moriesque homages (TLC's *Unpretty*), seething R&B grrrl rage (Kelis' *Caught Out There*) and lascivious uptown hymns to booty (Q-Tip's *Vivrant Thing*), Williams breaks decisively with hip-hop's territorial allegiance to the street.

In its place, he projects an aesthetic of ghetto fabulousness, a term invented by the Bad Boy record label CEO, producer and plutocrat Sean "Puffy" Combs. As a world-view, ghetto fabulousness epitomizes an early 2000s mindstate of hypercapitalist realism, replacing the mid-1990s ideal of the heavy-lidded gangsta with the archetype of the playa, weighted with "ice," plat-

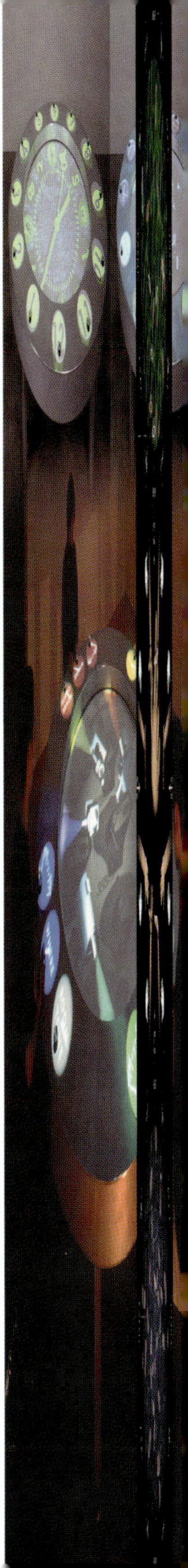

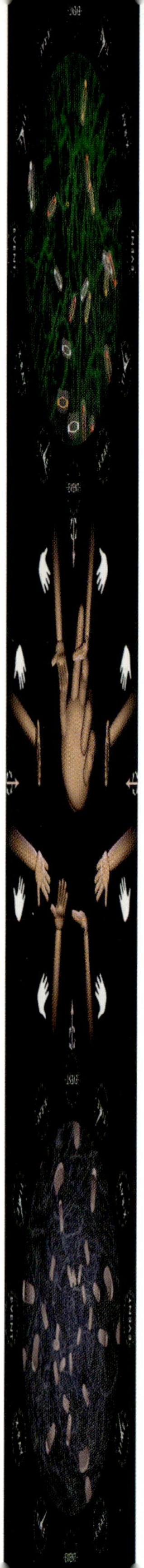

inum crucifixes, bracelets and necklaces, the baller who blazes and shines, driven by an endless appetite for unlimited luxury.

In particular, Williams' videos for the songwriter, producer, emcee and vocalist Missy Elliot and the emcee Busta Rhymes reveal a vision of ghetto fabulousness at its most rhythmatic. The Elliot videos *The Rain (Supa Dupa Fly)* (1997), *Beep Me 911* (1998), *She's a Bitch* (1999) and the Rhymes videos *Gimme Some Mo* (1999) and *What's It Gonna Be* featuring Janet Jackson (1999) therefore form the launch pad for an immanent analysis of the rhythm of vision in the Information Age.

Whatever movie you're watching, sound is fractionally ahead of sight, the ear always pilots the eye, vision always lags behind listening. The rhythmatic music video, in particular, insists on this aural advantage by turning a perceptual condition into its content, generating audiovisions, as the theorist Michel Chion calls them, in which you hear what you

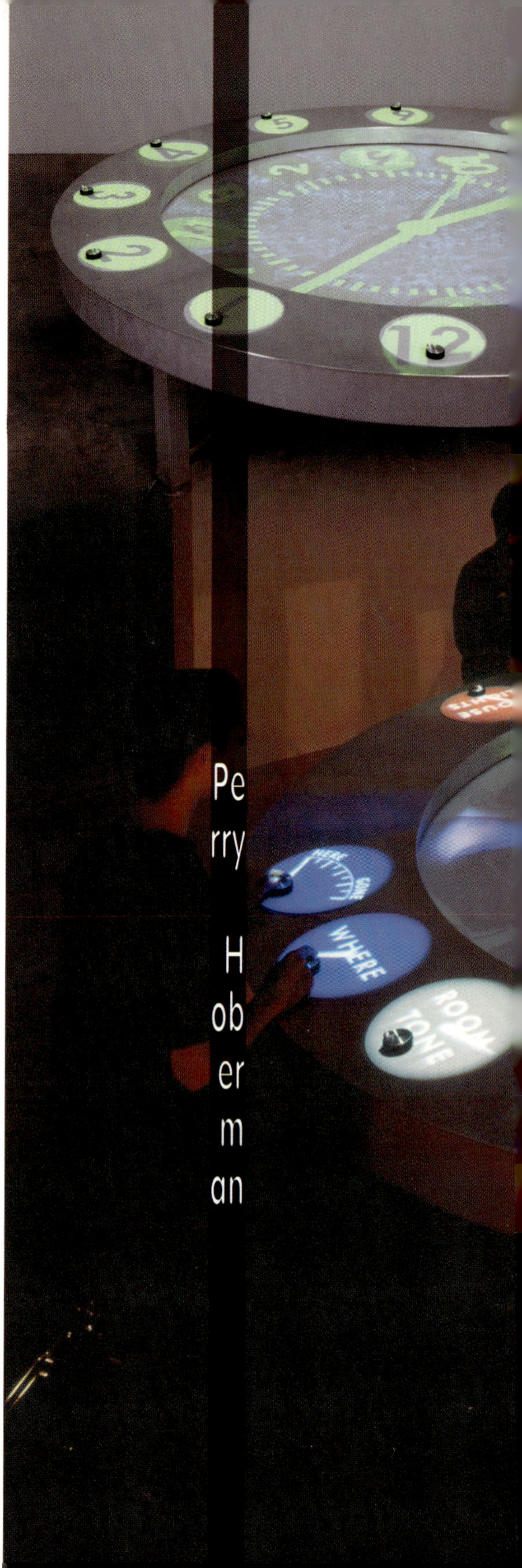

Perry Hoberman

The twentieth century has transformed our concept of time, and the interactive multi-user installation *Timetable* attempts to reproduce the manipulation of time – its shrinking, its recording and even its elimination – that technology has made possible.

In *Timetable*, an image is projected from above onto a large circular table. Twelve dials are positioned around the perimeter of the table. The functions each of these dials changes and mutates, depending on what is projected onto them at any given moment. Dials can become clocks, gauges, speedometers, switches, steering wheels and so on. A real-time 3D scene, projected onto the central part of the table, is controlled and influenced by the movements of the dials. Through the operation of these dials, images projected onto the table pass freely through the past, the present and the future, mutating as they go; the microcosm of time lies in the hands of the visitor.

Timetable

At the outset, the space of *Timetable* seems to be rational and unified, but the longer the piece is used, the more complex and multi-dimensional it becomes, as perspectives and timeframes diverge and split off from each other. *Timetable* attempts to make certain paradoxical (even impossible) pseudo-scientific concepts into concrete experiences, such as time travel, multiple branching universes, alternate dimensions and shared hallucinations.

The table itself represents a kind of giant immersive clock, but it could as easily be described as a board game without rules, a top-level meeting with

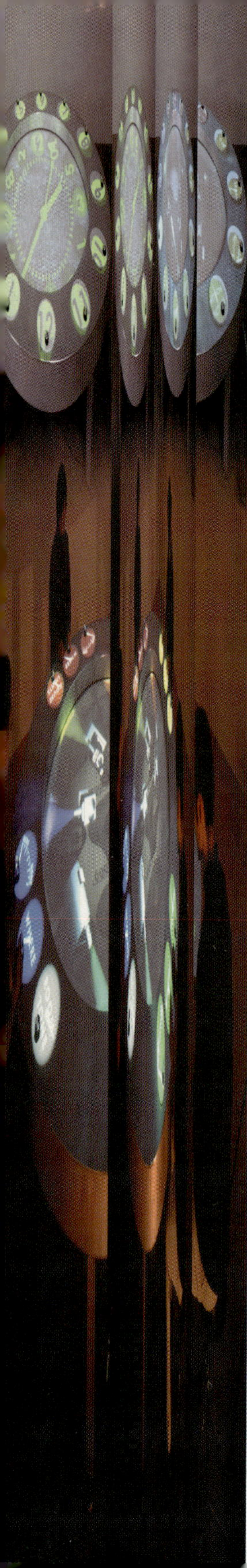

want to watch rather than vice versa.[4]

VISIONS OF RHYTHM IN THE KINEMATIC

Every music video visualizes its songworld; the modern dance video opens up another dimension by extending the kinematic, the field of movement, into the sonic, so that the image becomes "kinesonic," in Drew Hemment's term.[5] To understand William's kinesonic visions of computerhythm, it's necessary to understand his key videos as a trilaboration with Melissa Elliot who contributes the persona Missy Misdemeanour and the influential R&B producer Tim "Timbaland" Mosley, with whom Elliot cowrites tracks.

PNEUMACOSM OF HYPE WILLIAMS

Born from the merger of Brownian discipline with Kraftwerkian stiffness, funk is where the human and the machine meet and part exchange, a discontinuum between the organic and the mekanik, the rigidly human and the softly machinic. Back in 1996, Timbaland hyped the funk with his signature sound, an ultra-electronic hypersyncopation that reprogrammed R&B overnight, setting off repercussions throughout the late 1990s/early 2000s audioscape.

A Timbaland production such as the synthetic hypersoul of Aaliyah's *What's So Different* (2000) or Ginuine's *What's So Different* (1999) immediately arrests you with its stopstart supersyncopation. Mosley's digital age funk incited Williams' fascination with sonomotion, his vision of the digital image libidinized as pulsation and frequency.

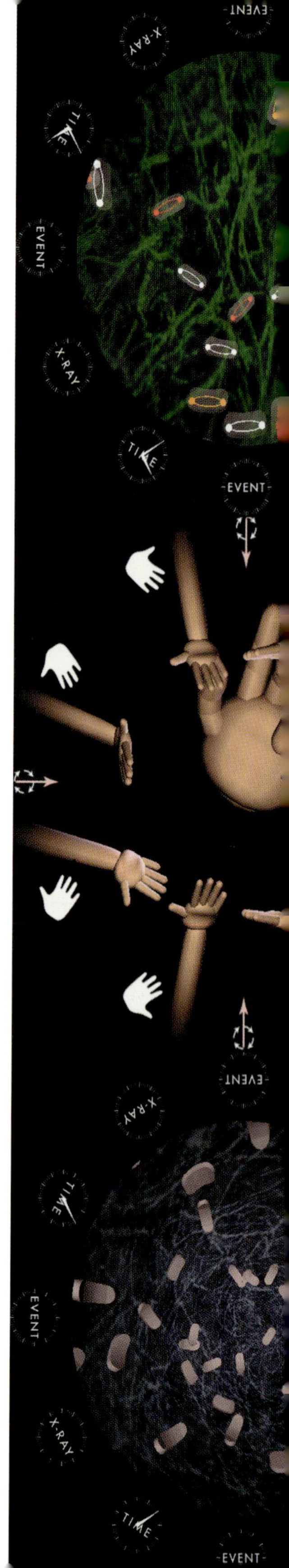

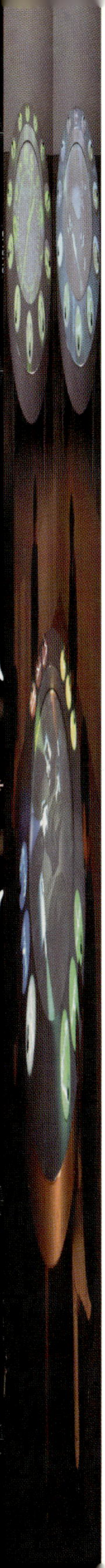

To assemble the landscape of synthetic percussion, that is, the syncussionscape of *The Rain*, Timbaland sampled the title vocal and reconfigured two bars from the chorus of Ann Peebles' 1974 synthetic soul classic *I Can't Stand the Rain*. Minimal yet weirdly huge, with pauses wide enough to park a Jeep in, the synthesizer tones in *The Rain* are rhythmelodic, simultaneously rhythmic and melodic. Listening to *The Rain* – formed from bass pulse, tick-tock syncussion and ultrastark hook processed into a half Moog-half woodblock twintone – is like braindrops falling off your head.

By artificializing R&B, *The Rain* announced a cyborg funk that allowed Williams to generate metal melodic machine worlds populated by humans modified by media. Robo steps and rotary hips: a Williams video grows a new human from the feet upwards. A Timbaland track moves with a stilted, lurching gait that Simon Reynolds terms "falterfunk." It's a series of hesitations that never fail to ambush you. Patterns are unresolved, incomplete, indefinite.

Rhythmatically speaking, it's cleverer than you or me, it's always wrongfooting you. Without warning, doorknocker snares double and triple in tempo: dot-dot-dash Morsecodes that pause, listen, then head off in another direction, bringing you up short, catching you out. Basswise, Mosley opts for spasms that sometimes double up the kickdrum sound, other times erupting suddenly from the giant spaces between the snare-steps, sliding the floor from beneath you, blindsiding you.

no agenda, or a seance without spirits. At the end of a century in which all our ideas about time have been shattered and radically reconfigured, *Timetable* is an attempt to play with concepts of time – to buy time and to spend it, to save time and to waste it, to find time and to lose it, to borrow it, to run out of it, to kill it.

Produced by: NTT InterCommunication Center [ICC] for ICC Biennale '99
Sound: Elliott Sharp
Code & Interface Design Assistance: Juha Huuskonen
Real-Time 3D Rendering Engine: SurRender 3D
Production Assistance: Scott Konzelman
Winner, Grand Prix, ICC Biennale '99

Perry Hoberman

Timetable

Throughout this treacherous rhythmscape, Timbaland prowls sotte voce, a creepy phono-stalker. Elliot herself doesn't flow lyrically so much as zigzag in a precise cadence, poised between emceeing and singing. Her sprechgesgange leaves space for what the composer Toru Takemitsu calls "vocalism," an indelible onomatopoetry of vrrrrooms, beep beeps, ugggghs, heees and brrrrrrs.

Elliot is what the drum 'n' bass producer Pascal calls a mind-stresser. She specializes in stressing the odd syllables in a word, pausing at the hinge points of syntax, then stre-e-e-tching the ending until the word topples off the beat into space. By accenting unanticipated syllables, she stretches and dilates space until syntax projects dynamically, trading with space, punch phrasing with the beats. All hip hop does this; Elliot does it asymmetrically.

Taken together, Elliot's cadence and Timbaland's programming mutually reinforce a new pattern of inhalation/exhalation. In their world, you're reprogrammed from the lungs inward, invited and incited to breathe and stop, as Q-Tip commands in a circulatory pattern that's both fluid and rigid, liquid and abrupt, stiff and loose.[6] These paradoxical patterns form the biomechanical diagram for funkatized computer music. They are a schematic of the twin illogic of today's modern dance.

In lyrically regressive, rhythmically advanced dance musics like R&B, Southern bounce and two-step garage, harmony and melody have fused to become harmelodies, texture and rhythm to become texturhythms. As cultural expression, music video choreography is ignored if not reviled as the nadir of ultrasexism, as a dead end of complaisant video-hos gyrating and lounging by gigantic swimming pools. If choreography is ever noticed, it's to disparage it as the epitome of uncreative corniness.

As Klaus Theweleit suggested, the dance medium "always displays the conscious cultivation of new images of the

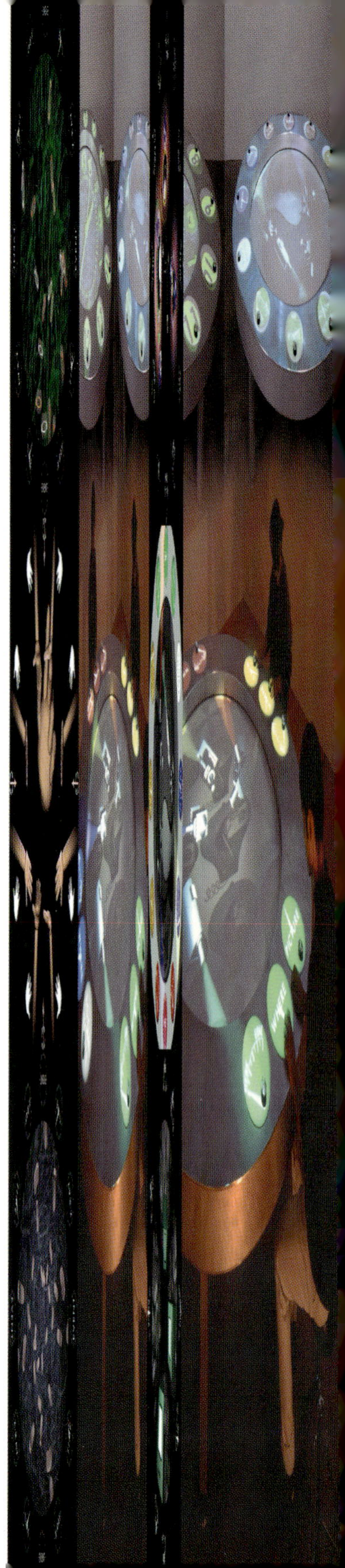

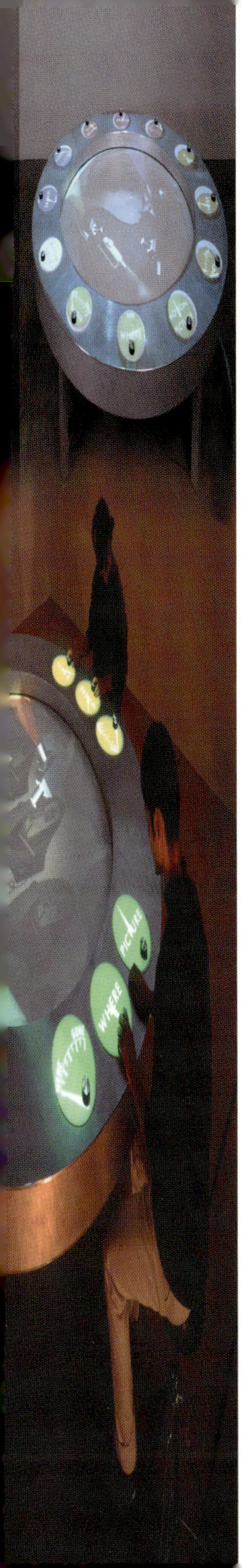

body."[7] A closer look at choreography in Williams' videos suggests that it functions as a medium within the video medium, not only for visualizing rhythms as human patterns, which is obvious enough, but for translating advanced polyrhythmic events into human ornaments. Not mass ornaments in the sense of the stadium gymnastic displays that Siegfried Kracauer noted in the 1920s. Nor quite the kaleidoscopic patterns of rhythm Busby Berkeley orchestrated on celluloid at the same time.

Rather, it elaborates special effects as cultural fantasies, delivering you comfortably into the moving vehicle of the impossible image. When digitally edited syncopation is translated into digital movement that is translated as human movement and then digitally reedited as unrealtime dance, an "artificial realism," in photographer Jeff Walls' term, ensues – a smooth delusion that happily blurs the distinctions between the organic and the computational, soft machine times and flexible carbon tempos.

The Hype Williams universe flaunts these qualities because it's a syncopescape, a five-minute hypersyncopated landscape in which everything has rhythmelodic properties: the camera angles and the optical filters, the lighting and the set design, the surfaces and the finishes, the costumes and the makeup, the limbs, the faces, the gestures, the expressions. In this world, hypersyncopation isn't so much illustrated as it is orchestrated. It assumes the capabilities of a motive force by animating an abbreviated world peopled by polyrhythmaddicts, worlds in which everyone and everything is in thrall to the dynamics of the digital.

The synchronization of syncopation is the motor of the dance music video. Look closely at *The Rain* and it's audibly clear that a twitch is a beat, a shrug is a kick and a nod is as good as a wink. Choreography, effects processing and musculature all fuse in an angular fluidity. Elliot's movements, all sudden twitches, abrupt lunges and insectoid pulses, update the early-1980s style of tic toc bodypopping, the dance which

animated the analogue motion of first wave electro.

Syncussion depersonalizes Elliot and her girl dancers, trapped in the doll's house of *Beep Me 911,* into woman-droids with hinged joints, in the grip of invisible forces greater than them. Their gestures – lower arms held at right angles, dipping from the shoulder, stiff-legged gait, inflexible turns – stage the rigidly robotic mindstate and bitter mood of the song's worldview.

Beep Me 911 syncopates and abbreviates the long line of geometric females from the Metropolis robot to Marie 1 and Marie 2 in Vera Chytilova's eerie 1966 movie *Daisies* to the 1970s of Bryan Forbes' *Stepford Wives.* Missy's girls join in a ballet rhythmechanique, rigidly embodying what Antonin Artaud recognized as the gestural music of "a falling foot, an arching knee, a constant play of mirrors where human limbs seem to echo one another."[8]

Welding the vocal science of the sampler to the editing/effect processing of the work station, the dance music video orchestrates a microphysics of gesture, a labyrinth of vocalization. *The Rain* demonstrates Elliot's zygomatic muscles becoming a facioplastic fantasy in time, a vision of on-beat rhythm. Her eyes do one thing while her mouth does another. When she leans into the camera her lips swell and quiver in an S-wave motion.

The image slows down to the weightless tempo of a glide-by shooting.[9] As she leans to the left, her eyes look right and bulge, slide sideways, look up from beneath her fake fringe as her lips struggle to suppress a laugh. In the electronic world of *The Rain,* she regresses to an artificial girlhood. On top of the hill "like Lauren," she smooths her wig, shakes it in her face, wipes it away, bats her eyelashes Diana-style.

Sunglasses inflate and mold the eyes into bugged orbs. From The Fly in *Car Wash* to Sly Stone, from Stevie Wonder to Miles Davis to Kool Keith, you could write a monograph on the shades in postwar African-American electronic music. As the *Supa Dupa Fly*, the personification of the song, its presiding demon, Elliot drastically reinvents this male tradition of looking fly while buggin' out.

Her eyewear fuses shades with helmets, headpieces with goggles, emphasizes finish and exaggerates frame into Technic 1200 toned tough reflective skins that wrap the spaces between cheekbone, nose and forehead. Concaved by Williams' goldfisheye lens, Missy becomes ultra-fly. Facing Puffy Combs, she tilts and cocks her head, reticulating rhythmic movement with an exaggerated alertness. Pam, the singer from Total, the Missy-produced girl trio, leans forward in a lazy curve. Her tongue, lengthy as a gecko, lolls out and slurps the air. In *No Scrubs* (1999) the cybER&B girl trio TLC become armbumpered, kneepadded, wallcrawling chameleons nimbly scaling the paneled surfaces of their platinum tubeways.

"On either side of a characteristic synch point," Michel Chion explains, "the capacity for temporal elasticity can become almost infinite ... hooking auditory continuity to visual continuity is what allows the time around it to swell, fold, puff up, tighten, stretch or on the contrary hang loosely like fabric."[10] Chion was pondering the dynamic edits of martial arts movies when he wrote this, but it fits the Williams aesthetic like a velvet glove. The parallels between the on-point slash and scythe of martial movements and the onbeat punch of breakbeats are voluble.

Maybe Missy Elliot's Michelin Woman suit in *The Rain* is so startling and so satisfying to see and feel because it translates sonic temporality into pneumatic tangibility. Glinting and gelatinous, it exaggerates the elasticity Chion hymns, crosswires sensations until you see the fabric of the song. Swathed inside her inflato suit, her limbs protrude like cats coupling in a four-cornered bag, like a starfish tussling with a telephone kiosk in a gloss black jellymold. She deflates on a steel gray plinth, softboned, head lolling, arms limp as

Dig
ital
ly
org
ani
ze
d
im
agi
ng

Kodwo Eshun

VISIONS OF RHYTHM IN THE KINEMATIC PNEUMACOSM OF HYPE WILLIAMS

razor-edged rotor blades swinging either side of her larval state.

Lip-synching to her voice at half speed means that her mouth lags behind playback. Typically Williams fluctuates the degrees of asynchronicity to infra-thin slices of time so that Elliot's mouth sometimes runs ahead of a micropause while a syntharmonic bass lurches forward. Conversely, she visually pauses as her cadence swerves sideways and a bass suddenly halts. A net of gaps, a skein of traps connecting the visual to the mobile to the now-diverging/now-converging rhythmic, opens up the dimension of the kinesonic.

On *Gimme Some Mo*, by contrast, Busta Rhymes' flow runs on in a series of rapid-fire lunges, syntactic strikes launched for optimal informational density. Williams often freezes a scene so that Busta halts, stranded on the verge of a new word. Vision pauses for a micro-tic as audio streams on, thus creating the paradoxical impact of a moving pause and the overwhelming sense that the visual is discharging the audio, dynamizing it.

It's the visual equivalent of the DJ technique of punch phrasing, where you delay the record on beat, wait a blink, then release for a Kapow! effect. At other times in *Gimme Some Mo*, the fermata explodes into a gliding slowness until the Versace-bright avatars float momentarily untethered from gravity.

The Williams syncopescape affirms the

Woody Vasulka

The dramatic moment of transformation into a binary code of energy events in time, as they may be derived from light, or the molecular communication of sound, or from a force field, gravity, or other physical initiation, must be realized in order to appreciate the power of the organization and transformation of a code. The process of analog-to-digital and digital-to-analog conversion envelops the internal digital-code operations, the state of the world, which is exclusively human-organized and cross-disciplinary. The unity of the coding structure has laid down an astonishingly versatile material from which codes are constructed and from which the hierarchical order of codes can originate.

These states of transformation exist in as many time domains as the generation, organization or processing of codes required for the media they represent. (A complex sound, for example, can operate in a lower time domain than a complex dynamic image, while other media – for example, printed text generation – seem more time-immune.) In this way, time assumes a new compositional meaning, a micro-compositional one, where control over the generation of an image can be exerted even in short or very short lengths of time. That in itself signals an urgency to define the craft in which the notion of time dominates (W.V. from *Syntax of Binary Images*, 1970s).

In the long view, these principles have consumed practically all my productive life. Adding the condition of real-time feedback, this basic and significant furnace

rhythmic qualities of everything. Therefore the dimensions of space take on an animated aspect. El Lissitzky called his constructed spaces pangeometrical because they were places where vectors took on the energetic quantity of lines of force.

Pangeometry comes alive in *What You Gonna Do,* where silver cubic grids permutate into a funky mathematics of syncopated space division. Janet Jackson's glutinous tunnel gradually sucks Busta Rhymes out of his cubic world. The platinum corridor undergoes hostile rhythm division, closing in on his knight avatar until he learns to become liquid.

Here, the sets are often more rhythmatic than the humans grown from them. Regan Jackson's aggressively pangeometric set design for *She's A Bitch* splices the pulsating fluorescent wireframes of *Tron* with the lethal interchanges of The Cube. A camera balefully prowls around Flavinoid lines of

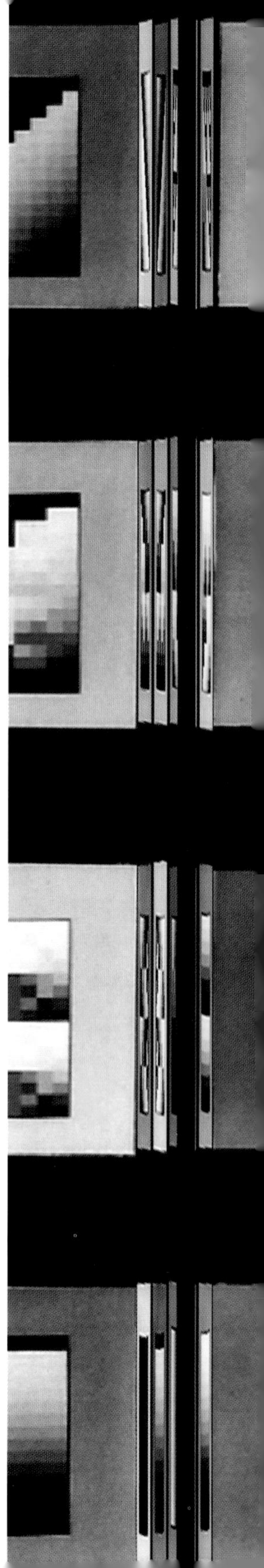

light, pulsing on/off across the horizontal while interlocking floor patterns fluoresce in a rapid eye network of triple optics. Submerged in blue darkness, Elliot's light-vectored gloves and neon-ringed breastplate wink off/on, alarming the cubed space, animating its hostility. Periodically the screen strobes, stepping up a retinal ferocity.

While *The Rain* takes its cues from Timbaland's micro hesitations, *She's a Bitch* animates stentorian string sequences and synth-harmonic low end with an intimidating thuggishness. As forbidding as *The Rain* is lightfingered, its chorus combines rhythmatic impacts with a nervous guitar twang and scuttling bongo-triplets. Oppressiveness resounds in her sullen menacing headbang to the loadbearing thud of Timbaland's beats.

In time to the ooomphs, the dancers, trussed and spiked in a humid second skin, grind their heels and twist the balls of their feet to the twang of the guitar,

Digitally organized imaging

Woody Vasulka

of systemic power, it has bonded me to a long and mutual custodianship. It has led to the construction of various environments in which the machine becomes the suitable confinement for the practice of each specific principle. Only much later did I begin to question this condition. For an existentialist, the illusionist purpose of this kind of servitude has no meaning. But perhaps that was just a glimpse of the future: We should give up the convenient, logical and purposeful life of servility to our next kin – the machine.

(Woody Vasulka, August 2000)

stomping on the giant island M platform. Vacuum-packed into a harnessed ultra-black exoskeleton, Missy holds her head, tilts it from left to right and twists it as if screwing it off her shoulders.

If the dance medium consciously cultivates "new images of the body," then the section of *The Rain* that shows Missy toppling and teetering suggests that she is being buffeted by the ruff ryde of a new rhythmic regime. On observing the Balinese Theatre in Paris, Artaud perceived a similar adaptation process. "They have their own way of regaining their balance" he noted, "a peculiar, arching, leg-twisting stance which gives the impression of a wet cloth about to be wrung to music." Like the Balinese, Elliot's droids are struggling to integrate a new behavior, to grow a new nervous system.

The opening scenes of *She's a Bitch* reveal Missy as a dreadnought, sailing down a black tube, black cloak unfurling silently like Darth Vader's vicious sister's. More Technics 1200 than human, her skintone is lit with silver until it emits a paradoxical black light. Retinal intensity is sucked into a vacuum and inverted until it illuminates everything as degrees of humid, indistinct black light. It's a world of service sectors and tubeways, tunnels and airlocked corridors where the distinction between walls and ceiling collapses in a continuously clad curvature.

Jackson fascination with curvature takes its cue partly from Mark Romanek's *Scream*

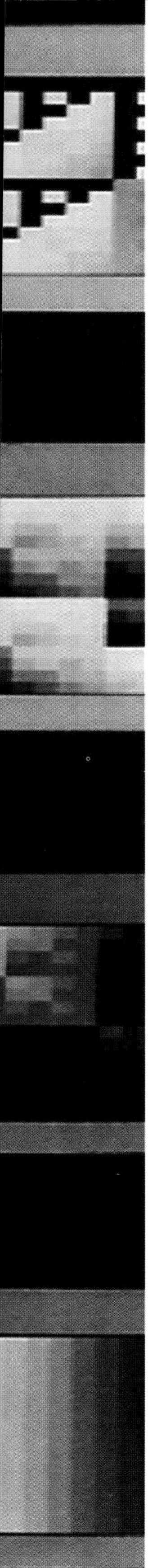

video for Michael Jackson, partly from Williams' colossal preference for the (gold)fisheye lens which picks up space and wraps it around his figures, enclosing them in a wide-angled aquarium from which they peer out at us. They home in on the camera, pulsating the screen, crowding and squeezing into the frame until it's on the verge of bursting, going pop. Back in 1993, De la Soul called this the Buhloone Mindstate, the sensation of a membrane swollen with desire, tangible with appetite."

As its greedy title suggests, the video for Busta Rhymes' *Gimme Some Mo* escalates this sense of a puffed-up life to monstrous extremes. Rhymes' seven-deep crew of MC allies and cronies are called the Flipmode Squad; accordingly, all events occur in the flip(ped) mode of the song's interior, a space that rotates around the royal axis of an unchanging yet endlessly listenable loop from Gus Van Sant's *Psycho* remake.

When the child Busta trips on a tree root, bumps his head and mutates into a monster boy, his alteration isn't synched so much as propelled by door-knocker snares and the adult Rhymes' terse, impatient "C'mon C'mon." Rhymes' pupils dilate, turn red, swirl and rotate. Leaning towards the maid, whose sheerly clad legs tower over him, yellow canines shoot from his lipless purple mouth. His right eye, left eye, nostrils and brow violently sproing from his face and he sprouts electric blue fur.

Polyrhythm incites monstrosity. It calls it out by its name. Busta, now Monsta Boy, is

Gimme Some Mo's (un)real face, the "fabulous" in ghetto-fabulous animated and amok in a world turned Pantonesque. As the maid scales the fridge to escape Monsta Boy, the camera waits for her. At the top of the fridge, her head broadens and squashes up against the frame. Her nose and mouth swell and flatten into a nostrilly, planar rhinoplasticity.

Her body is swallowed by the aggressively, exuberantly shape-changing world she inhabits. Far below, her red shoes taper into points. Space distends so Monsta Boy looking up at her from the checkered kitchen floor is banished to the vanishing point.

Busta as a swaggering cop, his elbow making a musical angle with its forearm, Busta in a blue zoot suit, Busta tied to a railway line, Busta in a lime-green suit splined along the curvature between wall and ceiling, Busta with a droopy moustache and sombrero, Busta as a flashwad tycoon shaking dead presidents at you, Busta obscured by high-beam goggles, Busta in a pink snakeskin top with hooped rings at the upper arms, Busta suitalooned in an inflatomuscular skin, Busta draped in a luxurious chinchilla coat that heedlessly sweeps the floor: Busta has selves to go.

Gimme Some Mo exemplifies ghettofabulousness in its perpetual parade of luxurious mutation fired up by continuous appetite. *Gimme Some Mo* is Hype Williams in excelsis.

References

1. Lev Manovitch, *What is Digital Cinema?*, from Peter Lunenfeld, *The Digital Dialectic: New Essays on New Media* (Cambridge: MIT Press, 1999).
2. Parliament, *The Motor Booty Affair* (Casablanca, 1978).
3. Dario Argento, *Cat o' Nine Tails* (1970).
4. Michel Chion, *Audio-Vision* (New York: Columbia University Press, 1994)
5. Drew Hemment, *On Sonomotion* (Mute, 1997).
6. Q-Tip, *Breath and Stop* (Arista, 2000).
7. Klaus Theweleit, *Male Fantasies* (University of Minnesota Press, 1987), 318.
8. Antonin Artaud, *The theatre and its double* (Tr. Victor Corti, London: Calder, 1970), Antonin Artaud, *On the Balinese Theatre*, 38.

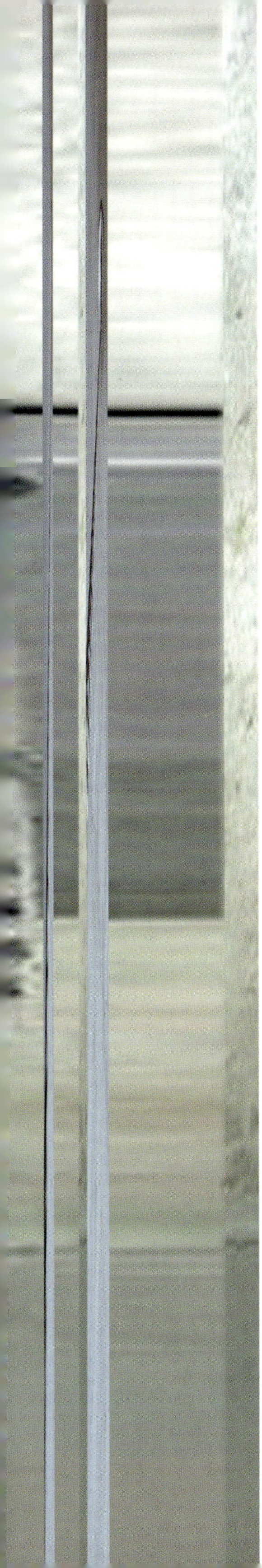

9. 2 Lone Swordsmen, *Glide By Shooting* (Slut Trax, 1998).
10. Michel Chion, *Audiovision* (Columbia University, 1994), 140.
11. De La Soul, *Buhloone Mindstate* (Tommy Boy, 1993).

Kodwo Eshun (1968) at seventeen, won an Open Scholarship to read Law at University College, Oxford. After eight days he switched to Literary Theory, magazine journalism and running clubs. He is not a cultural critic or cultural commentator so much as a concept engineer writing on electronic music in today's setting of science fiction, technoculture, gameculture, drug culture, post war movies and post war art for I-D, The Wire, The Face, Arena, Suddeutsche Zeitung, Die Zeit and The Times.

More Brilliant Than The Sun, his first book on sonic fiction, the interface between science fiction and electronic music was published in May 1998 by Quartet Books. Here he assembles an entirely new field of study which he terms sonic fiction: the intersection between science fiction and sound. Kodwo Eshun dismantles the mechanics of the "futurhythmachine" – the co-evolution of humans and machines.

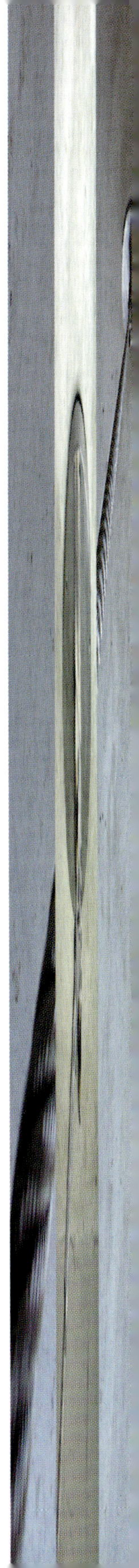

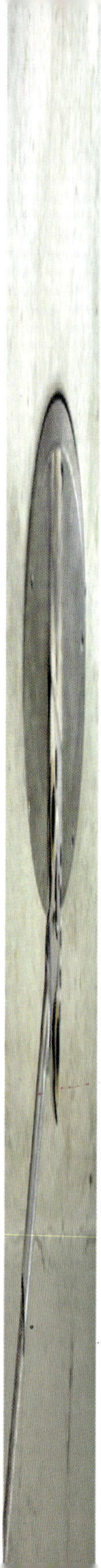

Robert Levine

TIME TALKS, WITH AN ACCENT

TIME TALKS, WITH AN ACCENT

Few would question that new levels of time pressure have resulted from the exponential advances in technology and communications that define modern life in much of the world. A century ago, technological advances such as the railroads and telegraph led to the establishment of standardized timekeeping. Today's global technology demands finer and finer timekeeping, tighter and more coordinated schedules and increased pressure toward make every moment count. When students from temporally lenient cultures study international business – most often at universities in clock- and schedule-dominated cultures – there is no question that emphases on behaviors related to the clock, time urgency, and treating time as money become the rules of play. It would not be farfetched to argue that there is something of a temporal colonialism being brought upon the world by economically influential governments, and even more by powerful international businesses.

Still, beliefs about time remain profoundly different from culture to culture. Research shows that cultural differences in time can be as vast as those between languages. In one particularly telling study of the roots of culture shock, sociologists James Spradley and Mark Phillips asked a group of returning Peace Corps volunteers

to rank 33 items as to the amount of cultural adjustment each had required of them. The list included a wide range of items familiar to travel paranoids, such as "type of food eaten," "personal cleanliness of most people," "number of people of your own race" and "general standard of living." But aside from mastering a foreign language, the two greatest difficulties for the Peace Corps volunteers concerned social time: "the general pace of life," followed by one of its most significant components, "how punctual most people are."

No beliefs are more ingrained and subsequently hidden by our cultural upbringings than those about time. Almost 30 years ago anthropologist Edward Hall labeled rules of social time the "silent language." These informal patterns of time "are seldom, if ever, made explicit. They exist in the air around us. They are either familiar and comfortable or unfamiliar and wrong." The world over, children simply "pick up" their society's conceptions of early and late, of waiting and rushing, of past, present and future, as they mature. No dictionary clearly defines these rules of time for them, or for strangers who stumble over the maddening incongruities between the time sense they bring with them and the one they face in a new land. I have spent the better part of the last two decades studying social time and its consequences around the world. Most of what I have observed leads me to agree with the writer Jeremy Rifkin that "every culture has its own unique set of temporal fingerprints. To know a people is to know the time values they live by."

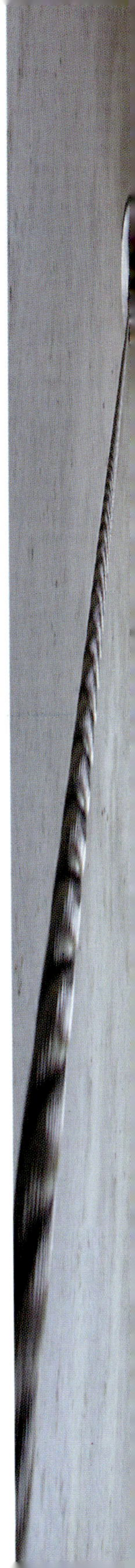

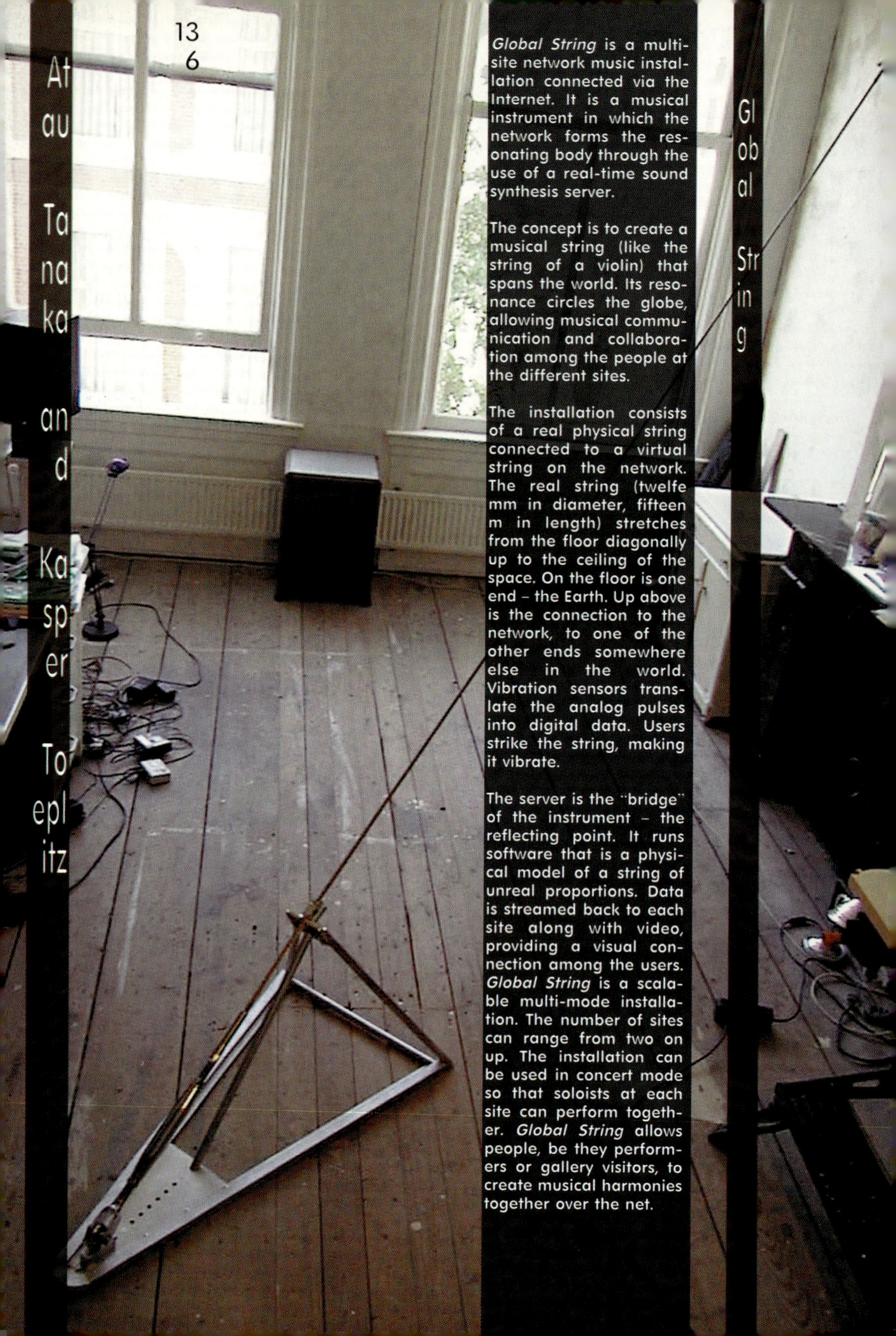

Atau Tanaka and Kasper Toeplitz

Global String

Global String is a multi-site network music installation connected via the Internet. It is a musical instrument in which the network forms the resonating body through the use of a real-time sound synthesis server.

The concept is to create a musical string (like the string of a violin) that spans the world. Its resonance circles the globe, allowing musical communication and collaboration among the people at the different sites.

The installation consists of a real physical string connected to a virtual string on the network. The real string (twelfe mm in diameter, fifteen m in length) stretches from the floor diagonally up to the ceiling of the space. On the floor is one end – the Earth. Up above is the connection to the network, to one of the other ends somewhere else in the world. Vibration sensors translate the analog pulses into digital data. Users strike the string, making it vibrate.

The server is the "bridge" of the instrument – the reflecting point. It runs software that is a physical model of a string of unreal proportions. Data is streamed back to each site along with video, providing a visual connection among the users. *Global String* is a scalable multi-mode installation. The number of sites can range from two on up. The installation can be used in concert mode so that soloists at each site can perform together. *Global String* allows people, be they performers or gallery visitors, to create musical harmonies together over the net.

Much of the world continues to live with minimal regard for clock time. In many cultures, the most important events in life continue to be governed by the clocks of nature – when to plant, when to sow, when to bring the animals to the fields and when to bring them home. Social life is more often than not scheduled by event time. Under this mode of timekeeping, events begin and end via unverbalized mutual consensus, "when the time seems right." The international business standards of clock time and calendar scheduling play a role in all of these cultures, of course, but often they do not have a dominant role.

Perhaps the most significant cultural difference in timekeeping is whether scheduling comes from the clock or from social events. Under clock time, the hour on the timepiece governs the beginning and end of activities. When event time predominates, scheduling is determined by activities. Events begin and end by mutual

consensus, when participants "feel" the time is right. They use the hour on the clock to schedule the beginning and ending of activities, or whether the activities are allowed to transpire according to their own spontaneous schedule. The difference between clock and event time is about more than just speed – although life certainly does tend to be faster for people on clock time.

Many countries extol event time as a philosophy of life. In Mexico, there is a popular saying: "Darle tiempo al tiempo," or "give time time." In other words, let time breathe – allow room for spontaneity and the unplanned to emerge by not overscheduling. In Trinidad there is a saying that "Anytime is Trinidad time." In Brunei, people often awake with the question, "What is not going to happen today?" Psychologist Kris Eysell was confronted by a variation on the African expression "Even time takes its time" as a Peace Corps volunteer in Liberia. Every day, as she made her eight-mile walk from home to work, complete strangers would call out to her along the way: "Take time, Missy."

Anthropologists have chronicled many examples of contemporary event-time cultures. Philip Bock, for example, analyzed the temporal sequence of a wake conducted by the Micmac Indians of Eastern Canada. He found that the wake could be clearly divided into gathering time, prayer time, singing time, intermission and meal time. But it turned out that none of these times were directly related to clock time. The mourners simply moved from one time to another by mutual consensus. When did they begin and end each episode? When the time was ripe, and no sooner.

Robert Lauer tells of the Nuers from the Sudan, whose calendars are based on seasonal changes in their environment. They con-

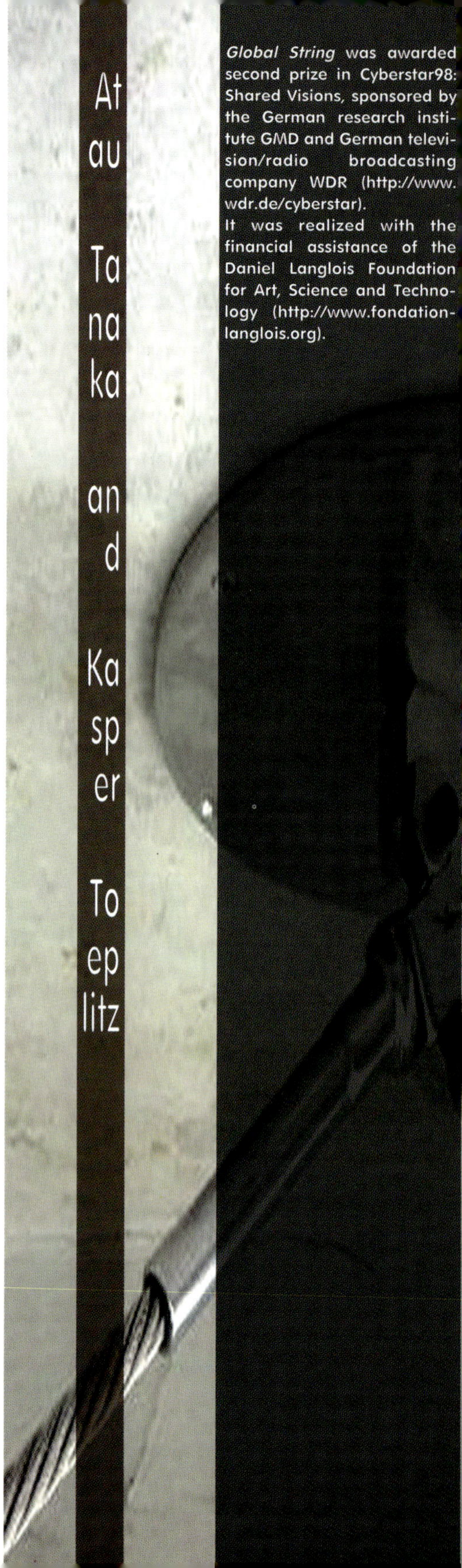

Atau Tanaka and Kasper Toeplitz

Global String was awarded second prize in Cyberstar98: Shared Visions, sponsored by the German research institute GMD and German television/radio broadcasting company WDR (http://www.wdr.de/cyberstar).
It was realized with the financial assistance of the Daniel Langlois Foundation for Art, Science and Technology (http://www.fondation-langlois.org).

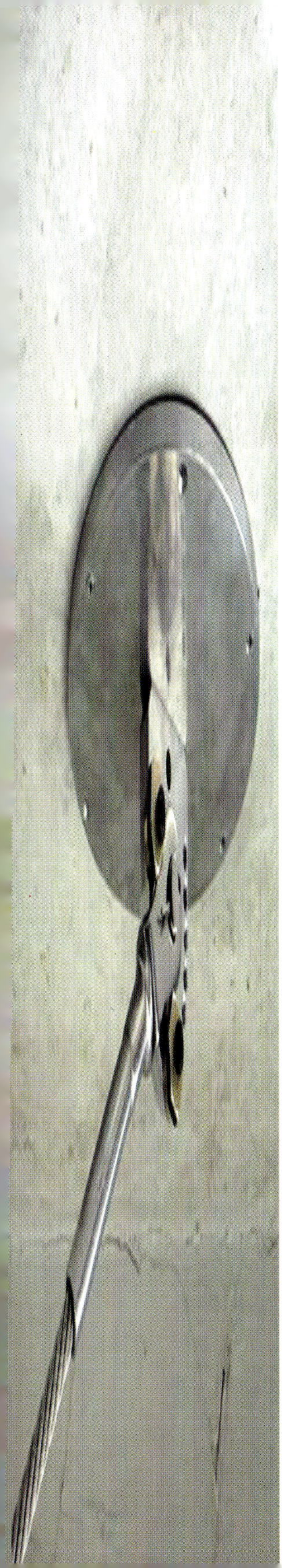

struct fishing dams and cattle camps, for example, in the month of kur. How do they know when it is kur? It's kur when they're building their dams and camps. They break camp and return to their villages in the months of dwat. When is it dwat? When people are on the move. There's an old joke about an American on a whirlwind tour of Europe who is asked where he is. "If it's Tuesday," he responds, "this must be Belgium." If a Nuer were asked the same question, he or she might answer: "If it's Belgium, this must be Tuesday."

Many people use their social activities to mark time rather than the other way around. In parts of Madagascar, for example, questions about how long something takes might receive an answer like "the time of rice-cooking" (about half an hour) or "the frying of a locust" (a quick moment). Similarly, natives of the Cross River in Nigeria have been quoted as saying, "The man died in less than the time in which maize is not yet completely roasted" (less than fifteen minutes). Closer to home, not too many years ago the New English Dictionary included a listing for the term "pissing while" – not a particularly exact measurement, perhaps, but one with a certain cross-cultural translatability.

Most societies have some type of week, but it turns out it's not always seven days long. The Incas had a ten-day week. Their neighbors, the Muysca of Bogota, had a three-day week. Some weeks are as long as sixteen days. Often the length of the week reflects cycles of activities rather than the other way around. For many peoples, markets are the main activities requiring group coordination. The Khasis of Assam, Pitirim Sorokin reports, hold their market every eighth day. Being practical people, they've made their

week eight days long and named the days of the week after the places where the main markets occur.

Natives of the Andaman jungle in India are another people with little need to buy calendars. The Andamanese have constructed a complex annual calendar built around the sequence of dominant smells of trees and flowers in their environment. When they want to check the time of year, the Andamanese simply smell the odors outside their door.

Monks in Burma have developed a foolproof alarm clock. They know it is daybreak, time to rise, "when there is light enough to see the veins in their hand."

There are groups who, even though they have wristwatches, prefer to measure time imprecisely. Anthropologist Douglas Raybeck, for example, has studied the Kelantese peasants of the Malay Peninsula, a group he refers to as the "coconut clock" people. The Kelantese approach to time is typified by their coconut clock – an invention they use as a timer in sporting competitions. This clock consists of half a coconut shell with a small hole in its center that sits in a pail of water. Intervals are measured by the time it takes the shell to fill with water and then sink – usually about three to five minutes. The Kelantese recognize that the clock is inexact, but they choose it over the wristwatches they own.

Some people don't even have a single word equivalent to "time." E.R. Leach has studied the Kachin people of North Burma, who use the word "ahkying" to refer to the time of the clock. The word "na" refers to a long time and "tawng" to a short time. The word "ta" refers to springtime, and "asak" to the time of a person's life. A Kachin wouldn't regard any of these words as synonymous with another. Most Westerners treat time as an objective entity; it is a noun in the English language. The Kachin words for time are treated more like adverbs. Time has no tangible reality for the Kachin.

Time Wars

Because cultural norms are so widely shared by the surrounding society, people often forget their own rules are arbitrary. As a result, we often misconstrue the intentions of peo-

ple with temporal customs different from our own. A particularly frequent source of mishaps involves clashes between clock and event time. Fortunately, most of our stumblings are limited to unpleasant miscommunications. When misunderstandings occur at a higher level, however, they can be serious business.

An example of this occurred in 1985, when a group of Shiite Moslem terrorists hijacked a TWA jetliner and held 40 Americans hostage, demanding that Israel release 764 Lebanese Shiite prisoners being held in prison. Shortly after, the terrorists handed the American hostages over to Shiite Muslim leaders, who assured everybody that nothing would happen if the Israelis met their demands.

At one point during the delicate negotiations Ghassan Sablini, the number three man in the Shiite militia Amal (who had assumed the role of militant authorities), announced that the hostages would be handed back to the hijackers in two days if no action was taken on their demand that Israel release its Shiite prisoners. This created a very dangerous situation. The U.S. negotiators knew that neither they nor the Israelis could submit to these terrorist demands without working out a face-saving compromise. But by setting a limit of two days, the Shiite leaders had made a compromise unlikely and elevated the crisis to a very dangerous level. People held their breaths. At the last minute, however, Sablini was made to understand the way his statement was being interpreted. To everyone's relief, he explained: "We said a couple of days, but we were not necessarily specifying 48 hours."

40 deaths and a possible war were nearly caused by a miscommunication over the meaning of the word "day." To the U.S. negotiators, the word referred to a technical aspect of time – 24 hours. For the Muslim leader, a day was merely a figure of speech meaning "a while." The U.S. negotiators were thinking on clock time. Sablini was on his own event time.

In Praise of Multitemporality

My own experiments have taken a more systematic – albeit perhaps more superficial – approach to measuring cultural differences in time. In these studies, my students and I have systematically compared the pace of life in large cities in 31 countries throughout the world. We have looked at indicators of time such as walking speed in main downtown areas, the speed of work in post offices and banks, and the accuracy of public clocks. Here again, it is clear that there are vast differences in the pace of life around the globe. Big cities in Western Europe and Japan tend to be fastest on our measures, while those in economically struggling nations (such as Mexico, Brazil and Indonesia) tend to be slowest. (The Netherlands, where measurements were taken in Amsterdam, came out ninth fastest (out of 31) overall on our measures. The people of Amsterdam had the second fastest walking speed, were fourteenth fastest on postal worker efficiency, and had the 25th most accurate clocks.) Even when comparing cities within the United States, we often found large differences in these behaviors. In my own home city of Fresno, California, for example, we found that people on average walk only two-thirds as fast as do pedestrians in Boston, Massachusetts.

Whether or not these are the best measures of the pace of life is open to question. What does seem to be clear, however, is that vast differences persist in how people around the world approach social time and the pace of life. This brings us back to the question of temporal colonialism. Will today's continuing technological advances and multinational powers produce a degree of cultural homogenization of time such that distinctive approaches to time will be lost?

To some extent, of course, the answer to this question is yes. There will be increased temporal homogeneity as surely as people in every corner of the world continue to draw on so much else of Western culture,

from music and literature to McDonald's and embarrassingly mindless television shows. After we accept this multinational trend as a given, however, I believe we are left with more worthwhile questions to deal with. The truly significant temporal issue that individuals and cultures face, I believe, is how to find a balance between traditional ways of thinking and the new values demanded by the new global economy. Too often we talk about these different belief systems as if they were a zero-sum game: Should I live by the clock or by my own personal metronome? Should I give in to the demands of making every moment count, or should I take each moment one at a time? Speed up or slow down? But do we really need to choose between competing options? In fact, I believe, the answers to these questions are both more complicated than simple binary alternatives, and at the same time the possibilities and opportunities abound.

There is an interesting concept in personality psychology known as psychological androgyny. Traditional research on psychological sex differences has treated masculinity and femininity as polar opposites. Early studies offered the unsurprising finding that stereotypical "masculine"-type personalities are more likely to succeed in situations calling for qualities like assertiveness, while "feminine" types do better in situations requiring such traits as nurturance and emotional expression. Since professional success has traditionally been associated with masculine skills, one result of this stereotype is that a long line of career women have had to confront doubts about their femininity – the more successful they were, the more they felt they were

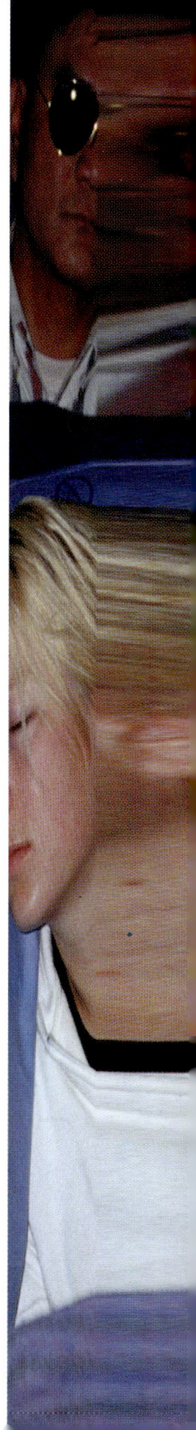

12th of Never

A photographer defines reality thus: anything that can be photographed is real. Photography is not a tool for duplicating reality in images, it is a tool for producing reality through images. This is not only true of traditional analog photography; it applies equally to Gerald Van Der Kaap's digital photography. According to "theorist of velocity" Paul Virilio, we no longer experience a landscape we fly over in a plane as real, but our body inside the plane is very real indeed. And what strange phenomena take place in our bodies as we fly from one time zone to the other! An airplane is a time machine, a machine "in between times," and digital photography is preeminently suited for recording the effects it has on our bodies. This is what Gerald Van Der Kaap demonstrates in the *12th of Never*. Poetry in machine times.

Gerald Van Der Kaap

TIME TALKS, WITH AN ACCENT

Robert Levine

looked upon as like men.

But a recent generation of female social psychologists – leaders like Sandra Bem and Janet Spence – have challenged the assumption that women's ability to compete in traditionally "masculine" endeavors must mean compromising their "feminine" side. It is they who have developed the idea of psychological androgyny. Psychologically androgynous people combine both traditional masculine traits (such as assertiveness) and feminine traits (such as nurturance) in their personality repertoire. The androgynous person is not a psychological neuter who falls midway between extreme masculinity and femininity, but one who has both strong masculine and feminine attributes at his or her disposal.

A number of studies have demonstrated the value of psychological androgyny. Whereas masculine types do better in traditional "male" situations and feminine types excel in "female" situations, experiments have shown that androgynous people – both men and women – are more likely to succeed at

both masculine and feminine tasks. It has been demonstrated, for example, that masculine and androgynous personalities are better than feminine types at resisting group pressure to conformity, but that feminine and androgynous people do better on tasks such as counseling a fellow student with problems. Androgynous and feminine spouses – both husbands and wives – also tend to have happier marriages. The androgynous person, in other words, has access to the best of both worlds.

Our approaches to time and the pace of life move in an analogous pattern. "The question is not just what floor of the building you're living on," as the transpersonal psychologist Ken Wilber puts it, "but how many floors you have access to as you negotiate your way through life." Many situations are best met by a temporal approach requiring a rapid pace of life – speed, attention to the clock, a future orientation, the ability to value time as money. Other domains in life – rest, leisure, the incubation of ideas, social relationships – are more adequately met with a relaxed attitude toward time. People and cultures that combine both modes in their temporal repertoires – or, even better, who can draw upon a multiplicity of modes – are more likely to be up to all occasions. Jeremy Rifkin speaks of the dangers of temporal ghettoes. People who are confined to rigid and narrow temporal bands are unprepared to determine their own futures and political fates. Multitemporality is the ticket out of these temporal ghettos. To have the ability to move quickly when the occasion demands it, to let go when the pressure stops, and to understand the many temporal shades of gray may be the real answer

to the question of "Which pace of life is best?" As Lewis Mumford wrote:

Though our first reaction to the external pressure of time necessarily takes the form of the slow-down, the eventual effects of liberation will be to find the right tempo and measure for every human activity; in short, to keep time in life as we do in music, not by obeying the mechanical beat of the metronome – a device only for beginners – but by finding the appropriate tempos from passage to passage, modulating the pace according to human need and purpose.

Like the psychological androgyne, the truly multitemporal person or culture does not simply fall in the average range, but has the ability to move as rapidly or slowly as is needed. A study conducted at the University of Michigan measuring worker satisfaction in a wide variety of occupations found that personal flexibility (versus rigidity) was an effective buffer against stress and job dissatisfaction no matter what one's occupation. The Italian who works hard enough to achieve, but who can decelerate to enjoy la dolce vita gained through his or her labors, possesses an element of this multitemporality. The Japanese worker who excels at both speed and slowness also understands the skill. This is hardly to say that all Italian and Japanese workers have mastered multitemporality. If anything, in fact, my own data highlight the price that many in these countries are paying for their rapid pace of life; it is no coincidence that coronary heart disease rates in Western Europe are some of the highest in the world and that suicide is a serious problem in Japan. But the traditional values in these cultures offer

potential templates – recipes of a sort – that illuminate paths by which mindful individuals may take control of their time.

The novelist Joyce Carol Oates wrote, "Time is the element in which we exist ... We are either borne along by it or drowned in it." How to be productive enough to be comfortable, to minimize the temporal stress on which this achievement is built, and to simultaneously make time for caring relationships and a civilized society – this is the multitemporal challenge.

Robert Levine is a professor of psychology at California State University, Fresno. His recent book, ***A Geography of Time*** (Basic Books), published in German under the title ***Eine Landkarte der Zeit*** (Piper), was awarded the Otto Klineberg Intercultural and International Relations Award. Parts of this article are adapted from the book.

Robert Levine

C H R O N O C R A C Y

Peter Weibel

CHRONOCRACY

Time Market is inscribed above the entrance to information society.

"The reality of time has been replaced by advertised time." (Guy Debord, 1967)

The turn of the millennium was a boom time for time. Time was pregnant with countless models: biological, cosmological, physical, astronomical and many others. In contrast to the popular philosophy of time, this study will focus on a single model of time: the social construction of time, time's economy. For we believe that the economic construction of time is the only relevant one, since it is the one from which all the other forms of time are derived. Our task will be to develop a theory which outlines the dialectics of the concepts of free time and production time, labor time and consumption time, and which explains how these concepts structure and dominate the whole sphere of life. We propose therefore to explain the functioning of society by means of a theory of time. This theory of time does not begin with natural conditions, however, but with specific social and economic conditions. This movement from natural to social time can be clearly observed in the function of the clock.

In the beginning, real events were counted and measured: the movement of the sun and the clouds, the burning down of a candle. The water clock and the grandfather clock counted and measured real, visible and physical things. Our clock, which is based on the movements of the stars in the cosmos, measures the length of the interval between two successive culminations of one and the same fixed star. This is the equivalent of one rotation of the earth,

one day, 24 hours, 1,440 minutes or 86,400 seconds. The time measured by the clock is thus incorporeal and abstract.

A clock counts only a certain class of events. It measures the length of an interval of time which remains constant. This enables us to tell the time of day. What is measured in the flow of time is thus not real events, but abstract entities like seconds, minutes and hours. The introduction of time was a process of abstraction. The intervals and lapses of time measured by the clock are of an abstract, formal, indeed mechanical nature. The clock has made time abstract and mechanized. Time is measured and represented by a machine, a technical mechanism. In truth, however, our concept of time itself is already abstract and mechanical. I can only represent the passage of time by a mechanical clock because our concept of time is itself already mechanical. Time is transformed by the act of measuring it. The measurable concept of time is the counting of hours and events. Numbers rule time. The moments of measuring time and counting the hours enable time to be expressed in terms of numbers. This is the basis of capitalism, which has recognized that time is not only countable but also profitable.

Under the pressures of countable and profitable time, time itself is reduced to mere production time. Where nothing is being counted (because no work is being done), time just stands still. Time begins passing again once the flow of money is resumed. If you are making money, you are also making time – producing it, in fact. Anyone who is involved in production is therefore in a position to buy time – in the form of credit, that is, which is a grant of time for a fixed period of labor time and life time. This is why it is also called a loan.

Only when time is considered in light of the unity of labor and time is it possible to speak of a waste of time, which is simply time during which no work is being done and nothing is being earned or otherwise acquired. Consumption, leisure time and idling are all time lost. Under capitalism, all non-renumerative activities are a waste of time. Money has been the real clock for quite some time. Every bit of time has its price. The worker sells his or her time, work time and liv-

ing time. The currency of payment is time. One who is paid for one's time pays with one's life. One pays for the time one has worked. Money buys the time that someone is willing to sell in the form of labor. Time becomes capital. Ever since time has been measurable, expressible in numbers and mechanized by the clock, it has been impaled on the stopwatch, rigidly controlled (for every second costs money) and expressed in time notes: time is redeemable. Time rings out in the cash registers. Correctly translated, the adage "time is money" means "time is a number" or "money is the commodity form of time." Value is brought into being by countable time. Time's value is variable; from the unskilled laborer through to the expert, time has a different price. How are values converted into prices? The famous transformation problem of economics finds its answer in time. For time is expressible in monetary and figures and numerals. Ricardo defined labor as value and time as its measure. Price is thus nothing more than the temporal form of value, and money is the value form of time. This is why values can change into prices, or rather why forms of value change into general money commodities, in whose use value the exchange values of all other commodities are expressed. Ricardo suggested this approach when he wrote: "I may be asked what I mean by value and how I come to judge whether or not a commodity has changed its value. My answer is that I know of no other criterion for judging whether a thing is cheap or expensive than the sacrifice of labor necessary to preserve it. Everything is

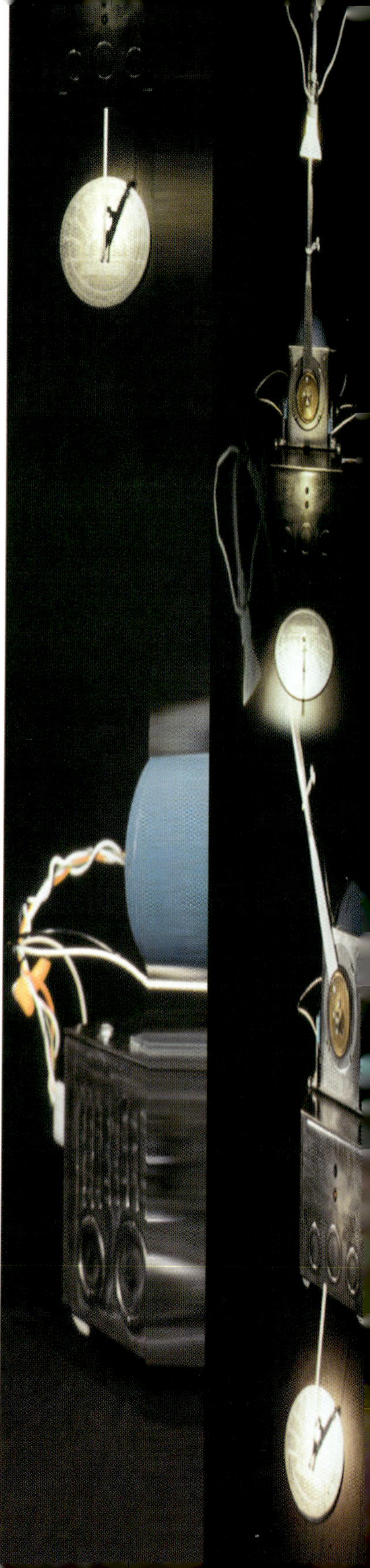

originally acquired through labor" (quoted in Pierro Sraffa, *Warenproduktion mittels Waren*, 1976, p. 159).

As Ricardo's successor, Marx defined commodity value in terms of the number of hours worked: "Money as the measure of value is the necessary manifestation of the immanent measure of commodity value, which is labor time" (Capital, vol. 1, 1962, p. 109). Time as a unit of labor measurement becomes the sole measure of value. Homo economicus is a creature of time. Space too turns into money for homo economicus, for space is merely the representative of time. In one of Raymond Chandler's novels, a landlord says to a customer who has been sitting at a table too long, taking up space and consuming too little: "Man, this is money space." First, time is money, and now space is money as well, for space too has been succumbing to the value form of money for quite some time.

"Time for sale" is posted above the entrance to industrial society, and trading in time is the business of the information society. Chronometry, or the measurement of time, is the precondition of a market economy in which money is the highest form of commodity. Thus when Frederick Winslow Taylor (*The Principles of Scientific Management*, New York 1911) and Frank and Lillian Gilbreth (*Fatigue Study*, London 1916) started time-and-motion studies as production engineers, they did so in the correct assumption that time was the most precious metal, the one invariable measure of value. The time-and-motion studies conducted around the end of the nineteenth century accompany an industrialization of time and

Ana Giron

Artificial Time

Much of modern life has come to depend on the accurate measurement of time. With the development of the Cesium Atomic Clock, we can now keep time to one millionth of a second per year. As technology has developed we have intervended in nature`s timekeeping process with the ultimate goal of improving on its perceived imperfections. In so doing, we have abstracted our sense of time from nature – what we live with today is predominantly a technological time.

Artificial Time is an interactive telerobotic installation for the web that explores our concepts of and relationship to time. A robotic arm, which consists of an armature with a halogen light, is connected to the web and acts as a light source that revolves above a sundial. By controlling the movement of the robotic arm, one is able to control the shadow on the sundial, thereby controlling the representation of time.

A video camera transmits the image of the sundial on the web. While multiple viewers can see the sundial, only one person can control the robot arm at a time. When one gains control of the arm, the time and location set on their computer is sent to the server which positions the robot accordingly. Anyone else who is connected at that time is able to see the location of the Exclusive Client as well as the initial time they connected. A second window with a Time Map is also part of the web site. It is a record of the last 24 connection times drawn in shades of gray from black to white where the last connection is in white.

The project, installed at a gallery, is being manipulated remotely.

are proof of the beginning of time's control. Timesmiths Taylor and Ford recognized that real power, the true bomb, is time. Time comes as a time bomb. The coming of abstract time coincided with the achievement of the abstracted labor of the conveyor belt, a labor stripped down into parts in the factory – dislocated, distanced and estranged.

Time-and-motion studies were explorations of capital, of the abstract value form of money, and they prepared the way for the subtle capitalism of post-industrial society. The process of abstraction initiated by exchange value, which gradually transformed objects into commodities and commodities into signs, this process of the dissolution of objects, has been so intensified in post-industrial capitalism – which is a feudalism of time – that money itself is disappearing because it still betrays too much of its origins in the object or commodity. In the course of the conversion of space into time by the faster machine, labor itself was turned into

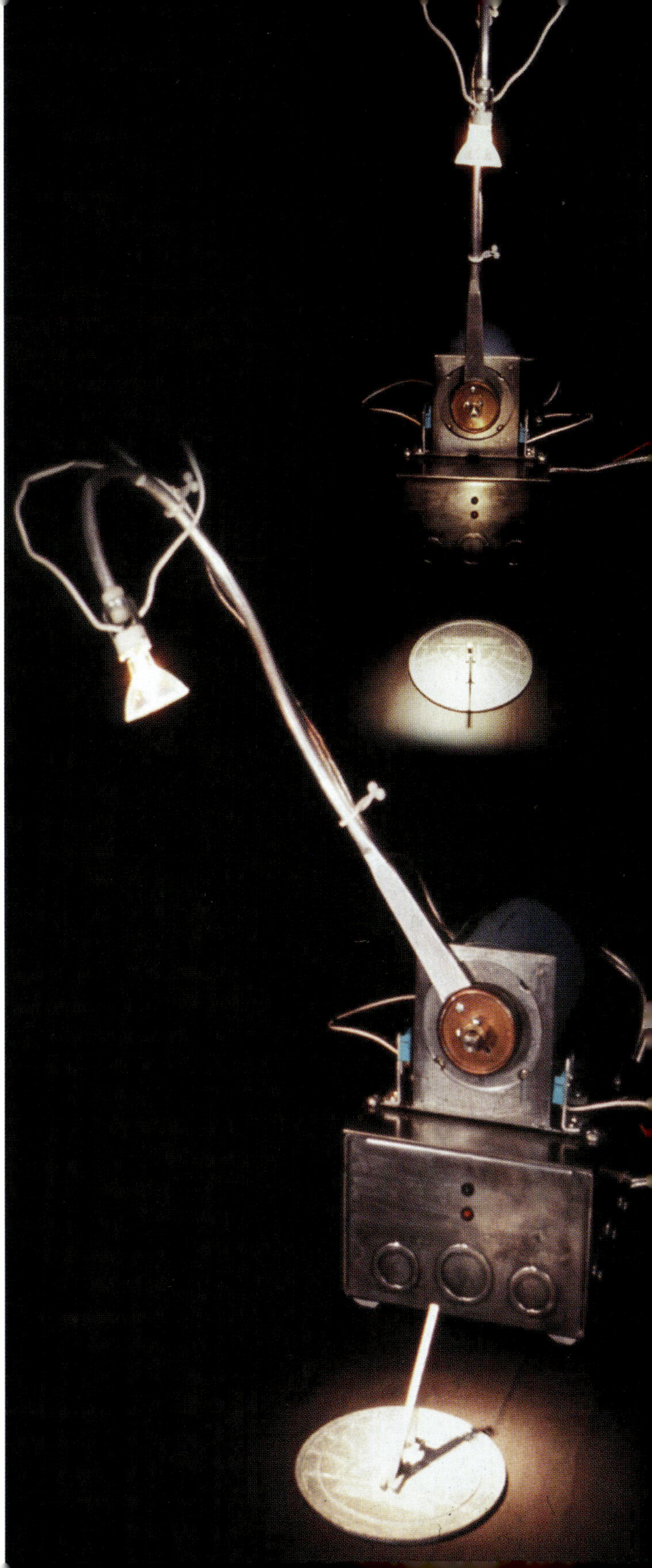

time. Not only did movement become independent of space, but the value of labor and the price of value thrust themselves forward as absolutes. This led to the independence of prices and the commodity of money, to the abstraction of money circulation, which became almost immaterial and unreal.

The stock market, stock market transactions, stocks and shares, forward exchange and foreign currency dealings, where money is exchanged for money and profits are created, not by some form of productive work but from mere differences in time (!) are testimony to this accelerated abstraction of labor which is wiping out labor itself. The pure money market is liquidating money – just as in the age of space space is disappearing. The emergence of the bank card, which has displaced money to such an extent that in the USA a person offering to pay with cash rather than with a card is immediately suspected of being a criminal, confirms the extinction of money as an object or a second-order commodity and verifies its promotion to absolute immateriality. After labor and time, money too has now become so abstracted that it not only vanishes as an object twice removed but, by a truly paradoxical twist, even becomes a gauge of poverty. The rich do not have money anymore, at least not in their pockets: they carry cards. The bank card contains a graphic notation of the hierarchy of wealth. It will be recalled that the multimillionaire Howard Hughes never had money in his pocket. In the better hotels in the USA you cannot get a room for cash: only a card will do. Only the poorest

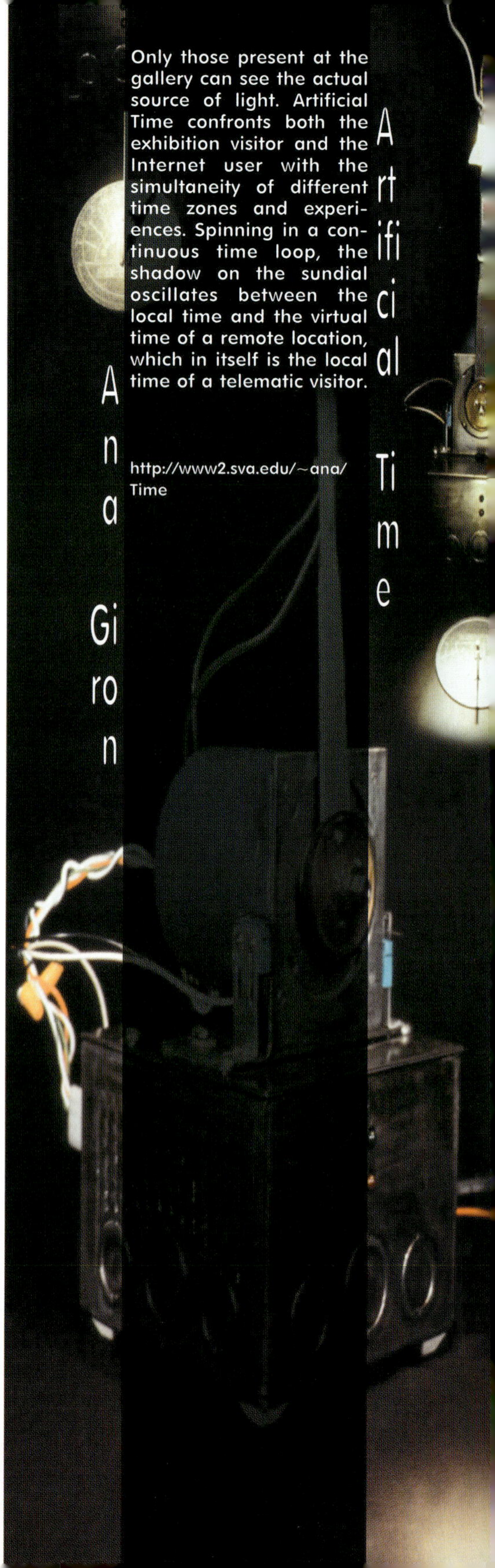

Ana Giron

Artificial Time

Only those present at the gallery can see the actual source of light. Artificial Time confronts both the exhibition visitor and the Internet user with the simultaneity of different time zones and experiences. Spinning in a continuous time loop, the shadow on the sundial oscillates between the local time and the virtual time of a remote location, which in itself is the local time of a telematic visitor.

http://www2.sva.edu/~ana/Time

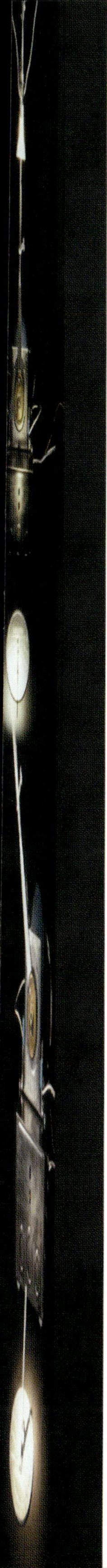

people actually have ready money. In the age of the bank card, which is the age of temporalized money, the person with cash is actually broke. Dematerialized money is the currency of the poor. Checks and credit reveal capitalism as a trafficking in time, as the product of the progressive abstraction and mutual independence of labor, value, time and money. Originating in exchange value, this process of abstraction has transformed the theory of value into the theory of price. The process has abstracted labor to the point of superseding it, so that within "economic calculation" (Charles Bettelhaim) there has been a shift from the production of commodities by labor to "the production of commodities by means of commodities" (Piero Sraffa, 1976). Under the capitalist mode of production and the circulation of capital, indeed, the economics of prices has become so detached from the reality of labor that Sraffa found himself compelled to turn to this structural mathematical model in order to explain the laws of the market. The economy, too, operates in a virtual mathematical space. Under the diktat of time and chronometry, the economy is becoming an eco-metry.

The final stage in the abstraction of labor is the present production of time by means of time. The economy subsists on the sale and investment of time (in the form of work time) by those who work in order to earn money to purchase their free time (in the form of commodities, leisure and the means of subsistence). Time is what is invested, bought and sold. This is why so-called options or futures offer the most lucrative deals. The highest, most abstract

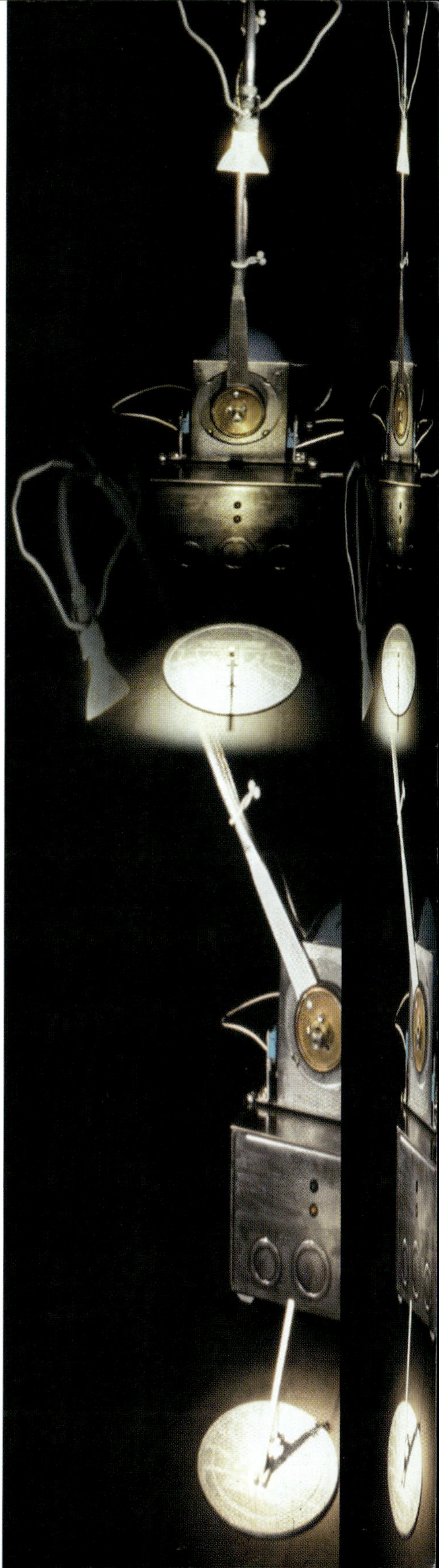

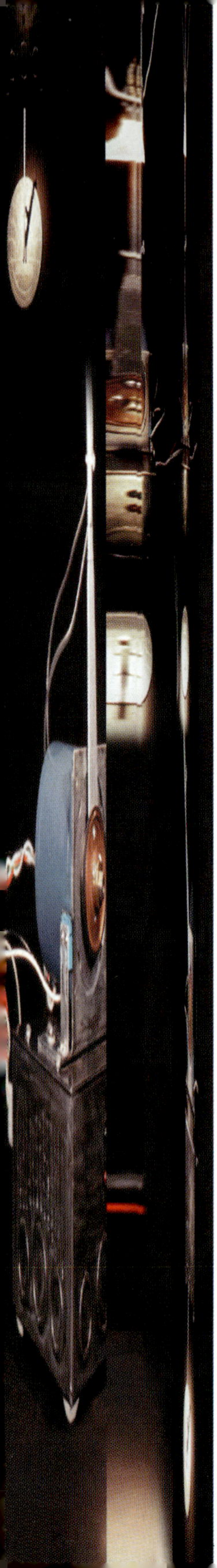

form of capitalism is the monetarization of time. This the logical consequence of the equation in which labor time and value time, time value and labor value were posited as the same. Even Marxism has failed to avoid this fatal prospect. The inflations and crises of capital are caused by implosions of time within economic calculation. In *L'atelier et le chronométre* (1979) Benjamin Coriat described the beginnings of chronocapitalism in Fordism.

The Taylorist atomization of the work process and its Fordist mechanical reconstruction in large factories led to a speeding up of productivity, in particular of the mass production of standardized commodities. A crisis of overproduction would have occurred had there not at the same time been mass consumption of commodities cheap enough to be purchased by workers. This is why Ford made the well-known statement that "our workers should also be our customers." Within a kind of self-regulating market, the workers were to a large extent also the consumers of the commodities they produced. On the basis of this mass production and mass consumption, huge reserves of capital were accumulated and the great American fortunes were made. However, once the household, the most important market for such mass products, became saturated with mass-produced goods, this self-regulation entered a crisis of overproduction. The problem of overproduction was exacerbated drastically by the replacement of people by machines in the automated production process, which was the second source of faster productivity. The workers made redundant by automation were left on the one hand with an superabundance of time at their disposal, and on the other hand no purchasing power since the profusion consisted merely of time in which to stand idle. A divide began to open up: the production of mass commodities was sped up and the mass of workers capable of buying them simultaneously decreased. One and the same cause, the machine, was responsible for both the rise in productivity and the decline in purchasing power, since the machines led to the dismissal of workers. The more machines produced, the more workers were "released" by mechanically automated production, and the more com-

modities there were, but also the fewer workers were earning enough money to buy and consume those goods. The contradiction is best formulated in monetary time. The workers were the consumers of the time they produced. However, once automation began to produce more and more time, the workers had less and less time to consume it. The result was overproduction not only of consumer goods, but also of time. This is why trade unions now no longer fight for a reduction of working hours, which was their original historical goal, but on the contrary, against the reduction of the working week being forced through in the industrialized nations by increased automation. The program now is neither the abolition of work nor the reduction of the number of hours worked, but the preservation of work time and work. The unions are using their power to bring time to a halt, to put it on ice. The problem of the consumption of goods only serves to conceal the problem of the consumption of time, the overproduction of time. The economic equilibrium, the self-regulation of economic growth, was thrown off balance by quickening time. The labor-value-commodity-time-money economic equation was destabilized by the time factor, by the mechanical speeding up of time.

In fully automated factories, inside the neo-Fordian work process, the speed of production is completely detached from the speed at which human beings work. Just as movement and time were once detached from space, and price from value, so now time is detached from labor. Exploded time (independent production speed) inserts itself into the game and dictates the rules. Just as space and time have entered into a new relationship in temporalized teletechnetronic society, so too have labor and time. Fordism's goal of using machinery to produce more and more goods in less and less time has blown labor apart, releasing the nuclear power of time. Taylor's atomized time was indeed the atomic bomb of time. Automation has produced too much time. It is an overproduction of commodities and time. What has been set in motion, therefore, is a complex juggling act of labor time and released time (analogous to the "released" worker, as a worker without work is euphemisti-

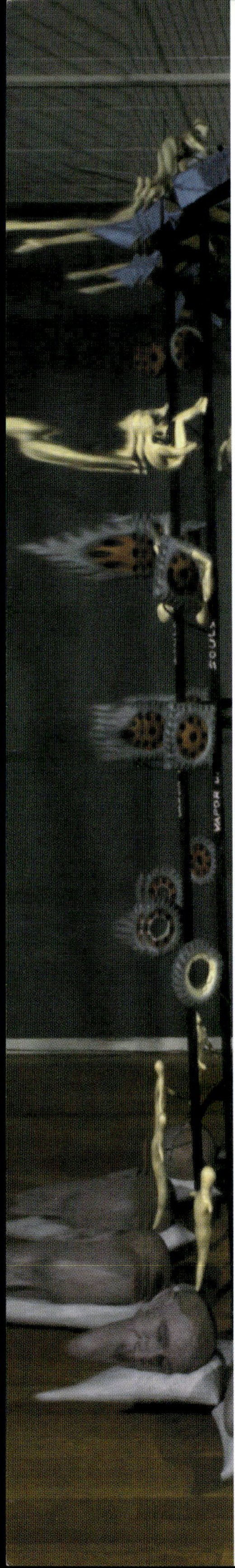

cally referred to nowadays), of spare time and free time, and of production time and consumption time. If time is money, then besides counterfeit money there is also counterfeit or simulated time; in the light of the practices described by R. Alquati in *Sulla Fiat e altri scritti* (1975), one could say "Fiat time." Protected by their unions, the Fiat workers very often absented themselves from factory work in order to get hold of some "free time." And this was also necessary, because wages were not high enough to finance the steadily increasing amount of spare or leisure time. For during this "free time," the absent worker could undertake work in the black economy somewhere else. Thus Fiat hit on the idea of hiring its own absent workers to work "black" in their own factories and paying them under the counter for the work they were performing on the side while they were supposed to have been at the factory anyway. This is tele-presence, simultaneous presence and absence, economic far-nearness. All parties have an interest in restoring the profitability of supposedly free time. It was at least cheaper than not producing anything and paying the workers in their absence, for these union-protected workers could not be fired and replaced. The time stored in the machine could not be made profitable without labor. The time saved became money again by giving the workers a little more money, even if it was money paid under the counter.

The new aim of Fordism is thus to produce a maximum of time (consumption) with a minimum of time (production) in order to avoid overproduction (of commodi-

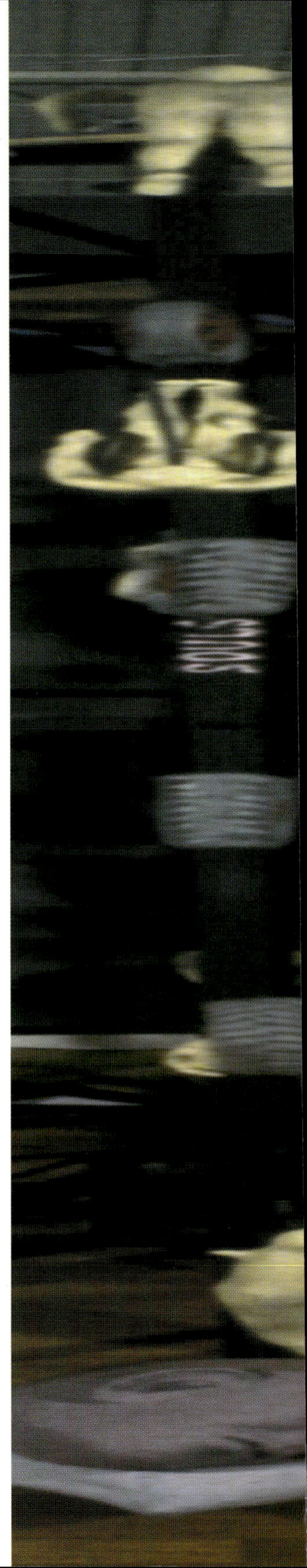

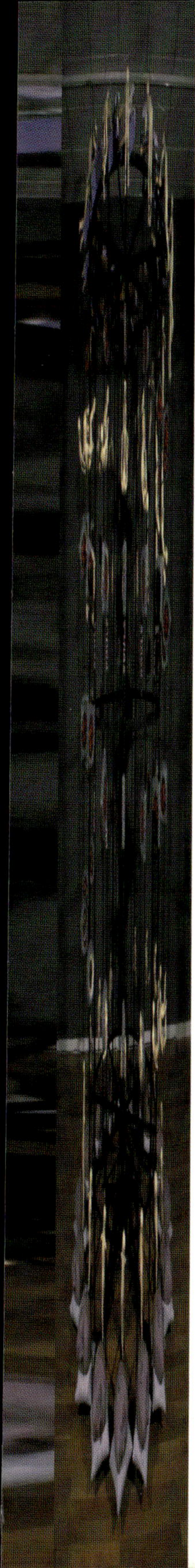

ties and time). The theory of "human capital," which makes everyone a producer (or artist), has represented the neo-conservative conception of homo economicus from Gary Becker (*Human Capital: A Theoretical and Empirical Approach,* 1964) to Joseph Beuys (*Kreativität alias menschliche Produktivität als Kapital*). When an individual becomes a producer of commodities, the value of those commodities is then measured by the amount of time the individual spends enjoying and consuming them. They are counted as consumed time. In a consumption-oriented society whose vector is the elimination of overproduction, it is no longer labor that is the only true source of a nation's wealth, as it was for Ricardo, but consumption. At least to the minds of the neo-conservatives.

The signifier "individual as producer or artist" masks the inversion "consumed time." For the reality is different, precisely because it is time that produces commodities, and thus consumed time, and precisely because time is the sole factor in the production of commodities, so that the degree of abstraction is reached in which – as already indicated – time is produced by time. A perpetuum mobile of time is the unredeemable core of neo-conservative economic theory.

For to make time, individuals must earn money, for time is, of course, money, and money is time. To earn money individuals must devote a portion of their time to labor. To prevent this time of labor from getting too long, and to ensure that he or she gains time from the production of commodities (consumption time), the individual

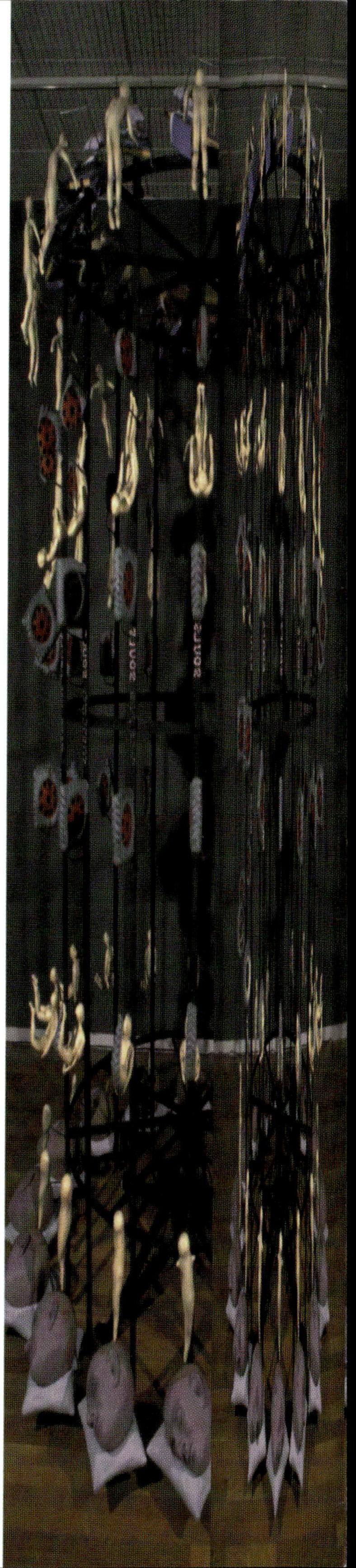

SOULS
SOULS
SOULS
SOULS

has to build machines that accelerate the process of production. That is to say, he or she must acquire knowledge. Again, this costs time; machines are thus stored and saved time. But in order to store this time, in order to shorten the period of labor by the use of machines, in order to save time with machines which produce commodities more quickly, the individual must first lay out or invest this time. In other words, he or she must both delay and cut back on consumption time. In reality, this gives rise to a new asceticism, an immense pressure of time. In order to acquire the high income that apparently promises more goods and consumption time, the individual must devote a major portion of his or her time to earning the money to purchase those machines that allow more time to earn money. On the other hand, if this individual's time is worth nothing, and his or her wages are already too low anyway, he or she will have more and more time to consume less and less.

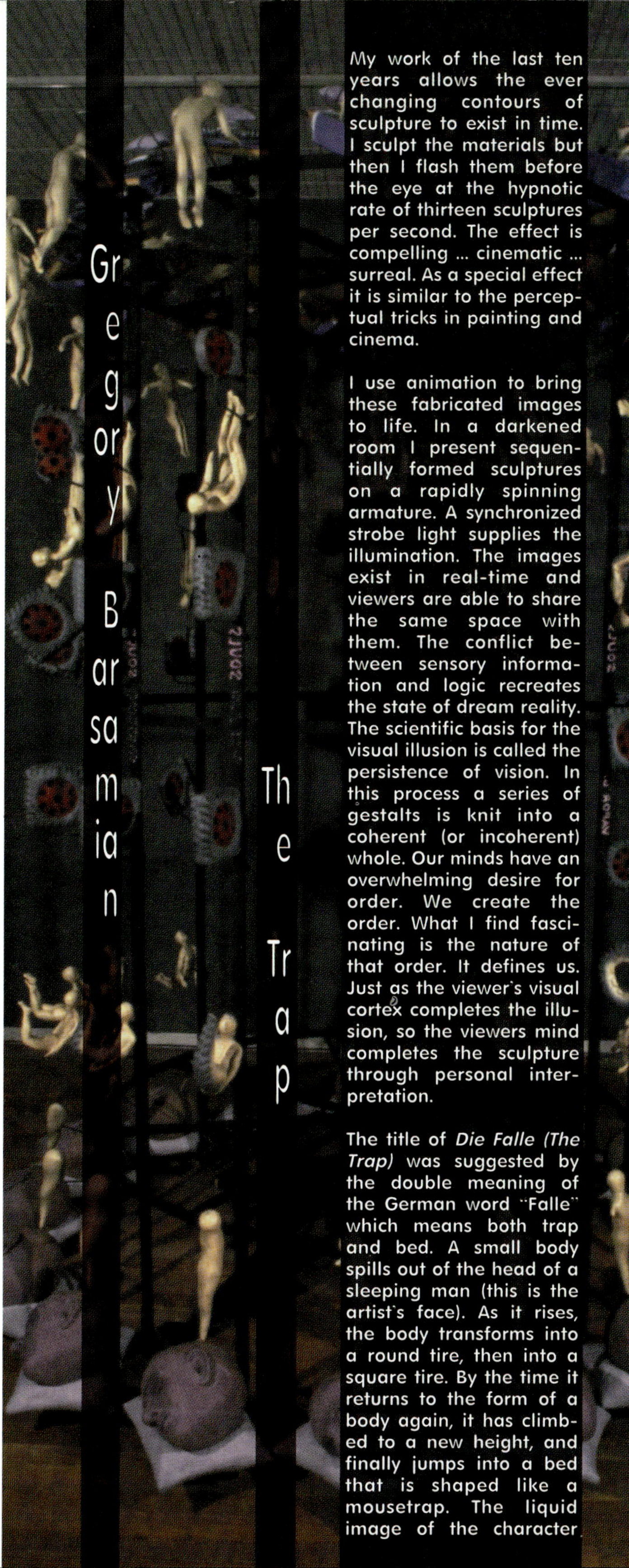

Gregory Barsamian

The Trap

My work of the last ten years allows the ever changing contours of sculpture to exist in time. I sculpt the materials but then I flash them before the eye at the hypnotic rate of thirteen sculptures per second. The effect is compelling ... cinematic ... surreal. As a special effect it is similar to the perceptual tricks in painting and cinema.

I use animation to bring these fabricated images to life. In a darkened room I present sequentially formed sculptures on a rapidly spinning armature. A synchronized strobe light supplies the illumination. The images exist in real-time and viewers are able to share the same space with them. The conflict between sensory information and logic recreates the state of dream reality. The scientific basis for the visual illusion is called the persistence of vision. In this process a series of gestalts is knit into a coherent (or incoherent) whole. Our minds have an overwhelming desire for order. We create the order. What I find fascinating is the nature of that order. It defines us. Just as the viewer's visual cortex completes the illusion, so the viewers mind completes the sculpture through personal interpretation.

The title of *Die Falle (The Trap)* was suggested by the double meaning of the German word "Falle" which means both trap and bed. A small body spills out of the head of a sleeping man (this is the artist's face). As it rises, the body transforms into a round tire, then into a square tire. By the time it returns to the form of a body again, it has climbed to a new height, and finally jumps into a bed that is shaped like a mousetrap. The liquid image of the character

Loss of time for some and loss of commodities for others are the consequences of the division, of capitalism's subsumption of the totality of time. Those whose time is expensive because they are "experts" will have to work more and more. Others, the unskilled workers, will be less and less able to work at all. This is the true face of the accumulation of time, as distinct from the accumulation of capital. "Capital accumulation will be for the individual nothing more than an increase of the number of commodities that save him the trouble of taking the time to consume them" (Eric Alliez and Michael Feher, *The Luster of Capital,* in Zone 1/2, New York 1986, p. 352).

Money is turned into time in two ways. Money crystallizes time as production time in the form of payment. Money earned is then time saved. As capital, money stores the time of commodity consumption. Capital becomes the bestower of time, time's provider (Gonzague Pillet, Roland Leinsburger, Aline Bourrit, *Les donneurs de temps,* 1981). Absolute chronocracy, the rule of time, has thus already begun. It is a new feudalism of time, in which there are time slaves and time masters, chained to each other in the common desire to make time profitable. Tele-technological acceleration (by machine) has made the most radical impact on the economy, creating monetarized time and temporalized capitalism.

Just as eleventh-century feudalism was a society of underfed poor and overeating rich, so the new feudalism consists of more and more consumption time (which is of course money stored and saved) for the rich and steadily less con-

sumption time for the poor (which is the equivalent of "free time" or time made redundant). If you do not have time in the sense of time as money saved, purchasing power, you can buy yourself some time. But what do you do if you have no money to buy yourself time and your desire for time stems precisely from the fact the you have no money? You simply sell your time. But how is this possible, given that we started out from the assumption that you have no time? In the age of the politics of space, you could borrow against your land. In the age of chronocracy, you can borrow against your time. The person whose present stock of time is insufficient sells his future time. He mortgages his future time, which is a time that will only mature as future. He takes out a loan or credit. He barters his time. The individual buys himself time now, consumption time, enabling him to buy straight away the goods he wants to consume and enjoy in selling future time. The time slave must naturally pay interest – interest on time. He will usually have to invest in, produce for, or pay the future a third more time than what the commodity would have cost him now. The individual thus loses time, life time, in this exchange of time in the form of a loan. You borrow time from the bank, mortgaging your life time to that bank – which for its part insures itself against your premature decease, your death before time, and you pay for that too – which enables you to buy now products you cannot yet afford because you have not yet worked enough for them, not yet earned enough money or produced enough time. The dual luster of

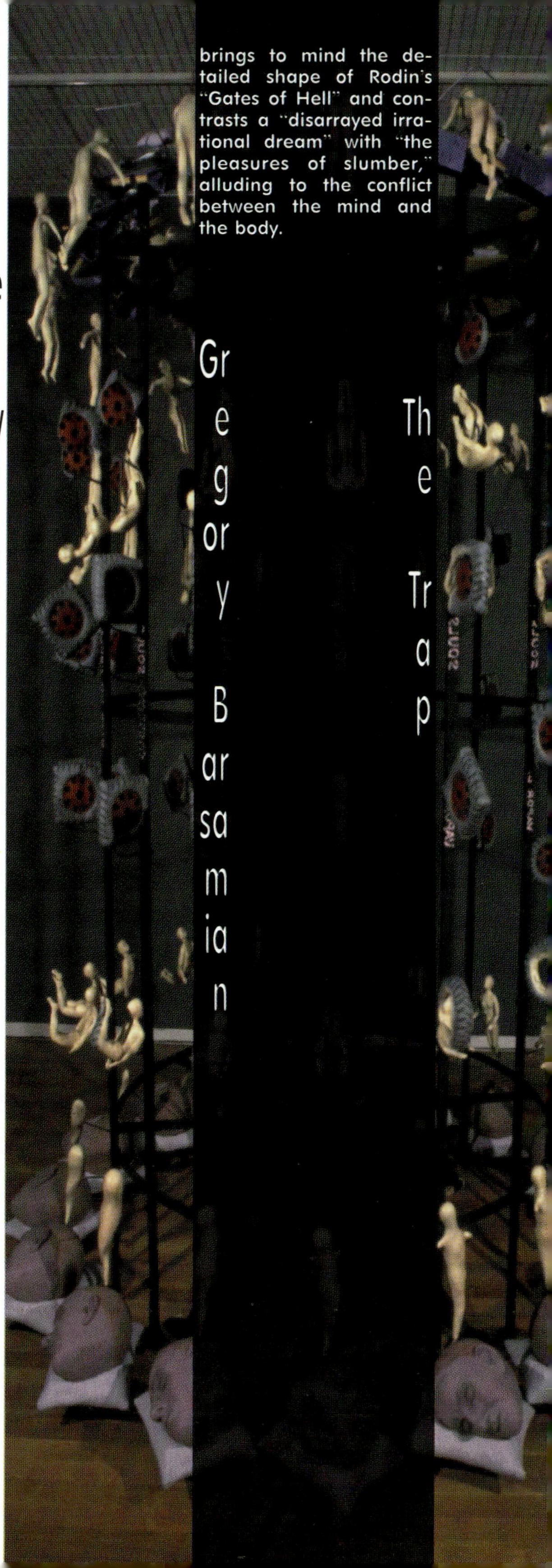

brings to mind the detailed shape of Rodin's "Gates of Hell" and contrasts a "disarrayed irrational dream" with "the pleasures of slumber," alluding to the conflict between the mind and the body.

Gregory Barsamian
The Trap

capitalism, time as the production of commodities and time as the consumption of commodities, has been split into two independent parts in the chronocratic society.

Borrowed and loaned time are to some extent simulated or counterfeited time. Today the actual wage of labor is loaned time. We can judge the extent to which we are already living under chronocracy from the fact that today everyone, private individuals and businesses alike, lives on loans and credit. Credit cards and the credit system are the signs of a "tele-economy," a "controlled economy." An economy which has reached such a degree of abstraction that it lives on time, and in which time is produced by means of time, must also be capable of manipulating the time worlds as plural time, rather in the way that it manipulates space and tele-space as plural space. Fractalized, movable, accelerated and decelerated time – time purchased, borrowed and earned – is the sign of the borrowing and lending universe of the chonocracy, the new rule of feudal time, of the time aristocracy, where everyone, from the individual to the great concerns, lives on bought, sold, borrowed, lent or simulated time. In this economy the present no longer suffices to produce the amount of time required: everyone needs more time than they have. That is why time is bought and borrowed for immediate consumption at the expense of future life time. Everyone offers life time as cover for their debts. The economy is ruled by surrogate time. Fixed-term debt identifies debt-burdened time as the new inflationary virus of the world economy, which is an economy of time. This is the real reason why chronological time, historical time and natural time – the visible forms of time – are past and gone, and why the techno-time of the electronic media is now the legitimate artistic form: the electronic media articulate the simul-time of the new feudal society, its character as a place defined by the borrowing and the granting of time, for, in place of the spatial depths of classical visual representation, the electronic screen is capable of imaging the virtually infinite depth of time, capitalism's apparently inexhaustible resource.

"Tempus fugit" necessarily predicates "Time is

money." The chrono-analyses of time management, the industrial structurations of time, time-and-motion studies (from Marey to Ford) have produced not only the enormous speeding of telecommunications, but also time and speed as the sole invariable measure. The teletechnotronic instantaneity of ubiquitousness has abolished all physical dimensions and all spatio-temporal distances. For the "annulment of time and space" (Carlo de Benedetti) by modern technology facilitates a new globalization, which no longer emanates from local conglomerations of production – topographical concentrations of an industrial sector, such as Detroit and Turin as car-makers – and their global sales networks, but from the concept of "flexible specialization" (Michael J. Piore and Charles Sabel, *The Second Industrial Divide*, 1984), in which not only mass consumption but also mass production are globally dispersed.

This is one answer to the crisis of the overproduction of mass commodities. Since the local work force is no longer numerous enough to buy the commodities it has produced, mass-produced commodities have been internationally standardized for transnational sale. This next necessary step was to transfer production from a local to a global setting: in another place, for example, the workers could be made to work faster, making it possible to produce more, and therefore cheaper, commodities in a shorter period of time. This led to the flooding of the market with East Asian products (from Taiwan, Singapore, Hong Kong, etc.), from shirts to electrical goods, manufactured under American and European license. The transnationalization of capital, production and consumption, the global market, ties together the strategies of the time technocrats. Michael J. Piore describes his concept thus: "The industrial world is in transition from a mode of production dominated by mass production to a mode which Sabel and I call flexible specialization. The underlying idea of mass production is the achievement of technical progress through dividing the process of production into a series of discrete tasks," just as the elements of a single movement were broken down into a series of discrete images. These specific, discrete tasks were carried out by specialized machinery and by workers who were specifically trained for this one operation. "The main economic problem with this was to create markets large and stable enough to keep these highly specialized resources fully occupied. At the micro-economic level this gave rise to monopoly or oligopolistic industrial concerns, and at the macro-economic level to the Keynesian welfare state." This economic equivalent of a cinematographic montage has been described aptly by Piore: "The characteristic institutional structures of mass production are fragmentizing and hierarchical. Each operation is isolated ... and only acquires its meaning (economic and social) when (graphically) integrated back into the product it of which it forms only a small part." The coordination required for the reintegration of these differently produced parts was naturally at first easier and cheaper to achieve from the beginning if "all operations are carried out in close physical proximity to each other, and we see how the mass-produced car is historically connected with urban conglomerations such as Detroit and Turin." In principle, however, standardized parts can in the long run also be integrated into a geographically "highly decentralized production process." Due to the recent new developments in tele-technology, "transportation and communication costs have fallen, and for this reason mass production has shown a tendency to be dispersed across very large geographical areas." Geographically dispersed production in the tele-technetronic topology versus the centralized production of the mechanical era expresses the distinction between industrial and post-industrial society, between the second communications revolution and the third. Constant product innovation is require to maintain the technological momentum. "Flexible specialization, which backs multi-purpose tools and equipment (poly-technology), and broadly trained skilled workers, against rather narrowly specialized workers and machines is, therefore, invading the domain of mass production. Flexible specialization is a technological mode of operation that deploys very general, multi-taskable resources to produce short-term specialized products. In extreme cases they are tailored to meet a single specific

requirement" (all quotations from Piore in Zone 1/2, pp. 432-433). Thus, the historical, mass-produced commodity (car) was built in a closely integrated physical and spatial environment (conveyor belt, factory, city). The mass-produced commodity of techno-time and techno-space comes into being in a decentralized, spatially and temporally separated and displaced production process because, along with the tele-technological cost-benefits, lower wages, lower employers' contributions and higher work rates easily offset transport costs. In this way, the political and social asynchronicity of third-world countries destroyed by colonialism is once more exploited. Economically speaking, the disappearance of space means that space has become cheap and the transport of goods costs almost nothing. Space and transportation are at least cheaper then time. Carl Sagan's definition "speed expands time to the degree that it shrinks space" throws instant light on the economic significance of speed. Hence the distribution of the mass production of commodities, from radios to television sets to cars, over large geographical areas. The parts of the "world car" are produced in different countries, and even on different continents. So not only mass consumption but also mass production is globally dispersed, for by destroying old natural scales, such as human work time, locally situated raw materials, spatial distances, weather conditions etc, modern technology has created a whole new economy of scale.

The diffusion of the space of production through tele-technology extends from the global macro-production of the transnational concerns down to the local micro-production of home-workers. A gigantic social "factorification" has taken place in which life in the city and life in the factory are rendered indistinguishable, and where the boundary line between work at home and work in the workplace has been erased. Together with the concept of "flexible specialization," information technology and telematic homework, this development has brought about a rebirth of the small and medium-sized factory. It is a sort of micro-business or underground economy whose earnings, despite their marginality, make a sizeable contribution to the functioning

of the economy as a whole, because they actually do comprise "free time" (low taxes, etc.) and are therefore strong producers of consumption time, of time as the power to purchase commodities, whose scarcities and deficits are the new form of inflation. The danger of talking about time as "human capital" and measuring everything in turns of human time is that it blurs and dissolves the boundary between paid work and home-work, work time and free time (this is already implicit in the "Everyone an artist" model), so that the whole of society becomes a single great factory, where the totality of private time is identical with capital time. For a discussion of the theme of human time, see Theodore W. Schultz *The High Value of Human Time: Population Equilibrium* (Journal of Political Economy, vol. 85, March-April 1974, p. 58), which complains of the asymptotic curve of the development of production time and consumption time, and Charles Busch, *La sociologie du temps libre* (Paris, 1975).

The destruction of the local mode of production of mass commodities by conveyor belt and factory, around which the masses of workers created cities, also destroyed those cities. The decentralization of mass production has also decentralized the cities, transforming them into suburbs. Another inversion is now added to those produced by speed which we have already looked at. First the fast machines produced the city, the cinematism of the city, but then acceleration became so great that it replaced distance with its instant ubiquitousness, so that space and local topology, the preconditions of the existence of the city, were destroyed. The Industrial Revolution produced the city; post-industrial society deterritorializes, depopulates and destroys the city. The tele-montage of global mass production, flexible specialization and the chronocracy of capital have enforced a process of deurbanization. Time management has finally wiped out topological accumulation; the city as the architectonic form of capital accumulation is gone. The decentralization of production, the transnationalization of capitalism have turned living around the conveyor belt and the factory into history – which is why hopeless armies of unoccupied workers are to be found sitting around Detroit today. "A sort of residing without residence" (Paul Virilio) is produced, rather like feudal nomadism from the eleventh century onwards. If then there was nowhere enough food, today there is nowhere enough work and (consumption) time. So today's nomad is constantly in search of them, particularly in the USA. Rendered obsolete by tele-technology, the material city dissolves into global electronic suburbs "where the Man without Qualities, lives as a nomad without even an identity" according to Marc Guillaume, co-author with Jacques Attali of *L' anti-economie*, in Zone 1/2, p. 439.

The decline of the cities marks the failure of scientific management and direction. With the dematerializations of tele-technology and electronic topology, with deurbanization and the disappearance of the cities, architecture entered a critical situation, whose neo-conservative solution was the emphasis of the facade. If spatial architecture and the city are disappearing,

the facade at least must be kept intact. "The appeal to history suggested by some of the experts of postmodernism is merely an excuse for ignoring the question of time, the régime of transhistorical temporality produced by the technological ecosystem," writes Paul Virilio in *L'espace critique* (Paris, 1984). The transformation of urban topology into electronic topology has outdated traditional architecture, like certain forms of agriculture, reducing it indeed to a mere facade. Technological, synthetic space-time allows material architecture no more than the scope to play with facades and to juggle with the history of urban elements.

We are living in a new feudal society of time, where time is conferred, bought and sold. In the age of time's dominion, the lord of time is the lord on high. Everyone is involved in the struggle to dominate, possess, conquer and master time, from surgeons to bankers to arbitrageurs. The arbitrageur earns his profits from buy-

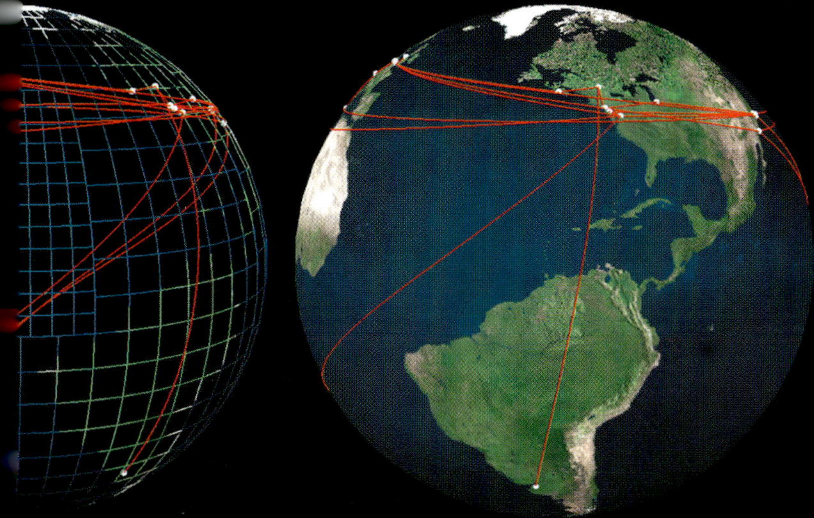

The Internet is an infrastructure of networked computers for the transmission of digital data. The lines and cables that connect these computers are not evenly distributed over the whole Earth, and the way in which the data travel through them is not instantaneous, nor do the packages always take the shortest routes.

Ride the Byte offers an impression of the complex structure of the Internet by visualizing the trajectory of individual data packages (bytes) sent from the exhibition site to another location on the globe. Looking down from a platform, visitors can see a projection of the Earth. On an LCD display, the visitor chooses one of a number of pre-defined Internet pages. A data package is sent to that Internet site and the route the data take is graphically depicted as a trace route, as a clearly visible track on the large-scale image of the Earth. The route is marked by the geographical locations and IP addresses, the unique addresses of each computer on the Internet, of the servers through which the data are transferred. At the end of the data's trip through the Net, the chosen Internet page is shown. As these trace routes accumulate in the course of the day, the pattern of the Net is woven onto the surface of the planet.

art + com

The transmission time of data on the Internet is strongly dependent on the speed allowed by the nodes and cables and by the amount of data traffic; as there is always a limit to available bandwidth, high data traffic can effect a slowdown, while temporary failure or congestion at certain nodes can necessitate the rerouting of data.

ing stocks and bonds, foreign currencies and commodities on cheap markets and selling them almost simultaneously on expensive markets. The arbitrageur thus takes advantage of the price differences obtaining on different markets at the same time, which are in principle time and place differences of the tele-economy. Power no longer lies with the ruler of space, but with the ruler of time. Time is money and power. The philosophy of first strike which came into being during the Cold War in the 1950s clearly articulated this change. Dominance over time rather than territorial conquest was the new goal of politics. The Strategic Defensive Initiative (SDI) follows directly from this philosophy of first strike. Since the terrestrial terrain has become unimportant in the age of chronopolitics, it is simply abandoned, and the theater and place of war switches to the heavens and goes into orbit. The idea is to be so fast that the enemy can be defeated in the air before landing on the ground. War in the space age is a war without space. Terrestrial warfare, which is a warfare of space, becomes a warfare of speed and time. The strongest is the fastest. SDI is only the belligerent form of the chronopolitcs and chronocracy that have already dominated society for some time.

Those who control time while it is being measured also control events taking place in it. They control the worker who is paid according to the measurement of his time. The feudal ruler of time, the owner of time as capital, lends out the time of his employees. Precisely in the information economy, where the commodity is relatively

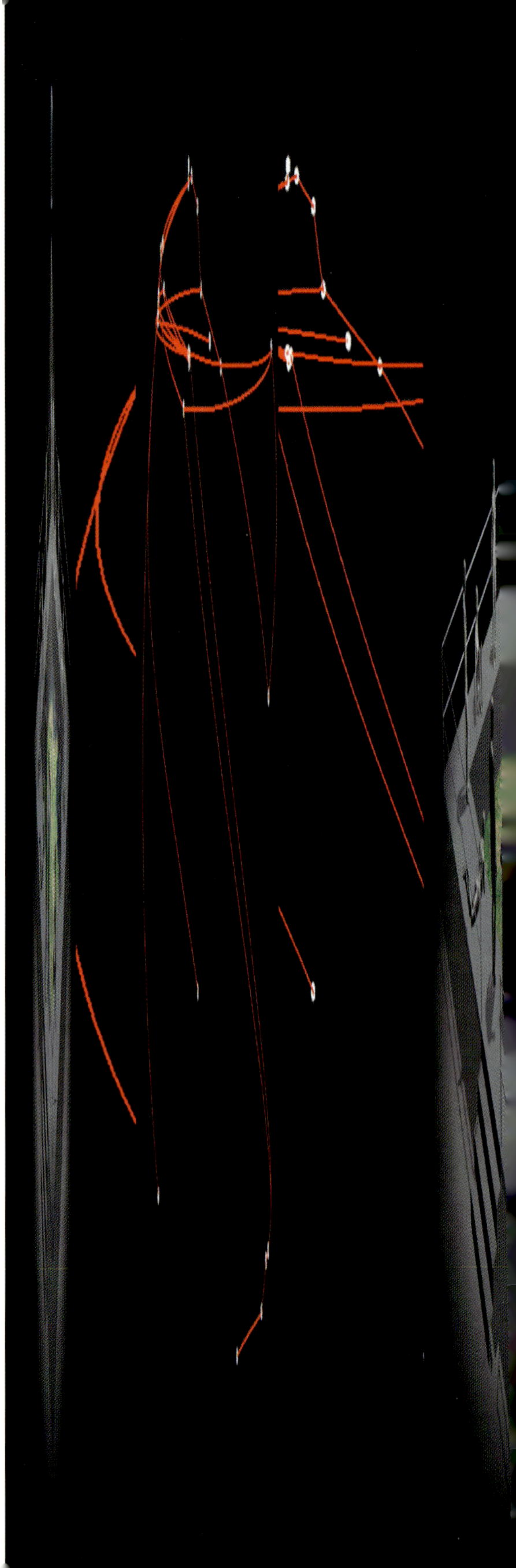

Ride the Byte visualizes the ever-changing spatio-temporal structure of the Internet, indicating both its massive size and its technical idiosyncrasies.

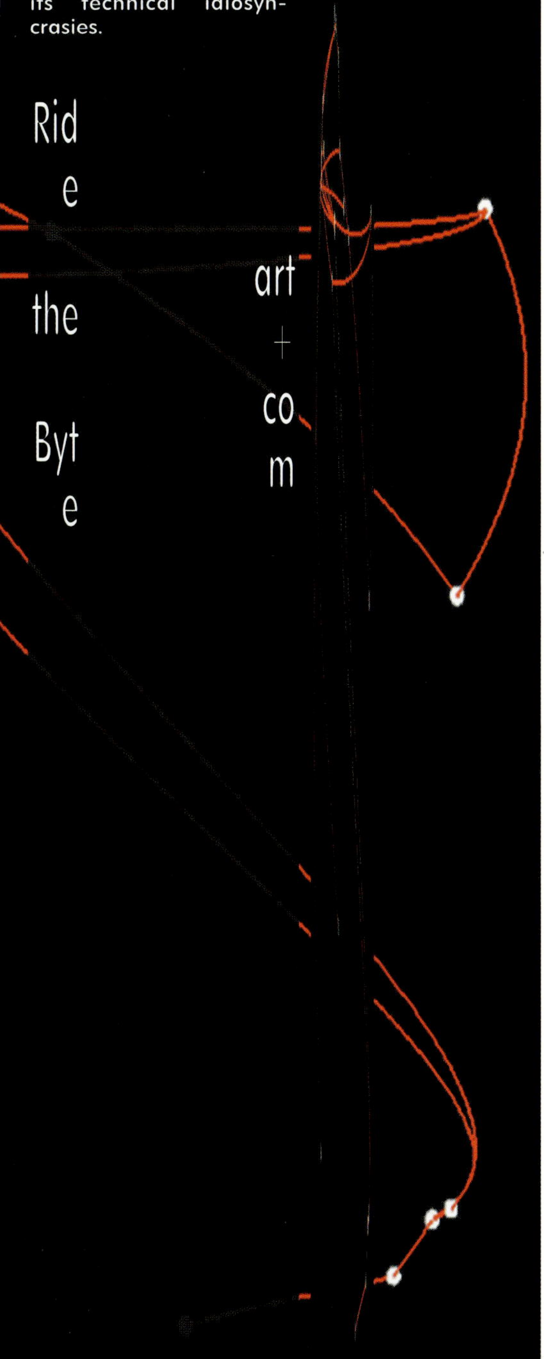

immaterial, and where specialists and experts have a high time value because their special knowledge cost a lot of time to acquire and was paid for by the firm to whom they belong, employees are loaned out on fixed term contracts to firms that cannot afford to train their own permanent experts. Trading in futures with human capital is the face of reality, you Beuyses – and Beckers. There is a new court society of time, with time masters and time slaves. Socially unconscious though it may be, the dominant form of society today is the courtly culture of time. The chronocrats are much cleverer at exploiting their slaves than the machines ever were. From machine slave to time slave is a small leap in the feudalism of time. The quickened journey's end is "the Court of Time." For this reason, it seems to me that a revolt of the slaves is called for in the society of feudal time, like the one that has already begun in culture.

Today the accelerated images must be made accessible to the masses. For, like the railway barons of earlier days, today there are the computer czars and princes who heap up quick millions with accelerated image machines. The price of high-performance computers must come down, as electricity did in the past. The bondsmen of time rehearsed the revolt using cinema, the proletarian art form of time, but it failed because capitalism is still in possession of its double: time. The cultural struggle around speed continues, however, while the chronocrats sit in the opera houses and buy paintings – for on their own admission, they prefer an aesthetics of stillness, stasis, stability, and an art that is "timeless" – the

slaves enjoy the moving pictures. Painting has become part of the court-and-salon culture of the chronocrats who, because of the logothetic masking of the contrary signifier, must naturally repudiate the art of the present time. If you are living at the center of time, everything else may be relegated to the periphery of time. The timelords of the jet sets and the databases, who swindle time's slaves out of their time with spare time in which they sell them what they themselves produced themselves in their labor time while the nobles of the chonocracy took it easy, are creating new suburbs, which are no longer urban spaces but suburbs of time, the first circles of time.

Time and acceleration have become the driving social factors, from artificial insemination to artificial image, from the economy to art, for the tele-technetronic speed-up has laid hold of all social vectors, so that time is monetarized, space is teletransported, capital is temporalized and images are digitally accelerated.

Peter Weibel was born in Odessa in 1944 and lives in Karlsruhe (D) and Vienna (A). He studied literature, medicine, logics, philosophy and film in Paris and Vienna. His Doctoral thesis was on mathematical logic (modal logic). Since 1976 he has lectured at many universities in Europe and North America. After working as the artistic director of the Ars Electronica in Linz (A), he was chief curator of the Neue Galerie am Landesmuseum Joanneum in Graz (A). From 1993 until 1999 he was the Austrian commisioner of the Biennale di Venezia. Since then he has been working as chairman and CEO of the ZKM/Center for Art and Media Karlsruhe (D).

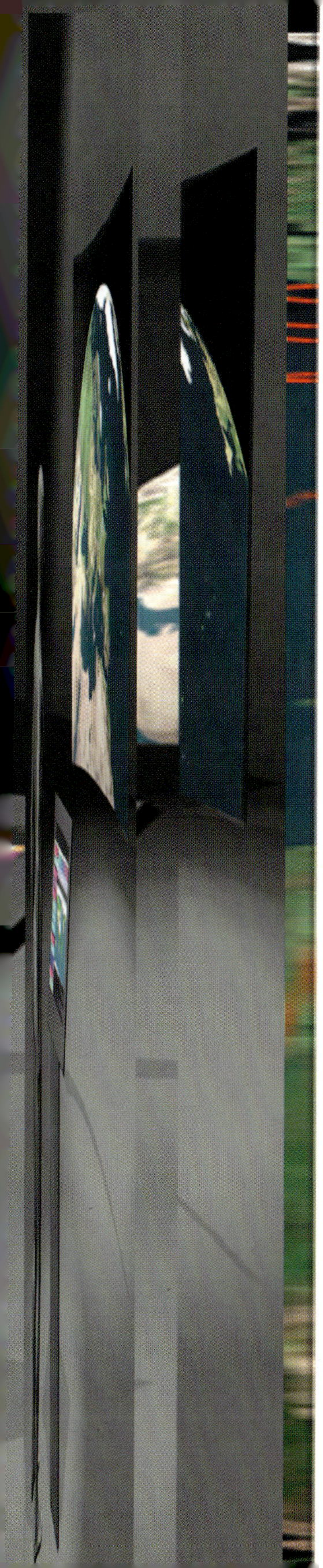

Peter Weibel

An interview with Æ

by Nicole Gingras

TESLA THE MACHINE-TIME OBSERVER-OPERATOR

Æ's Sparks series is a modular independent video production which finds its inspiration in the life of inventor Nikola Tesla (1856-1943), who was born in Smiljan, Croatia, and died in New York. His fervent intellectual activity placed him and his contemporaries at the source of alternating current, the induction motor, the transmission of electromagnetic waves and the fluorescent lamp.

How do you situate the series you are currently developing about Tesla in relation to previous works you have developed separately or together, not under the name of Æ? I am thinking of Timepiece *(1996),* Tempus Erit *(1993) and* Ouverture phénoménale *(1991), works that already had a strong connection to an exploration of time through a philosophical approach, and also the notion of energy applied to space, people, animals – elements we don't talk much about these days.*

The general intention of Æ and the present series is to reignite a living link with the phenomenology of the electronic medium as an art form, a psycho-/physiological experience of our modern technological unconscious.

It's in direct continuity with our interest in the perception of space-time, the positive distantiation that permits an eagle-eye view of existence and impermanence. Since 1990 we have realized that we're not interested in personal anecdotes but in science, philosophy, art and shamanism. We always hope to look (video) and hear (sound) through different scales of perception other than the anthropocentric realm of representational thinking. We use symbols and physiological responses to create emotional responses; we try to situate ourselves in research and experiences that let nature and electronics speak for themselves and not of us as artists.

Why focus on this man?

Tesla had concrete and optimized solutions for the beginning and future of an industrial world. His ideas were beautifully utopian, humanist and definitely not based solely on the capitalist ideology that sealed our world and put us deeper in slavery to production, production, production. He had a heightened perceptual system and lived through multiple shamanic ordeals (near-

The Mirror

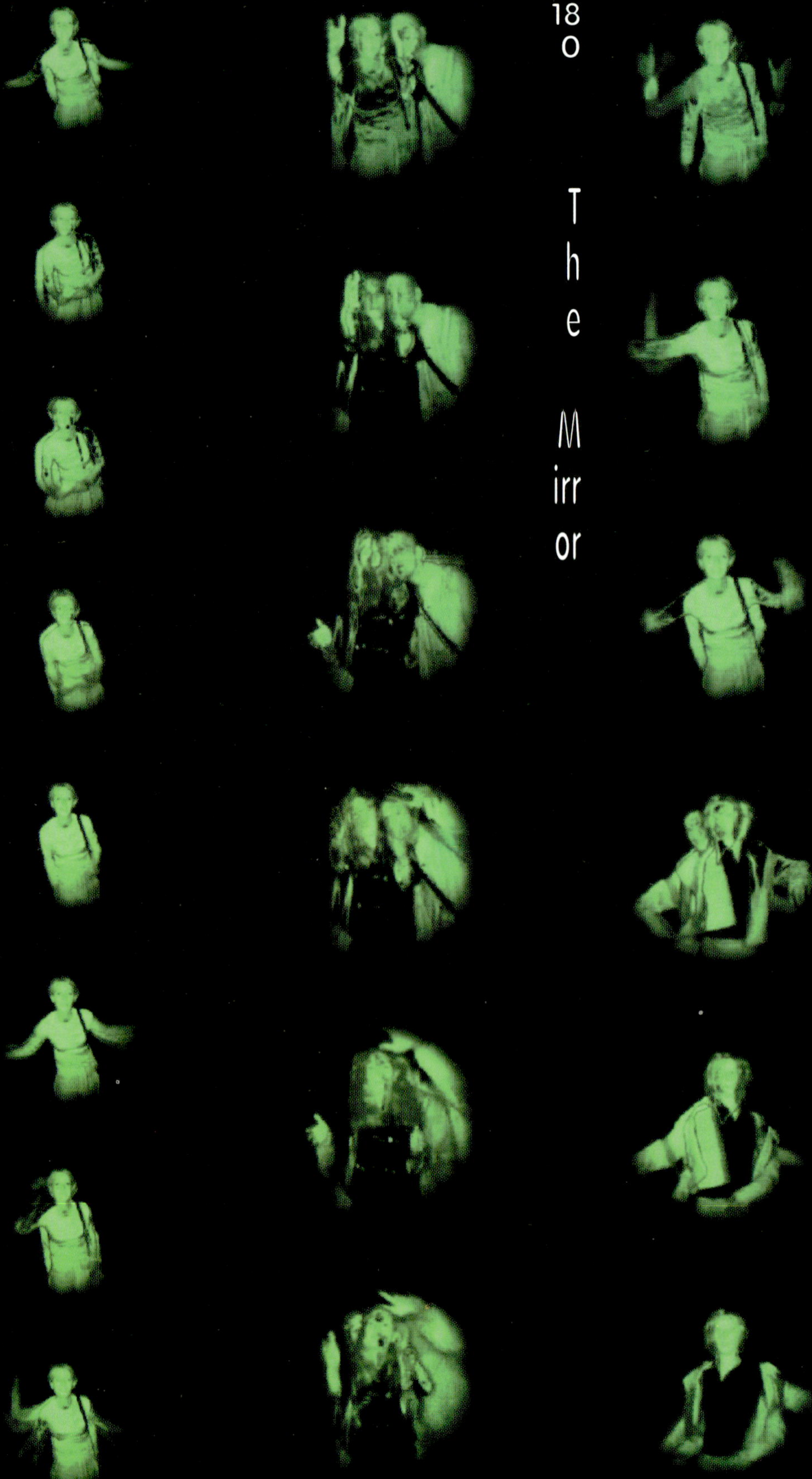

Ikuo Nakamura

I used to look into my mother's mirror when I was a child. I remember how frolicsome I was, playing alone in front of the mirror. And now I don't remember what I saw through that little mirror. (Ikuo Nakamura)

When looking into a mirror, we see a flat yet highly accurate real-time reflection of ourselves and the things around us. The interactive video and sound installation *The Mirror* takes this experience and recreates it in a more complex form: the viewer sees herself three-dimensionally, she sees herself in the present and in the past, and she hears the interference between these images of past and present.

The installation uses lasers and Holographic Optical Elements to produce a three-dimensional representation of the viewer. This representation can be seen floating in the space in front of the viewer at about one meter's distance from the Holographic Optical Element (HOE), which works like a lens by using a laser as a light source. Additionally, the visitor's movements trigger sounds which, like the live video image, are processed by the installation's computer in real-time.

By posing and moving in front of *The Mirror*, the visitor sees how her now breaks free and creates a distance from her past, which is distorted, shifted, lost, or fades away at each moment. At the same time, the interference between the now and the past can be heard as rustling noise. When the visitor stands still, the projected image fades, yet as she moves again, *The Mirror* projects its hybrid layering of time, space and sound.

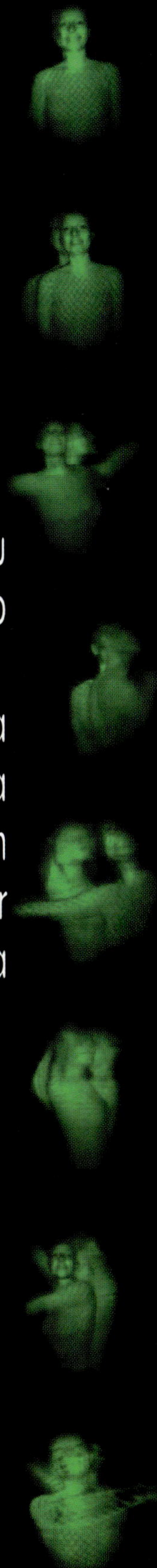

S8P ANTENNAS' TRANSMISSION

Æ

death experiences, sensory overload, sleep deprivation) throughout his life. The sheer number of patents that he registered in the USA is a testimony to his genius and constant activity. His work has been hidden from collective memory for economic, political, short-sighted reasons since the moment of his death (in 1943) during the Cold War, when one could say that some of his patents were studied and used in experiments for warfare activities still in use today.

Tesla had a complex persona, and as a visionary, he would not let himself be bound by normality. He was attuned to and guided by the physical laws and ideas which led him to a singular experience of the world.

We have come across many books, some of which were written by him; there are many scientific, esoteric and Tesla coil hobbyist Internet sites; he has been adopted by UFO believers, is revered by contemporary electrical engineers and physicists as well as music composers. His influence on all these people reflects his work, his far-reaching inventions and his heuristic methods of contemplation.

Could you say a few words about this artist/scientist's inventions?

Envision, in 1900, the transmission of electricity without wires, a carbon button lamp in which the ultra-hard carbon structure would be dissolved under high-frequency oscillations; a hand-held self-oscillating mechanism that would resonate harmonically and sympathetically with architectural and telluric materials to the point of creating earthquake-like chain reactions; utilization of the earth's geo-electrical properties in conjunction with the electromagnetic excitation of the ionosphere to create a permanently charged environment for the propagation of energy, intelligence, or a worldwide individuation system of communication, printed or otherwise; radio-controlled teleautomatons; all of this not tested on paper but experienced firsthand with ultra simple apparatuses in secret labs at the beginning of the century. Tesla, the machine-time observer-operator ...

We think that the observation of nature could be the key to solving most of our ecological problems. Tesla was a scientist/artist who took all his technological

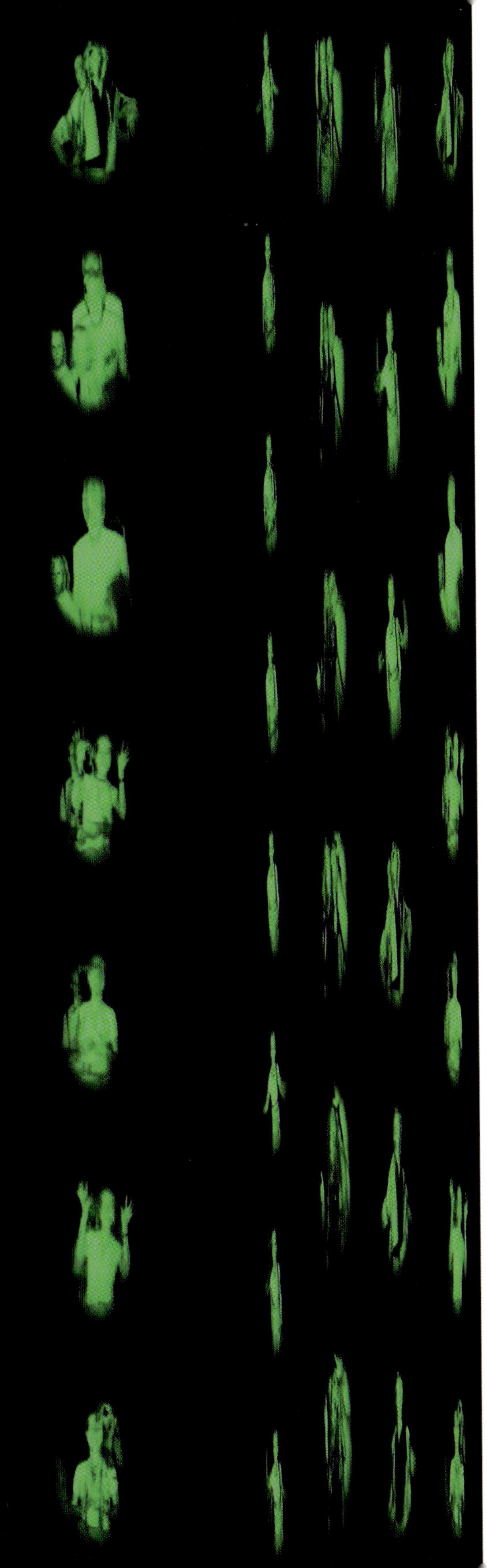

inputs from nature as an optimal self-regulated dynamic time machine.

So you respond to this side of him by the shots of nature under water, for example, which are in some way a moving parallel to the images of some of his inventions.

The nature images were included to emphasize the fact that nature has its own system of communication and electronic transmission. Antennas are not a new idea. Also, the shooting took place in a Biodome, a man-made museum of nature, recreating different ecosystems (tropical, boreal) ...

For me, Tesla represents a very eclectic mind which was misunderstood and also repressed, an eclectic mind which we still need around us now, in our predictable world.

His personality and accomplishments are overwhelming to artist and engineer alike. Even in doing some light research, one could associate almost every sphere of our electronic world with Tesla. It is almost unbelievable to realize that he originated so many of the applied electromagnetic inventions we use today.

Sometimes it is very puzzling the way you associate images with each other and/or place images and sounds together. In some way we could say that the unconventional essay structure of Sparks mimicks the eclecticism of Tesla's thinking, in terms of nonlinearity. You provide a fascinating collage of elements, testimonies through an approach which has affinities with documentary without being one, with a portrait of an important inventor without being impressionistic, emphatic or, even worse, hagiographic. Through the various elements, the various points of view of people in different fields (philosopher, engineer, members of his family) you develop a complex portrait of this man in multiple, shifting facets.

' We looked at his life and experiences as a nonlinear analogy of our own experiences with the digital medium. We definitively wanted to privilege a multifaceted point of view, leaving room for interpretation. As soon as we saw the complexity of the subject, it grew as multiple rhizomes, spreading even into a political realm which we had not foreseen in the beginning. We became overwhelmed by the vast quantities of information, and also we felt the need to respect the various groups and individuals who expressed their ideas, support and knowledge. We realized that instead of explaining everything, we had to go back to our basic root, the experimental genre.

Let's talk about the project in its totality: the idea of the units being shown separately, together, associated in a different order, information units distinct from each other but also combinable ... Was this "possibilité de combinaisons" planned from the beginning? This is very clever. And I could foresee possibilities ad infinitum. This goes for the work in itself but also

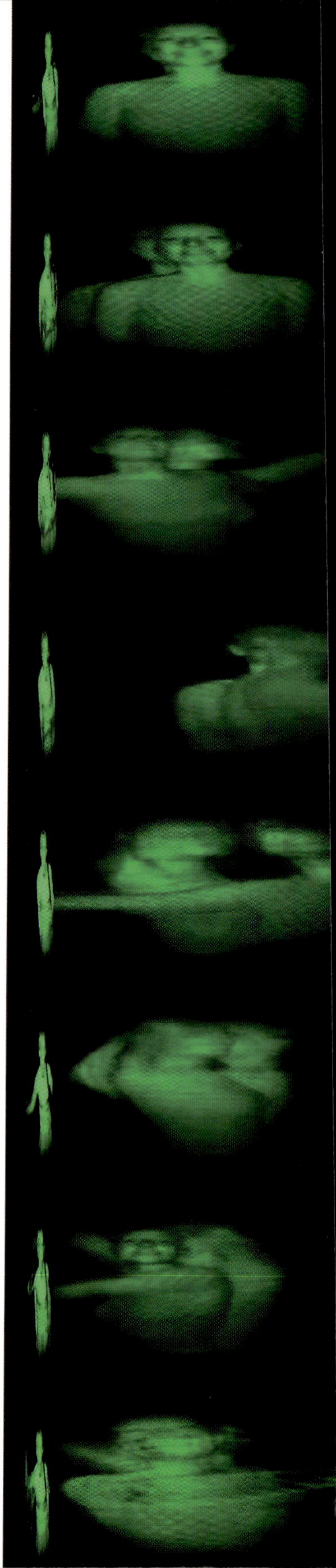

applies to the way the work could be presented – multiple apparatuses are possible.

Yes. In the beginning, there were eleven "sparks," each of very short duration. In the end, there will be only five capsules. Our way of working with this subject has been heavily influenced by our individual practices as video editor and audio engineer, so we were enchanted by the advent of miniDV, which permits high picture quality and multiple versions without generational loss. We have already made two 25-40 minute performative versions and a CDR remix of the original soundtracks, and in the end the single-channel modular series will be around 50 minutes. This was unthinkable for us even a few years ago.

We have considered doing another live version which could be produced with MAX-MSP, such as recombining the music and image in real-time in front of the viewers. This same software could also be applied to an interactive installation, where viewers could choose topics in their own rhythm …

The sound in relation to the image. How were these various soundscapes developed? What was the approach in collecting sounds, and later in associating or mixing sounds for this work?

A lot of the sounds were generated from physical analog modeling, filters, feedbacks and intermodulations at the interstice of their internal electronic limits and behavior, glitch, amplifiers distorting, concrete sounds originating from Tesla coils, shortwaves, machines, et cetera … Very old shamanic instruments-concepts (drum and digeridoo) made in plastic and PVC were recorded for some meaningful parts of the series. The assemblage, DSP, mixing was done solely

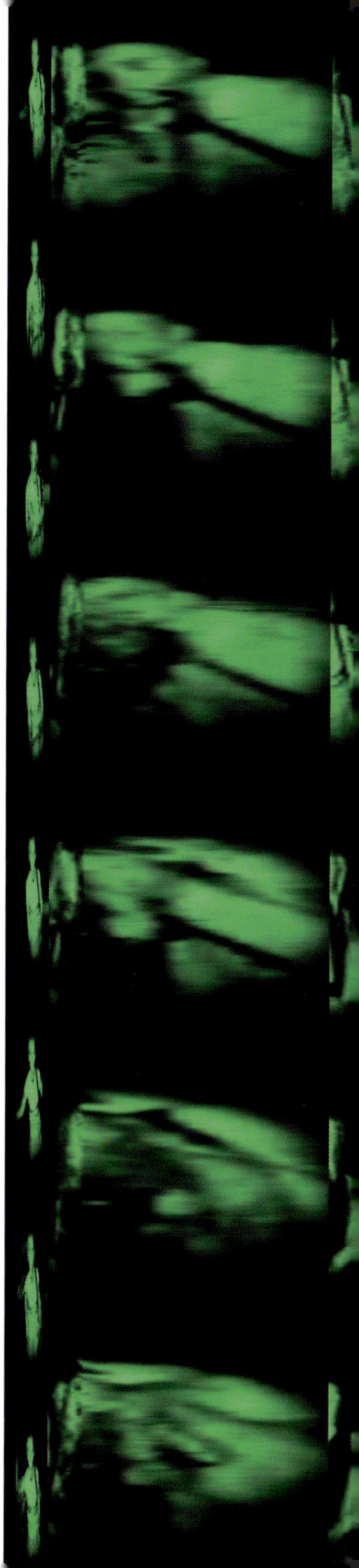

on a personal computer. *S1 Tesla and His Time* and *S8 Wardenclyffe* were constructed around the structure of the interviews and image composition, whereas *S8P – antennas, transmission* (live performative segment) was composed before the picture edit.

There is an extreme fluidity between aural and visual material in this work which, among other things, offers the viewer a mobility to reflect on some concepts discussed by the interviewees. It is a very creative space. This fluidity has to do both with space and time, I would say. In other words, it seems to me you are approaching various zones of invisibility as if to parallel "invisible" phenomena that were parts of Nikola Tesla's life and research: pointing some of them to us without describing them or freezing them into arrested time. In some way, these facets, an impressionistic or mosaic approach, brings Tesla into the present.

Yes, we always work with the premise that research, readings, moments of trance in the making of our audiovisual work will pierce the form to create other meanings and heightened perceptual experiences for the viewer. There are always a lot of coded

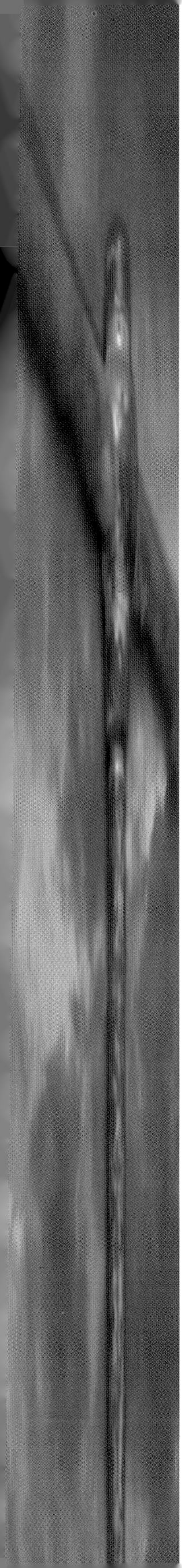

symbols and encrypted systems in our interpretation whether it is geometry, bindrunes, time concepts, color or numbers. It helps us to structure our thoughts, and we now have the confirmation that people get those impressions positively without us having to explain them. This way of communicating, invisibly, in silence, is very exciting for us!

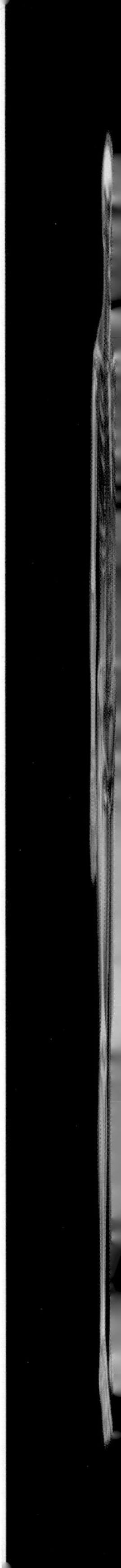

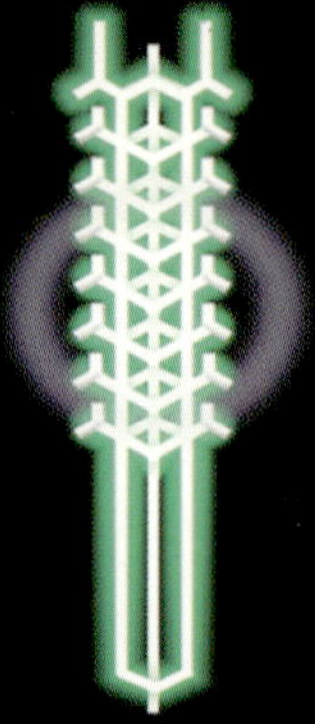

Æ

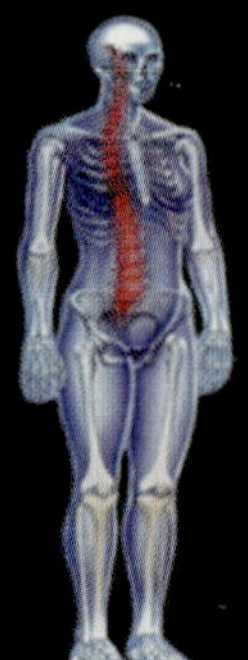

S8 P ANTENNAS, TRANSMISSION

In 1996, Æ was initiated as a research and communication unit based on an artistic and philosophical exchange between artists Gisèle Trudel and Stéphane Claude (who have worked creatively together for the past nine years), with the regular participation of other collaborators. Æ is a more anonymous framework consolidating their interest in an ecological awareness in the use of technology as echoed in the arts, science and traditions of shamanism.

Nicole Gingras is a writer and an independent curator living in Montreal. She has produced various digital art, film and video programs and solo and group exhibitions which have toured in Canada and Europe. As a publisher, she has been producing monographs and artists' books since 1996.

First published in:
Poolside, Fall 2000 issue, Winnipeg, Manitoba, editor Stephen Lawson.

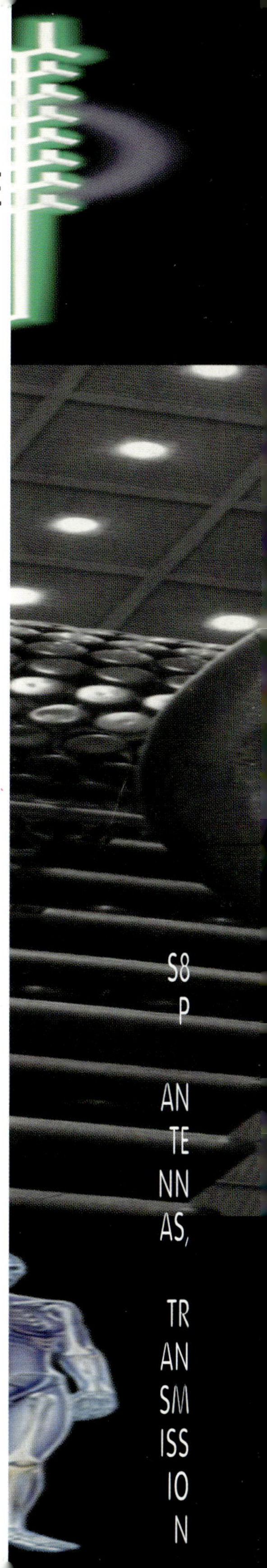

Colophon

Editorial team: Joke Brouwer and V2_Organisation

Design: Joke Brouwer

Translations: Leo Reijnen (Dutch-English) and James Lynn (German-English) with thanks to Laura Marz.

Project descriptions by Arjen Mulder (Kaap, Kölgen, Soppela, Ujica), Yukiko Shikata (Maebayashi) and the artists. Editing by Andreas Broeckmann.

Special thanks to Detlef Linke, Mark Taylor, Francisco Varela, Arjen Mulder, Andreas Broeckmann and Marjolein Berger.

Cover Photo from Martin Reinhard and Virgil Widrich.

Available in North, South and Central America through D.A.P./Distributed Art Publishers Inc, 155 Sixth Avenue 2nd Floor, New York, NY 10013-1507, Tel. 212 627.1999 Fax 212 627.9484.

ISBN 90-5662-189-0

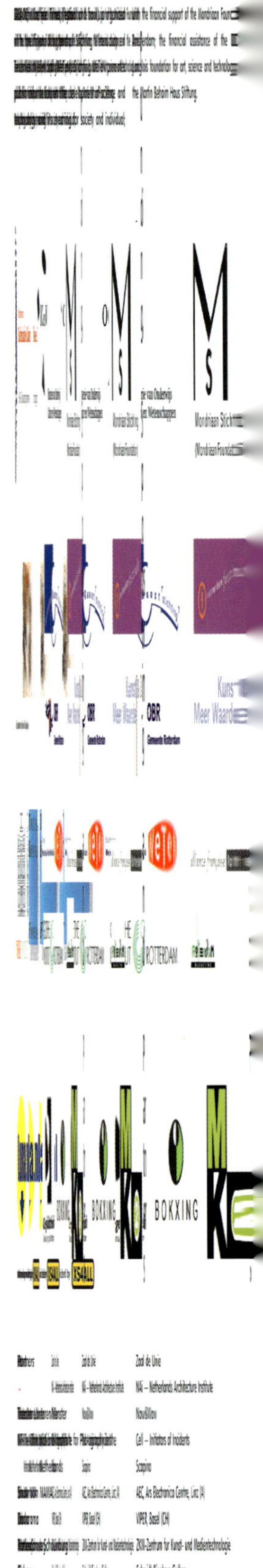

Subsidizers, Sponsors and Partners

DEAFOO, Machine Times (festival and book)

is organized with the financial support of Stichting Wetenschap en Techniek Nederland (WeTeN). Stichting WeTeN promotes public information on the development of science and technology and its meaning for society and individual; with the financial support of the Mondriaan Foundation, Amsterdam; the financial assistance of the Daniel Langlois foundation for art, science and technology and the Martin Behaim Haus Stiftung.

Ministerie van Buitenlandse Zaken
HGIS-Cultuurprogramma

OCenW
Ministerie van Onderwijs Cultuur en Wetenschappen

Mondriaan Stichting
(Mondriaan Foundation)

la fondation Daniel Langlois
pour l'art, la science et la technologie

Rotterdamse Kunststichting

rotterdamfestivals

OBR
Gemeente Rotterdam

Kunst & Meer Waarde

VSB FONDS

Thuiskopie Fonds

Stichting Wetenschap en Techniek Nederland
WeTeN

alliance française Rotterdam

GOETHE INSTITUT ROTTERDAM

Stichting Bevordering van Volkskracht

Rotterdam Marketing

Luna.nl

A.B.-geluidstechniek
Aleidisstraat 3 • 3021 SB Rotterdam

BOKXING

MK2

streaming media services provided by XS4ALL

Partners

Theater Lantaren/Venster
NFI – The National Institute for Photography in the Netherlands
Showroom MAMA
Dodorama
Rotterdamse Schouwburg
Calypso
Zaal de Unie
NAi – Netherlands Architecture Institute
Now&Wow
Scapino
AEC, Ars Electronica Centre, Linz (A)
VIPER, Basel (CH)
ZKM-Zentrum fur Kunst- und Medientechnologie
Schmidt-Bingham Gallery

w
w
w.v
2.n
l/d
ea
f